THE ACCIDENTAL FEMINIST

*The Life of One Woman through
War, Motherhood, and International
Photojournalism*

TOBY MOLENAAR

Arcade Publishing • New York

Arcade Publishing books may be purchased in bulk at special discounts for sales promotion, corporate gifts, fund-raising, or educational purposes. Special editions can also be created to specifications. For details, contact the Special Sales Department, Arcade Publishing, 307 West 36th Street, 11th Floor, New York, NY 10018 or arcade@skyhorsepublishing.com.

Arcade Publishing® is a registered trademark of Skyhorse Publishing, Inc.®, a Delaware corporation.

Visit our website at www.arcadepub.com.

10 9 8 7 6 5 4 3 2 1

Library of Congress Cataloging-in-Publication Data is available on file.

ISBN: 978-1-62872-410-3

Printed in the United States of America

To my children, Cathy, Marc, and Laura. And to Stanley,
still my friend, without whom this book might
not have published.

Les souvenirs sont cors de chasse
Dont meurt le bruit parmi le vent.
Guillaume Apollinaire

I thank my editor Jeannette Seaver, as well as Lawrence Malkin
and Ulf Skogsbergh for all their help.

Portrait painted by Mati Klarwein
Photographed by Ulf Skogsbergh

CONTENTS

PREFACE

As a child, walking to school, I used to chant names to myself, counting them like prayer beads: Samarkand, Zanzibar, Timbuktu, Kyoto and Surabaya. I had only a very vague idea where these places were or what they stood for, but I knew that one day I would go there. They were all still to come, the years of travel and discovery, of living and loving, the wonder and the sorrow of it. Seeing the golden stupa in Boudhanath, the white egrets in the flooded forests of the Amazon, or looking up at a star-filled Saharan sky, I would recognize the images of my childhood dreams.

More than forty years as a photographer have left me with a sizable archive. The pictures show me people of the deserts or of the misty rains, bringing back sights and sounds, smells and colors. The articles were written for publication and often screen my private emotions. The notes, scribbled in haste as an aide-mémoire to myself—*I should, I have, I must*—carry a sense of urgency tied to a specific moment. If together they form the texture of my life, they also remind me that memory is selective, biased and manipulative.

Memories, wrote Apollinaire, are the "call of horns, their echo silenced by the wind." Even fantasy finds equilibrium between memory and lie. When I consciously search for images I become one with what emerges. I am there again, at that point in time, and find that all has remained unchanged. The child, the girl, the woman that was I is still within reach.

ECHOES

In my dreams, I often have a husband. Not a new one, but a comfortable amalgam of the old ones. Perfectly nice, he seems to be au courant with my current life and I never have to say, "Oh, of course, that was not with you!" Sometimes he lingers a little after I wake up, but by the time I carry my coffee cup through the garden, down to the water's edge, I am alone to enjoy the clowning cormorant and the squabbling gulls. Actually, during the day I hardly think of any husbands and definitely not of the first one. He happened so long ago, long before Mallorca, Paris or Long Island and I seem to have left him behind somewhere. Except for unbidden snippets of memory recalled by such odd things as the sound of Swiss church bells on a Sunday morning, or a dead kitten in a trash can.

I was born in Holland, where although some of my ancestors built the massive windmills that dot the lowlands, most of them chose the sea. There was a fishing fleet that followed the herring; others built ships and repaired them. My grandfather built ship's cabins of deep red mahogany, my father was one of the youngest officers in the merchant marine, my brother chose the navy before he decided to make his money elsewhere and a grandson recently graduated from the Marine Academy in New York, thus continuing the albeit thin line. I was told a great-grandmother used to sail with her husband across the Channel to deliver fresh vegetables to England. Sailors of the small fleet would grumble, as that was "not done," but she was the captain's wife and she did. I like to think of her standing beside her husband, skirts billowing, watching the daybreak over England's coast, young, happy and alive.

I grew up in the noisy seaport of Rotterdam. Our house stood in a quiet tree-lined street with neatly trimmed hedges. Just behind our garden gate a narrow path lead to a dike beyond which stretched the empty *polders*, flat and windswept, the meadows furrowed by weed-covered ditches, where silver herons stood silent sentinel. A Dutch landscape scrawled in thin chalk. My brother and I gathered clumps of pearly frog's spawn in an old casserole and emptied them into the small pond in our garden; by early summer, they grew into a mighty chorus, invading the rest of the neighborhood. We jumped the *sloten* with long poles, fell in, disappeared under the jade-colored lichen into the mud and came up black and smelly. These ditches and the canal a block away from our house, where we skated in winter, were the nearest my everyday life then came to promises of oceans, deserts and jungles. But already my memory nudges at other images.

My grandfather used to visit an old sea captain of whom I was secretly very scared because he would take out his false teeth with horrible pink gums, thinking it amused me. He also had a blue and yellow parrot that sang Italian arias and swore in Spanish, or so I was told. It slept in a large round cage on a faded green velvet pillow but flapped around freely during the day, talking to itself in the mirror and screeching for sweets. Perched on the back of a chair it moved in small sideways steps, nibbling its clawed foot and quickly turning its head to give me a jaundiced look. It twice bit my finger. My sister said I would get rabies and die foaming at the mouth, but I always went back. Not for the bird, I realized later, but for what I thought it had seen.

I remember crossing silver bridges in the city, swift water rushing with the tide, forests of slender cranes swinging their loads into holds and white clouds that were always moving. I remember as a small girl spending a day on a tugboat of my father's shipyard guiding a cruise ship into port, about twenty miles along the shifting sands of the river Meuse. All that afternoon boats hooted and bells clanged, men were calling to each other, there was the smell of brine, the sun was on the water, a long leash tied me to some metal railing and I had never felt so free. It was almost dark when we returned and the pilot climbed down from the cruise ship. Its lights reflected in the sky, I heard music, voices, and the hull above us loomed as high as a mountain. I looked up and wondered, "Where has it been? What strange places did it see?"

GROWING UP

My parents

Until the war—World War II, that is—changed it all, life was simple and rather predictable. We were a large family with six children, siblings who quarreled and made up, parents who despaired and were proud of us. We went to school, celebrated birthdays and waited with all the other Dutch children for Saint Nicolas (rather than Father Christmas) to bring us presents. We must have seemed a rather typical, somewhat noisy but closely knit family. I have a different memory.

As far back as I can remember I had a sense of not quite belonging, of being not quite like the others, of being slightly in the wrong. I had an older sister and brother. After our mother died at my birth, my father married again, a pleasant-looking woman with bright red hair, called Susanna. The three younger children from the new marriage formed a little clan of their own, closely protected by their mother. My stepmother did not have any problems with my older siblings, but could never bring herself to accept me. She had known my mother well and knew how deeply her death had affected my father. Was I a constant reminder of how happy they had been? To everyone else, I was a child among others and she was my mother. I always knew that I had none.

It was my paternal grandmother and my young aunt Adry—just a dozen years older than I was and tending to treat me like her favorite doll—who gave me affection, guidance and protection. Their house was near ours. I had lived the first years of my life in their care and now spent much of my free time with them. Looking back, I know my stepmother was not a mean or evil person. She was a good mother to the others and later, as a grown-up woman, I would understand better how difficult it must have been to marry a young widower with three children. Still, she made my childhood miserable with endless small hurts. The small offhand remarks, the ever-present suspicion and slight exasperation in the voice—what did she do *now*?—the head turned toward me as a reflex when anything had been broken, gone wrong or been lost. The putting down of those qualities I *did* have and the rejection of gestures of goodwill on my part. Where, then, was my father in all this? He was kind to us, but we saw him only at the evening meals or on weekends, when last week's warmed-up quibbles between a wife and an unruly child must have seem trivial.

I loved school. It was a place where I could be myself, where I was judged by my curiosity, my willingness to learn and by my grades. I spent most of my free time reading and early on learned to lose myself in the world and company of those who peopled the pages. I had found a corner in the living room, behind an armchair, where I would sit on the floor with my book. My father walked by and let me be; my mother would find me and tell me to clean up my room or help do the dishes. When I graduated from junior high as youngest and first of my class, speaking four languages and showing no interest in domestic matters, she registered me in a girl's school where I would learn how to hem napkins and set a nice table. My grandmother did not allow me to whine, but this was a matter of my education. My parents were summoned and I changed schools.

My grandmother was my example and my conscience. I muddled through many small ordeals on my own, because I knew she would be there come real need. She spoke little and at times could seem somewhat distant. Once, having taken a close friend to visit her, the girl asked me, "Your grandmother does not like you either?" I stared at her and she said, "Well, she just calls you *child*! That is like saying cat or chicken!" I really had no answer. I only knew that my grandmother called no one else child and I firmly believed that to her I was the only child in the world.

One beautiful morning in May, war broke out. My father and I climbed to the attic and watched the German parachutes floating down, white specks glinting in the early sunlight. They looked like puppets dangling from an umbrella, and years later, I could never see Mary Poppins without thinking of them. Planes roared overhead, one burning Junker passing straight over our house, almost touching the rooftops. I heard the eerie wail, saw the black crosses painted on the wings, the red flames engulfing the plane, the pilot in the cockpit. I knew something terrible was happening, but had no idea what. I was eleven years old. During the next few days, the radio repeated information and instructions. The German army had invaded Holland; the Queen said that the royal family was leaving for England. An announcer told us in a very serious tone of voice to tear up bed sheets and prepare bandages for the wounded, pack an emergency suitcase, and no standing around in groups in the streets. The *Queen* was leaving? What emergency? What wounded? The following days brought the thunder of continuous cannon fire, explosions and air raid sirens. Searchlights scanned the night skies, three slender waving fingers of bright light reaching up to trap the silhouette of a silver plane. I saw dogfights between Dutch and German planes without ever knowing who was friend or foe, which went down and died.

In an effort to keep the German tanks from advancing, fertile polders were flooded with seawater, something incomprehensible to Dutch people. There was fierce fighting on several fronts, and the

Germans set an ultimatum for surrender. The time had not expired when pilots received their orders and the bombs fell on our city. We did not live in the center and our house was spared, but the explosions echoed through our quiet street and huge columns of black smoke uncurled like gigantic thunderclouds against a red sky. Clouds that brought no rain, but greasy black ashes and thousands of small scraps of paper fluttering down like a ticker parade. I remember saving some half-burnt pages bearing the letterhead of the *Statendam*, proud flagship of the Holland American Line, anchored in its homeport. The heart of the city went up in flames, thirty thousand houses lining wide boulevards and narrow medieval streets, the wharfs with their warehouses and dockside bars and cabarets, dozens of churches, schools, theaters, factories, banks and hospitals. A thousand people died and more than eighty thousand were homeless. It was a scene of total war and destruction. There was the smell of charred and burning things and the very air tasted bitter on the tongue. We children looked to the grown-ups to make sense of it all, but they turned to each other, the same disbelieving horror showing in their faces.

With Rotterdam burning and the German threat of other cities facing the same fate, Holland capitulated. The war had lasted five days and our lives were forever changed. We saw our first refugees, followed by armored cars and columns of young Germans on their heavy motorcycles fanning out through the streets, soldiers putting up official announcements in German and Dutch. The beginning of the occupation. The gray-clad soldiers with guns and bayonets, wearing black boots with iron nails and belts with shiny buckles pronouncing "*Gott mit uns.*" (God with us.) The anonymous faces under square gray helmets, within days to become such a familiar sight.

Several bombs had hit the zoo, and escaped animals added their own phantasmagorical note to the ruined and smoldering city. Lions roared in residential areas, an elephant stood looking forlorn at a bus stop, after having stripped all the trees in the little square. Wolves were hunting in the parks, while in our own gardens smaller wild creatures slipped through the evening shadows. In one absurd instance, a confused ostrich flapped hissing down the aisle in a nearby crowded church and attacked an unsuspecting priest, pecking furiously at his embroidered robe and chasing him around the altar. The zookeepers struggled to lure their charges back into improvised shelters, whereas the Germans shot the animals at sight. It did not make much difference; in the end, most animals starved to death or fell prey to survivors, whether men or beast.

We learned to live with coupons and identification cards, curfews, the wailing of air raid sirens and the BBC news heard on hidden radios. The strange thing was that many people pretended nothing had changed and continued to live as they had always done. But things had changed, even for us, the children. With schools destroyed or used as German barracks, we shared buildings in different parts of town, walking past smoking ruins, skirting still standing walls, their empty windows staring like hollow eyes. We rarely had a full day of school and established values or old rules were no longer valid. A boy would tell of family arrested during the night as an excuse for homework not done. He lived next door to me; we had heard nothing and no one had been disturbed at all. People did disappear; teachers present one day might not return the next.

If books and other school materials were scarce, the lack of food became ever more serious. From the first year of occupation, the Germans began shipping the harvests and manufactured goods of the Netherlands to the Fatherland, leaving the local population to survive on a minimum. Soon reserves ran low and people scrounging for food did things they could not have imagined doing only months ago. I saw one of my teachers, a respectable middle-aged family man, searching through the garbage bins outside the German barracks. My mother exchanged jewelry or embroidered sheets for a pound of butter or a loaf of bread and soon we would be grateful for plain boiled potatoes. My youngest brother used to infuriate me by pushing his one thin slice of cheese further and further back on his one thin slice of bread, leaving the cheese for last and saying, "I still have some and you don't!" Once we received a bag of oatmeal from friends in the country, which was a real treat. My mother was a very mediocre cook and tended to burn our porridge as well as leave lumps in it. I worried about it all night. Coming down the stairs that morning and looking forward to a rare, real breakfast, I was met by the smell of burned milk and I could have cried for anger. I was hungry, but I could not finish my plate. She punished me for wasting food.

As time passed, there were odd things one barely noticed anymore, such as the brown packing tape or cut up newspaper strips glued to the windows to limit bomb damage. At first, they were just there to keep the glass from splintering, but slowly the strips began to show designs and patterns and I remember the absurd pride people took in comparing the windows, as if it were a flower contest in a Swiss mountain village. As there was not always enough light to study by, my older brother Cees rigged up a bicycle on a stand, its dynamo-lit lamp pointed at a table. We children took turns on the bike, which made for great blackmail possibilities: you help me with my homework or I might just be too tired to make the bulb do more than glow a little. He also put together a carbide lantern with a tin can, a wick and some smelly paste, such as miners have used of old. (Many years later, with a small shock of recognition, I would see these very same lanterns used by fishermen along the coast of Java.) It produced a dismal little flame, smoked, stank and—to my secret glee at my mother's predictable hysteria—tended to blow its lid midway through the evening meal.

This brother, Cees, two years my senior, had always been closest to me. As long as I could remember we had shared our secrets and he could wipe out my hurts with his funny crooked smile and a little nudge, saying, "Hey, let it go." Then, one evening, he did not return home and we waited, as did all families to whom that happened. A friend brought news: Cees had insulted a Dutch Nazi on the tramway, the argument turned into a fistfight and he had been arrested. Several weeks later a short note came from a work camp called Kraft Durch Freude, (Strength through Joy), saying he was well and that we were allowed to write. I did, almost every day, through months that saw some of the loneliest times of my childhood. None of my letters ever reached him. Eventually released, he went underground until the end of the war. Later, living very different lives in different parts of the world, we lost our close touch, but he lived a full and happy life. When he died, ill and almost blind, I was there in time to say goodbye and grateful for it.

During the first few years of the war, some simple pleasures remained. When the canals and lakes froze over, we brought out our sleighs and skates. Iceboats sped, horse sleighs jingled and on Saturday the city's canals became a festive place. The light of lanterns tinseled the sparkling ice, neighbors gathered at stands that sold hot milk spiced with anis and popular sticky sweets, called *polka bits* for no reason I ever discovered. The youngest children pushed small wooden chairs to keep their balance, the older ones formed long lines, laughing, swerving at high speed with irons screeching in the turn. My grandfather carved me pair of wooden skates that looked like small boats curving upward in front, which were my great pride. It was a timeless pleasure, a Dutch painting come alive, happy little figures, wooden skates, red woolen hats and mittens, barking dogs and all.

One early morning in spring, a young teacher took us to see the tulip fields. Silvery light turned grasses and slim church spires into Rembrandt etchings of our flat, pencil-stroke land. Pollard willows lined the creeks, the wind caressed clouds and water, gently moving. The veils of mist drifted away toward the sea, leaving behind a vast expanse of color. Deep purple next to shimmering white, bright red flowing into pink, brassy orange fading into pale yellow: the flower fields of Holland. Touched by the new sun, the colors blazed, and it seemed to me then that this small corner of my world laughed for joy.

I remember the small bookstore on the street corner, which continued to double as a lending library until the very end of the war. It was an important part of our lives. In our family some could sing, some made music, but everybody read. On Saturday morning, some of us would stagger home with stacks of books chosen from the family list. I see my father crossing the room, glancing at the books on the table and finding him two hours later, one knee on a chair, totally engrossed in what might as easily be a novel, the latest science magazine, or a history of the Children's Crusade.

For a while, there was still music in our house. My mother played the violin, my father the organ and the piano. He sang in a choir and friends performed together in each other's homes. I have a memory of sitting on our kitchen doorstep while in the living room piano and violin joined with the soprano of a well-known Dutch concert singer, Jo Vincent. A small group of neighbors gathered at our garden gate while her voice, for which the *Lieder* seemed to have been written, floated through the trees, leaving an illusion of beauty and peace.

As time went by, most of these small joys slipped away and the younger children hardly remembered an earlier way of life. A world with oranges and bananas, hot water and fresh-smelling soap, a world where one played with toys and wore new clothes. Needles and thread or shoelaces became luxuries. I remember dying a piece of string with black ink and proudly using it to tie a pair of brown boy's shoes, the only pair I possessed. I could tell a Spitfire from a Messerschmitt by the drone of their engines, I had the best shrapnel collection in my class, and no, I did not play with dolls. Growing up fast, we watched the adults, who seemed mainly occupied with survival. There was no indication that this would end. Children live day by day, a year is a lifetime, and soon we did not really imagine a time when there would not be a war. More and more families were trying to leave the starving, bombed-out city, its people's faces reduced to bristle and bone, marked by hunger, scabies and dysentery. A place where children knew not to ask any questions about a prostrate form on the sidewalk, so prettily covered with a blanket of last night's snow. A city where Jewish friends wore yellow stars sewn to their clothes, where neighbors disappeared and German army trucks rumbled through the streets at night, whether loaded with soldiers or prisoners was anyone's guess. The trees in our street had long been cut down for firewood, as were garden shacks, wooden fences and sometimes doors or window frames. There was not always gas or electricity to cook or heat. My mother would partially cook a stew of turnips and frozen potatoes in an iron pot and place it in a box filled with straw, where it continued to simmer. The tramways lacked the electricity to run and were for the greater part dismantled, the cars sent to Germany, the copper wiring used to make bullets. Trains had mostly stopped running when part of the personnel went on strike to protest the persecution of the Jews and never really functioned again.

There came a time when neither rationing cards nor money could coax any food off the empty shelves. As children often had a better chance to convince a farmer or shopkeeper, we roamed the suburbs and nearby villages in twos and threes, hoping to bring home a head of frozen cabbage, a few onions or a loaf of bread. My older sister Adry was a very sweet but not at all an aggressive person; my brother was still in a prison camp, so it fell mostly to me, with my younger brother, to scrounge for food. One dark evening after curfew, we ran into a German patrol outside the city limits. They looked us over, two children with a small sack of flour, and told us to climb into the back of their truck. I fell on top of some people already lying there, people who seemed to be tied together, people who moaned. I tried to sit up and look, but a soldier pushed me down with the barrel of his gun. Every movement I made seemed to hurt someone else and I had no idea what was to happen to us. The truck drove back to the outskirts of the city, where we were told, "GET DOWN, NOW!" Standing in the empty street, I watched the truck with its wretched load of human torment, despair and death drive off and tried to understand what had just happened. Why would they let us be witness to that and allow us to go free?

Had they picked us up and then did not know what to do with us? Did they simply not care what children saw? They hardly could have meant to give us a friendly ride. In that truck? My brother—all of ten years old—just asked what happened to our bag of flour and did I know how to get home. We huddled in a store entrance until morning and walked. On September 5, 1944, after the invasion of Normandy, the Allied forces actually came so close that people in Rotterdam lined the streets and climbed on rooftops to welcome them. Waving flags, they jeered and threw stones at the German soldiers and the local Nazis who tried to leave the city by any means, cars, bicycles, horses or on foot. The Allied advance slowed down and the next day saw all those enemies return to be with us for many more months and taking revenge for the humiliation.

It was during those few chaotic days of promise that life became at times surrealistic, although I would not have known to call it that. My stepmother's mother died. She had been living in a nursing home for several years, and her death was not really a surprise. The family was getting ready to attend the funeral when, at the last minute, no more than one vehicle was allowed to accompany the hearse to the cemetery. My father and uncle joined the minister in the carriage. On the way back, a police officer warned them that the main bridge they had to cross might be blown up any minute. The panicked drivers whipped the horse-driven carriages in a crazy Wild West chase through the streets, when my uncle suddenly noticed that there was a coffin bouncing around in the back of the hearse. Rattling along on the cobblestones, the driver shouted back angrily that he knew nothing about it; coffins were expensive and hard to come by so the gravediggers sometimes simply slipped the body into the grave and resold the coffin. I overheard my father discussing it with my uncle, wondering whether it could possibly have been my grandmother's coffin. I do not think anyone ever told my mother, but it was a rather strange funeral.

My father was a kind man and I loved him, but I did not really know him well. Not until we set out together on the desperate and near-fatal journey in that last bitter winter of the war, a voyage still referred to by my family as the "hunger-journey." The idea may have originated on Christmas Day. Earlier that year my aunt Adry had been arrested as a member of the resistance and taken to the infamous Oranje Hotel, the name given by the Dutch to a Nazi jail, hidden in the dunes of Scheveningen near The Hague. We later learned that she had been warned to leave town: her group was betrayed and her fiancé shot. She did not flee, knowing only too well what would happen to her parents if she did. Neither did she dare to warn them, afraid that they might react as if they had known of her involvement, which they did not. She stayed home and waited for the Gestapo to arrive. I have often tried to imagine what it must have been like for that young woman, waiting through the night for the knock on the door. Adry opened to uniformed men, snarling orders, accusations, and the first beating. Hurt and bleeding, she was taken away. Years later, she remembered odd details: one of the men grabbed her bicycle from the hallway and an old fur coat hanging in a closet. She said that even at that terrifying moment, it had struck her as absurd. Liberated at the end of the war, she had spent more than a year in prison, mostly in solitary confinement, with all the horrors that implies. Through time, we grew close far beyond the family ties, and all my life I would measure decisions by her courage and faith.

My grandparents were heartbroken and blamed themselves for not having been more aware. My grandfather was a tall, dignified-looking man, white-haired with bushy black eyebrows and a voice that carried. In his grief, he took to walking back and forth in front of the German headquarters, harrowing the guards, airing his rage and his hatred to anyone who would listen. It took all the persuasion power of my grandmother and the rest of the family to convince him that his demonstrations were no help to his daughter and could only lead to his own arrest or worse.

On Christmas of 1944, we still had no news of Adry and my grandparents agreed to come and spend the day with us. Not that there was to be any kind of celebration. Most days now we fetched our meal in the public soup kitchen, established in our old school gym. Standing in line, clutching my casserole and ration card, I listened to people speculating on the contents of the big containers: pureed tulip bulbs, the ubiquitous beets and grass. They were mostly right, but I once saw my mother crying out in shock and bursting into tears, when the ladle brought up a scrap of well-boiled piece of grayish fur with something like a tail. We did not eat that day.

On this Christmas Day, the metal bins actually proffered a mash of sauerkraut, potatoes and tiny shreds of meat *Weihnachten* bringing out the sentimental side of our occupiers, I imagine, but we accepted the miracle and were shamefully, hungrily grateful. My grandmother was a formidable matriarch who always managed to restore a sense of normality whenever my small world started to tilt and slide. Rustling long black silk skirts, she now sat at the head of the table; watching the plates with their wretched portions. She ate nothing and said nothing. My father watched his family, ate nothing and said nothing. Soon after that memorable meal, a decision was made.

Thousands of people were already fleeing our city, hoping to find some distance or shelter from hunger, sickness, air raids and fear with family or friends. The plan was for my father to take my two younger brothers, Gerrit and Dick, to friends in the country, hoping to leave them there until better times. Moreover, I was to go along for the ride, or rather, the walk. I have never really understood why. Did he initially mean to leave me there as well and things turned out differently? Did he need me, at the age of fifteen, as an older sister for the boys? Someone in case something happened to him? Someone to be there on the way back? I cannot remember asking then or later. As we set out on that bleak morning in early January, not one of us, not even my father, could really have known what was lying ahead of us. It was one of the coldest winters on record and would later be known as the *hungerwinter*, the Dutch famine of 1944–45, in which over twenty thousand people starved or froze to death.

We must have said goodbye, but I do not see us wave or the door close. First setback: our means of transportation, a rickety car with a few gallons of gas, paid for as the treasure it represented, did not appear to pick us up the meeting point, a few miles out of town. We soon realized there was no sense in waiting. We had some luggage we would not be able to carry very far and a small tin of cold boiled red beans as our only provision, but my father and I knew that at this point we could not turn back. It was sleeting, freezing, the water already soaking through our surrogate leather and cardboard shoes. In short, a situation so totally absurd, hopeless and miserable that for the first time I began to realize how desperate my parents must have been to consider such a plan.

We started walking, the first steps on a journey that would take us hundreds of miles through a war-torn countryside. Trudging day after day along nameless roads, along with other families loaded with their most cherished possession. People pushing baby carriages, the stronger encouraging the very old and very young, the children's frightened faces. All are familiar images today, where we see the fugitives of wars, earthquakes or floods, whenever we turn on the news. Back then, for us, living in a small, well-organized and recently prosperous country, it was a first time, firsthand. And what crushed us with calculated and deadly contempt was neither nature nor warring factions, but Nazi insanity.

We begged rides with trucks that ran on potbelly stoves burning firewood, slept in barns and empty classrooms, received shelter or continued our search. We were stopped by men in the black uniforms of the Organization TODD, hunting for foreign labor needed in German factories. My father had escaped the large November raid in Rotterdam, as he was over forty years old—the official limit being any fit male between sixteen and forty—but would that rule mean anything here, out developed a pitiful limp whenever anyone in uniform appeared in the vicinity. As we moved away from the larger towns and deeper into countryside less touched by war and occupation, we sometimes managed to buy some food, but the ever-hungry boys often suffered stomach cramps. The famous beans had long gone, mostly eaten by Gerrit during a miserable night spent in a schoolroom. A group of exhausted people sleeping on benches, head on folded arms or sitting on hard chairs against the wall, neck askew, mouth agape. It smelled of wet dog, of woolen socks drying near the only stove. My father told me later that he had seen the small hand repeatedly opening the bean tin, but he could not bring himself to stop the hungry child. I just felt a sort of wry acceptance. While scrounging for food I had already learned what hungry people do. Young Dick complained, loudly.

We traveled on through peaceful countryside, villages and forests with sudden stretches of purple heather and farms with low-slung thatched roofs. Scenery I had always associated with summer and holidays. The air smelled different and strangely familiar until I remembered that here fireplaces and stoves burned peat, neatly stacked blocks cut from the nearby bogs, the smoke spreading like a delicate veil over fields salt-white with frost. I also recognized the pungent smell of sugar beets boiling in bubbling cauldrons to make molasses, which had become a valuable barter item. It reminded me of rare Saturday treats when my father, who was an excellent cook, produced high stacks of the thinnest pancakes for us children.

Odd things happened. A small gray military car passed and stopped about a hundred yards ahead of us. A hand waved us on from an open window. I looked at my father, but it made no sense to run from a car on the open road, so we shuffled and stood. A uniformed arm reached out, opened the back door and a voice said in German, "Get in." Warily, the four of us squeezed into the back seats, not knowing what to expect. A big man of about fifty, gray-haired, the heavy silver chains of the German MP (Feld Gendarmerie) glinting on his chest, turned to look at us. "You looked as if you could use a ride. Where are you going?" Surprised and confused, I looked at my father, who nodded. I realized that he did not want to let on he understood perfectly, so I gave the name of a village in the direction of our travels, but not our real destination. The officer was delighted that I spoke German, and I will never forget that strange ride. It was as if we were traveling in a cocoon. No one mentioned war and hunger; no one asked why we were tramping down this winter road, obviously far from home. There was only this friendly, superficial conversation between two uniformed enemies and a young girl, about daughters, schools, snow and Christmas. And very long silences that made me think of thin ice over black running water. We passed through "restricted zones" that housed bases for the V1 rockets the German were firing at London and Antwerp at the end of the war. No one said as much, the officer just told us to slide down in our seats. Having taken us well over thirty miles, they let us off outside the village, as if they understood that stepping out of a German car would not endear us to the local population. We walked on in confused silence, as there was really nothing to say. We later realized that they actually had made a detour, leaving the main road to bring us closer to our destination.

The last part of the seemingly endless journey we spent in the back of an open milk truck.

Huddling together against the freezing wind we saw roads, farms and meadows go by, measuring every mile by what it would have meant to walk them. At a bridge, German soldiers stopped our car and ordered Gerrit, the taller one of my brothers, to get down. He fairly fell off the truck, too frozen to move a limb. My father, jumping down with him, immediately explained that the boy was not required to carry identification and too young to be taken for labor, but it took a lot of "*Schnell*" and "*Ausweis*" and "*Schweigen*" (yes, they did say things like that, just like in B movies) before we were allowed to continue on our way. After that encounter, the truck driver had no wish to get involved with any more authorities, so we walked the rest of the way. Our unsuspecting friends, who had received none of our letters accepting their offer of shelter, were all and more we could have hoped.

Once the boys were settled in, however, and we had recovered for a few days with decent food and sleep, my father saw we could not impose any further. Other refugees hidden in this and neighboring farms had a far greater need for protection and our presence could only put them at risk.

We set off together, facing the same road once again, this time walking several hundred miles not away from the war, but back to it. The strange thing is that on that desperate return journey I remember often being happy. I remember walking through forests magic with sunlight on snow-laden branches and singing birds. With some food in our bags, wearing old newspapers inside my layers of clothes, my wool cap topped by my father's fedora, I actually had a sense of well-being. There were moments I felt as if we were on some sort of a dreamlike adventure totally removed in time, with no connection to the real world, as if we could just keep on walking and surviving without ever having to reach a specific place. Alone, my father and I talked religion, history, dreams, music and family. He told me about joining up as a young officer, choosing to ship out to Indonesia mainly because men in our family always had. (A great-grandfather brought back an Indonesian wife, who bore him several children and died very young. I always thought it must have been the cold climate and all those big Dutch people.)

I told my father about school and friends, about my studies and my dislike of the church. "The promise of being reunited with those you have lost is a powerful thing," he answered. When I asked him if he believed in an afterlife, he said, "No, it is not something I count on. I have learnt to deal with my blessings and my losses here." I remembered then that, when a minister advised him after my mother's death to find comfort and consolation in prayer, my father supposedly answered: "Comfort is a warm bowl of soup on a cold winter night. Thank you for your visit."

On this, our only journey together, he was patient and sometimes very funny, and I loved him. For the first time in my life, we spoke about my mother. He told me small stories, details about the way she looked, that she spoke several languages and had a good singing voice. How she took my sister for a walk in the stroller and finding a set of keys on the street, duly took them to the police station only to find out when she arrived back home, that they were her own. Small and unimportant stories, but they made her come alive to me, who knew hardly anything about her. What surprised me was that she sounded so very young, which of course she was. I asked about the why of death and he gave me the classic answer: it gives meaning to life.

He told me about my maternal grandparents, whom I only vaguely remembered. "Your grandparents died several years ago. They were wonderful people; you should have been closer to them and I regret it. In the beginning it seemed that there would be room for all of us, but we grew apart." I understood, but even then, I did not touch on my relationship with my stepmother. Should I have accused my father? Brought up the petty injustices and the nagging unhappiness that made me feel more at home, more loved in my grandmother's house than in my own? Did he not know? How, coming home with my pocket money's ten cents bunch of flowers to apologize for talking back, or whatever the quarrel had been, I could still see her dump them in the trash can, hear the lid clanking and her voice, "Did you think it would be that easy?" My books and school papers thrown out onto the balcony the very day it rained, for not having cleaned up my room. Making me wear a horrid green dress, a re-made hand-me-down from an old spinster cousin, for weeks on end, every day again, until I refused to go to school in it. Had I really expected him to explain it all away? Why could I not tell him even then? Did it all seem pathetic, petty, once away from home and told aloud? Did I remember my own rebellious attitude? Was I afraid to break the spell?

We trudged on. At one point, my father bought two old bicycles, which should have been a great boon, but with the snow, the icy roads, and the freezing wind they soon became something we mostly pushed. Days were short and traffic almost nonexistent now. The war was intensifying and coming closer every day. Cut roads and blown-up bridges made for long detours in unfamiliar countryside. Thus came the inevitable evening when, having lost all sense of direction, we made a wrong turn and fell into a deep snow-covered ditch. I woke to see my father lying close by, his face covered with blood, his bicycle partly covering him. I clawed and crawled my way over to him, shouting and shaking his arm. When at last he opened his eyes, he told me to leave him there, to find the next village where I would be safe. I realized I could not possibly move him by myself. I do not want to remember the panic and desperation that made me climb out of the ditch and start walking. My pitiful little flashlight hardly helped, and I just stumbled along and called for help. Who or what sent the only farmer likely to be on the road in the entire region that evening? The clop-clop of the horse's hoofs seemed like a hallucination at first, but the cart came closer, its dangling lantern more miraculous than any star, the man a savior. We dragged my father and his bicycle into the cart, tied mine with a rope to the back, and I rode along, wobbling, tottering, pulled by the horse. Arrived at the farm we were fed bowls of soup, given blankets and a place to sleep in the barn. My father was hurt, but mostly he was totally exhausted. Lying buried in the hay next to the cows, their moving and chewing seemed the most reassuring sounds I had ever heard.

We continued our homeward journey, on foot, floating down a river in a leaky barge and riding a freight train that sat on a siding for hours to make room for troop trains. Allied planes duly strafed it and we jumped to safety. Huddled in the frozen grass we watched our train turn into an inferno of soaring flames and looked up at the endless flow of Allied planes on their way to bomb Germany. Caught in long streamers of light, in an assault of golden bubbles, they passed through the vault of the searchlights, trailing colored strings of flak. Every so often one would fall without a sound, streaking earthward like a flaming meteor. A bright, moonlit winter night, filled with horror and terrifying beauty. Saint-Exupery would write, "Each burst of a machinegun or rapid-cannon fire shot forth hundreds of these phosphorescent bullets that followed one another like beads on a rosary. The bullets were transformed into lightning. And I flew drowned in a crop of trajectories as golden as stalks of wheat. I flew at the center of a thicket of lance strokes. (…) Each square hit by a fragment of shell sank into the hull of the plane like a claw into living flesh. (…) What's that! The plane has been hit, rammed hard; I thought. It has burst, been ground to bits . . . but it hasn't; it hasn't . . ."

We arrived home, absurdly clutching a package of dry sausages and a small bag of cornmeal.

Looking back, it seems incomprehensible that my parents could have allowed it, but a few weeks later, I actually set out a second time on that very same journey. Our friends in the country sent a message that neighbors had offered to shelter my elder sister (also called Adry) and me. We were to return home, together with our brothers, once things got better.

It was a completely insane venture, but we both believed we could do it. The situation in the city continued to deteriorate day by day. We were young, two sisters together and I supposedly knew the way. This time, the two of us set out on one bicycle. A small suitcase was tied on the luggage rack of the back wheel, so whoever sat on it towered ridiculously high above the one who was peddling. The rear tire burst the very first day and an ingenious boy in a garage replaced it with a piece of bright green garden hose. Although two girls found shelter somewhat easier than a family of four, we were never sure of finding a place to sleep. Remembering a good, old-fashioned hotel from pre-war days, we found it closed, although the restaurant proudly offered a thin broth and a slice of bread, served *comme-il-faut* with small linen napkins and crystal glasses, for which they charged us most of our small fortune.

In a nearby town, a minister and his wife took us in for the night. They also served us a plate of stew and country bread, which was a wonderful treat but my stomach was no longer used to "real" food. It gave me terrible diarrhea. We slept on the third floor and the only toilet in the house was all the way downstairs. I have hardly ever felt as ashamed and humiliated as when my sister helped me crawl down the unlit, steep staircase, wiping them with an old newspaper. There were also small, ridiculous adventures, such as the time that we could not stop the bicycle and literally scooped up a German officer standing straddle-legged in a square. He was very young and the whole thing so obviously an accident that it had no further consequences. We were lucky and it could have been very different. Once, given shelter in a barn and sound asleep in the hay, the farmer walked in reeling drunk, thinking us an easy prey. All we could do was run away, shoes in hand and pushing the bicycle down the road.

We never reached the village of our friends. Arrested by soldiers at a roadblock for lacking any valid travel permits we were held in a schoolhouse with other people, some of whom had been caught with black market provisions. We had done nothing wrong and thought we would be let go the next day. But no, an army truck took four of us— two older women and ourselves—to a military field hospital, hidden in the forest near the German border, where we were set to work. During that time, I became familiar with fear and death, with hatred and compassion on a level far beyond my age and understanding. I was carrying buckets of bloody waste in makeshift operation rooms or following an elderly nurse on her night watch, walking through dark, barely lit rooms where the very air seemed to be sated with the terror, the nightmares and dreamscapes of feverish patients. I watched burned and mutilated young men—German soldiers and a few captive Allied pilots alike—hold on to life through long nights, only to let go toward morning. Heard them cry out in horror when the stump of an amputated leg moved by itself or the fact that they were blind suddenly struck home. Held a burn victim, wrapped in bandages like a mummy, who came stumbling out of his room into the lightless corridor, the only sounds his muffled moans and the crash of the inevitable fall. In this place, young men died agonizing deaths for the monstrous delusions of a mustached dictator in a brown shirt, a band with swastika around his arm. Our small world became a theater of human suffering where all in our closely shared nightmare simply lived from day to day, hoping to survive, and accepting that many would not. Between rounds, I would sit in the dark corridor, hands folded in my lap, trying to remember other places, and the voices of people who loved me. Dealing with these traumatized young men, I realized early on that my own fear was contagious and learned to control it. I did faint once, falling down a flight of stairs with a bucket of waste and landing on top of two corpses waiting for burial. I was so young; it simply made for coarse jokes and friendly ridicule by the rest of the staff.

There was a young German soldier, a wounded and shell-shocked patient, who often disappeared and roamed the woods. He would come in for food at odd hours, wearing parts of his uniform mixed with pieces of civilian clothing. During the night shifts, I had sometimes seen him sitting at a patient's bedside, singing softly, or just wandering through the halls, talking to himself. Some called him a deserter while others just shrugged their shoulders, but no one really paid much attention to him. One early evening, walking to our sleeping quarters along the narrow path that skirted the forest, something hit me very hard in the back and slammed me to the ground. When I came to, the boy was tearing at my clothes and raping me. He was very strong, his blue eyes crazed, saliva and sweat were dripping on my face, and his gun was squashed on my chest between us. It was over in minutes. Standing above me, he fastened his belt and reached down to help me up. The gesture was made in a totally matter-of-fact way, neither friendly nor threatening. He gave me a little push with his gun into the direction I had come from, turned his back on me and walked away. I remember looking down and seeing my underpants caught around my ankle. Shaking them off, I left them lying in the road, but after a few steps I actually went back and, in some crazy sense of propriety, stuffed them in my pocket. Hurt, dazed and frightened, my face and hands scraped and bleeding from my fall on the gravel, I stumbled back to the hospital, found an empty room, an empty bed, and huddled under the covers until morning. I did not tell anyone. I had no one to tell. My sister Adry was a kind-hearted girl who panicked easily and although she was the older, I had more often been the one to comfort her. I did not quite take in what had happened to me and I had no way of putting all this into perspective. Against the fabric of our daily lives, woven from suffering, fear, mutilation and death, it must have seemed of little importance. I said I had tripped on the path in the dark and did not tell anyone. I did not know how. Not then. Not until I realized I was pregnant. A German doctor performed the abortion on a table in a small outbuilding and I had no idea what he did, nor did I allow myself to think about it afterwards. It seemed to me I was watching from a distance, from somewhere outside the room, like something that did not really concern me. I was back at work the next day. My sister was in shock and cried for days and the few people who knew sympathized with me, but in a place where doctors and nurses lacked the most basic supplies to save limbs and lives, a simple interrupted pregnancy did not make great waves. A minor event, and dealt with. Most people knew about the deranged boy; we sometimes heard him empty his gun at his private demons alone in the woods at night. Now, because of me, they would be a little more careful when walking the short distance to the other buildings.

I never saw him again, and I, too, believed I had put that experience behind me, safely wrapped, sealed and buried. I had washed off the stickiness and a little blood, I had an abortion and the issue was closed. I was convinced of that until, many years later, on a peaceful Sunday morning at the Gare d'Austerlitz in Paris, an ambling drunk stumbled into me, pushing me hard from behind. The next thing I knew, the man was lying on the floor, while I kept hitting him over and over with my umbrella, cursing him in *German*. Bystanders took me away, shaking, retching.

I realized that I had not really come to terms with that part of my past after all.

The months went by, carrying the rumors of Allied victories. We knew the war was truly over when most of the German staff fled overnight, taking those patients that could be moved, to make their way across the nearby border. The next day Canadian tanks and soldiers on heavy motorcycles—the young men on the motorcycles again—entered the courtyard of the hospital. Adry and I were asked to stay on as translators while waiting for some organization to help us get home. This time we did not have the courage to face the chaos that was waiting out there. When I caught a cold that developed into pneumonia, the Canadian army doctor gave me a thorough checkup. A young, compassionate woman, she asked questions, and I told her my story. She assured me that the abortion had left no permanent damage. She also said I had gonorrhea. Two days later, she handed my sister the signed and stamped approval forms for our repatriation through Red Cross channels. To me, as behooved a true fairy, she gave me a small glass tube filled with a newly discovered magic potion, called penicillin.

Entered in the system for displaced persons, we were shuttled from camp to camp, sleeping on straw in churches and schools, sharing food with people newly freed from labor camps, from forced work in German arms factories or coming out of hiding after months or years of underground existence. Until finally, one early evening, we descended from yet another truck in our damaged and liberated city. Typically, at one point I had leaned out of the back to look where we were going and hit my head at a gatepost. I therefore arrived home with a tremendous black eye, just turning purple and yellow.

In those early post-war years, life went on or started anew. Most people managed to fit in, their past nicely dealt with or not. My brother Cees came home and joined the navy. My sister's fiancé had returned from forced labor in Germany and they were getting married. They seemed happy and full of hope for the future. For me, life at home had not become easier, my stepmother no more able to accept me now than she did before. People around me did not seem to realize that I was no longer a child. I had seen things many adults never imagined and sometimes felt as if I did not really have the right to be still alive. There were now two kinds of people: those who had gone through too much and others whom the war had more or less passed by. As for me, of all the things I lived through few had marked me as deeply as having seen my father give in, if even for a moment, to despair. What made it so hard, his despair had also been mine.

SWITZERLAND

Ivan Doggwiler

I continued to live at home, but did not have a close relationship with my younger half siblings. Actually, we would not really get to know each other until we were all adults, married with children and living very different lives. At the time, I stayed apart. I was growing a shell of self-discipline over a barely controlled chaos. Until one evening at dinner, my brother asked me to pass a plate and I burst into tears, lost in such wretchedness, I could not stop crying. My parents could not understand: the war was over and life was getting back to normal, so w*hy was she crying now?* I went to stay with my grandparents, who might not understand either, but at least did not patronize me as a hysterical schoolgirl.

Not long after, friends introduced me to a young man from Switzerland, a young man different from any I had met. Clean-cut, handsome, well dressed and intelligent, Ivan talked ideas, books and travel, a world I had only dreamt about. He asked questions, but had no real relationship to our everyday life, to the things we lived with or still did without. He was quite simply *Swiss*. He was doing research for a story on the occupation, and I showed him what war and the Germans had done to my city. For a week, we saw each other every day and I tried to explain what I could. We went for walks and talked for hours, fell in love and wrote long letters after he left. Soon, ready for a new life, I traveled to Switzerland on an au pair student visa.

The young couple I worked as an au pair for owned a bookstore and had two small children. They were kind and tried to make me feel at home. The woman taught me how to prepare Swiss dishes, took me on excursions and to local theater performances. It was an odd, but pleasant experience to live in a small Swiss village, where nothing much happened. I had never seen real mountains before. Now I learned to ski. As was the custom with au pair girls, I went to school part time and had time free on weekends to spend with Ivan. I had never known young girl's romance and my only experience with sex had been anything but romantic. I had dated, danced and dined, but shied away from any closer contact. Leaving my country made it easier to cross more than one border. We were young, he was my first lover, and we were happy. Still, I never told him or anyone else about the rape.

I met his parents, who were not thrilled with the idea of a foreign daughter-in-law. From them I learned that his name was really Johann and that he changed it to press home his pro-communist leanings. Just recently, attending a youth forum in Prague and speaking at a conference, Ivan had made unflattering remarks about Switzerland. The newspapers back home had picked it up and blasted his disloyalty to his country, which did not go over well with the family. To me, he shrugged it off as unimportant and as I never saw him take any strong political stand after that, I believe the whole thing was a passing phase, meant to *épater les bourgeois*. He did not turn back into a Johann, however.

We married in a simple ceremony and moved to a small town called Solothurn. I learned to speak Swiss German, traveled the country and made new friends. It was a very different life from what

I left behind. Ivan worked at the local newspaper, and I found a job at the library. I also volunteered as an extra in the opera, singing in the choir, bustling about on stage, feeling important and very pleased with myself. I was nineteen years old. Leaving a war-torn country for Switzerland was both a dream come true and a real culture shock. Everything here was whole and beautiful. I walked wide boulevards with luxurious shops, the parks were full of flowers and the lakeshores housed clean, happy ducks. I saw an unscarred world filled with well-behaved, well-dressed and well-fed people, who were at times somewhat self-satisfied and even a little smug. I was not uncomfortable with them. The discrepancy was between having lived with death on intimate terms and worrying about the niceties within Swiss society. I was truly grateful to be here, but the experiences I could not accommodate into my new life sometimes bred a feeling of impatience, a slight disdain even, toward the smooth and polished environment. People told me with great sincerity how difficult the war had been, living with rationed coffee and only a few eggs a week. Young and curious, I soon discovered there were many things that were "not done" and at my age found it difficult to conform to any rules when I had seen all my childhood principles ignored, broken or betrayed for the most conflicting reasons. Life had taught me different values from those considered acceptable in Switzerland at the time. Without an established, conventional framework, I was left to rebuild what had gone or search for one of my own making.

Ivan had visited my ruined hometown. He had written an article on how the Germans, realizing the war was lost, systematically mined Rotterdam's harbors, intending to eliminate the long-standing rival of Hamburg and Bremen. Could I therefore expect him to understand what it was like to live one's childhood in an occupied country? How could I explain memories I lived with but could not share? Ivan and I went to see a movie about children growing up in London during the war. A girl stood in a ruined street amidst piles of rubble; balconies were hanging by a beam and collapsed walls showed rooms with furniture like a look-through dollhouse. I watched the screen and the stench of what burned in those houses stung my throat. I remembered the touch of cold wet ashes and felt again my own desolation, standing under a drizzling rain from such a grey sky. Could anyone who had not been there feel that way? It made for loneliness at times.

I had left my country willingly, even gladly, but in doing so I had stepped out of the charmed circle, the *we*, the *us* and the *ours*. I did not realize at the time that from here on I would always be a foreigner. I never again lived in a country of "my own." I think my roots started to spread sideways rather than reaching down, more like a strawberry plant than a carrot. Close friends became as important as family. Colors, sounds and smells replaced the flag. Even today, I find it easier to ask friends who live a thousand miles away for a favor than to knock at a neighbor's door. At the inevitable Where are you from?" I tend to feel a small, silent shudder. I feel as if people are really asking "Who are you?" and to that I have no simple answer.

Meanwhile, everyday life was pleasant enough. We were a young Swiss couple with now two small children, Cathy and Marc, earning enough to pay for babysitters and buying free time to spend evenings with friends. I spoke the language fluently and we had moved to Bern, thinking a larger city might be more exiting to live in. Ivan again worked at the local newspaper, I again in a library, of the university this time, and went to evening classes. I modeled on runways when the fashion shows came to town, typed theses for medical students, and translated film scripts for pennies. Bern in the fifties was very much alive, a center of existentialism as Zurich had been of Dada, and the theater was as avant-garde as one could find anywhere in Europe. The German versions of Eugène Ionesco's *"La cantatrice chauve"* and Picasso's *"Le désir attrapé par la queue"* saw their first performances on the small stage of the Kleintheater in the Kramgasse. Ivan did the photography and I helped with stage design and costumes. We had a large circle of friends and there were always things to do, places to go. I sang in a small jazz band, just for fun, and

all of us went to hear American musicians like Bill Coleman and
Joe Turner, who played in the fancy Chiquito club, but would come
downtown afterwards to jam in a basement until morning. Joe became
a good friend and we spent time together going to the flea market,
visiting galleries or having a sausage with Swiss *rösti*. (Thirty years
later, I would see him in a piano bar in Paris and tried to remind
him of those early Swiss days and our favorite song. He smiled a
faraway smile, and continued playing with one hand—the famous
left—holding a full glass in the other.)

I mostly liked living in Bern and still tend to think of it as a
reassuring place, its history alive in medieval towers and Renaissance
doors, in richly carved facades and windows overlooking stone-basin
fountains. Walking home on late winter nights, the pierced arches of
our covered sidewalk throwing a scalloped light on the snow-hushed
street, it became a world of timeless beauty. The old town, where we
lived, was the center of the city's social life. We met our friends in the
Café de Commerce, a small restaurant tucked away behind the old
clock tower in the Rathausgasse, where through the centuries people
hurrying by have looked up to see the turning bronze figures strike
the carillon. Run by two Portuguese ex-waiters who knew absolutely
everything about everybody, it served the best entrecôtes in town. The
clients were mainly local artists, writers, actors and musicians. Meret
Oppenheim would be there and Jean Tingueli, or Friedrich Dürrenmatt,
who had just scandalized the public with his play *It Is Written.* Not long
ago someone sent me a book that called our fifties Bern's "wild years."
I did not think them wild, but there was a sense of urgency in the air,
of exuberance. People created and experimented. For a costume party,
Meret sewed me into a black cat outfit that I had to wear for two straight
days: there was no way to take it off without cutting it up and nobody
wanted to ruin it. It was quite beautiful and, had I saved it, might have
earned its place next to her fur teacup in the MOMA.

Some of the friendships continue today. My friend Idh has been
like a sister to me since I can remember and it has never changed.

For morning coffee and croissants, I would often go to the local café, throwing dice for the bill with Sonia. Blond, beautiful, she might walk in, fur coat over long flannel nightgown and slippers. In bourgeois Bern. She later moved to Italy, acted in Cinecitta and married Boris Carmeli, a successful opera singer; they live happily in Rome, and we are still close friends. Boris was born in Eastern Europe. His parents fled the Nazis to Italy where the boy Boris was caught in a raid, shipped to Drancy in France and from there to Auschwitz. Tall and strong for his age, he was set to work and survived. He went to Israel, studied music in Milan and settled in Rome. A few years ago, he was invited to sing for the Pope, and I saw the concert. When it was his turn to be introduced and kiss the papal ring, Boris gently pushed up the sleeve of his tuxedo jacket, presenting instead his bare forearm with the tattooed number of his concentration camp youth.

It was in Bern that I first became interested in photography. Steffi was a German-Jewish orphan adopted by a wealthy Swiss family. Bright, funny, she was also an excellent commercial photographer. As she did not like to work alone in public places, she dragged me along to photograph store windows, expensive cars, or people trying out some new American product. I learned more from working with her than I did later in photography courses. Lesbian, a curious mixture of shy and outrageous, she had her own private circle of friends besides our larger group. In those pre-AIDS days, most of our crowd smoked, drank and slept around and no one judged the other's lifestyle, unless it made for some good gossip. Steffi got involved with group sex and drugs, appearing late mornings looking gray, depressed and totally disgusted with herself. "What is it about handcuffs, coke and whips? I don't get any pleasure out of it, I think that bourgeois crowd is a hypocritical bunch of perverts and still I end up there," she would say, hugging her first beer.

One evening shortly before Christmas, she joined us in the Commerce and asked if anyone could lend her some loose change. "What for?" said an American student friend, rummaging through his pockets. "For my gas stove," she said. "It works with coins and I only have two francs. It won't be enough to commit suicide." Laughter, applause and exit. Toward morning, the police woke me up: neighbors had smelled gas, and our friend was dead. The parents came to bury her. Nice, straightforward people who had given her a good education, a generous allowance and were proud of her slick ads in the glossy magazines. They blamed themselves. They could not possibly have imagined the world in which this daughter had gone astray, and none of us tried to explain. I too blamed myself. We all did.

Ivan and I played house, but the more we learned about each other the more we realized how unsuited we were as partners. People do meet, by chance, fall in love—or think they do—and marry. An ardent reader of Nietzsche and Schopenhauer, he accepted mainly their negative attitude, the "what wants to fall, one should also push" theory, whereas I am less inclined to give wobbly things the final shove. The breakup was hardly due to a different childhood or philosophy alone, but the result of a day-by-day disastrous process. The time came when we barely talked, where he chose to work nights, whereas I turned to my own work, friends and to my children. I was not a born mother, but I loved my children and made every effort to be what they needed. Cathy and Marc were loved and well cared for. They were also far too young to understand the falling apart of our marriage.

Ivan had often talked of working in the French cinema noir. I suggested therefore that we should move to Paris, where he could study film and we could both find some work. His reaction was total refusal, mixed with a deep resentment about "being stuck with a family." He began to drink in weekend binges and became violent. I started, even then, to write about my childhood experiences, only to be told, "What makes you think you can write? You always think you can do anything." Which was of course exactly how I did feel. I was young, curious about life and still full of hope. Why should I not believe that I "could do anything"? We stayed together mostly because neither one knew how to make a fresh start. Bound in a web of mutual hostility we seemed to be unable to stop this sliding into nowhere. We were now just two people who were bad for each other. He slept with our babysitter and spent weekends away from home. There was an issue of group sex, which I refused to take part in and turned my dislike for him into revulsion. Instead, I took lovers of my own.

I did not talk of this with my friends. There was a rather rough workmen's bar a few houses down the street, and I fell into the habit of sitting by myself at a small corner table and writing letters to Adry, my aunt and confident back in Holland. Sitting there, drinking beer and chasers like the rest of the clients, I was slowly sinking into a depression. There came the day the police picked up my husband for suicidal behavior on a bridge, the day he set fire to our library, the evening he took the sleeping children in the car and drove off like a demon. There was the winter evening—the children spending a rare weekend with the grandparents in Lucerne—when coming home from the theater I faced a locked front door, the key not in its usual place. It was near midnight and very cold. A dark-haired woman stood under the arch and said, "I saw your handsome husband leaving, but he was not alone. Why don't you come with me?" I knew she lived next door, we had exchanged good-mornings at the bakery, but I did not know her or anything about her. Making coffee, she offered, "You can stay here, but when I have a client you'll have to wait downstairs." It was too cold for her to wait long and clients were scarce, so we spent the night talking.

Not long after a friend suggested casually that I might want to give away my cat. My cat?? He refused to say more and I shrugged it off until some weeks later, I found the bedspread torn and the kitten missing. I discovered its broken body in the trash can. I stood staring at my small pet, its eyes half closed, its shiny fur matted and all life gone. That night, facing my empty marriage, I finally accepted that this was madness. Who was this person? If he could do this thing, he was capable of hurting the children. Everything that had once been worth holding on to now was soiled, broken and degraded. The only thing I regretted was that I had taken this long to accept it.

I managed to reorganize my life, moved to Zurich with my children and filed for a divorce. Taking the sole responsibility for our lives was at once terrifying and exhilarating, like getting on your skis for a steep run down an unknown trail. It set me free.

I had known Hubert for years; we were the same age and had the same friends. Bachelor, a collector rather than an artist, he lived within a few minutes' walk from us, in another one of Bern's arched-covered streets. Our affair did not cause the breakup, but without him it would have been longer and uglier. He helped me move to Zurich, where I found an apartment in Küsnacht, a pretty village on the lake just a few miles outside the city. The rooms were large and sunny, there were trees all around; we were living in the countryside with the city but minutes away. Ivan never paid the child support the judge had ordered and I did not ask for it. It was probably the wrong decision but somehow I was too proud to ask for money from a man for whom I now had no respect and with whom I wanted no contact. I first worked as a model for the couturier Jacques Heim, but soon took a job with Swissair that allowed me to work evening shifts and be home part of the day. Akka, my young Dutch cousin, came to live with us, taking care of Cathy and Marc. She loved the children and we became a new family. The children seemed happy in their new nursery school and loved living so close to the lake. Just below our building stood an old landing jetty from where we could wave to the ferry. It was not an official stop, but if the captain saw you and was in the right mood, he would steam over and pick you up. The children would jump up and down, wave and holler and thought it total victory if they made the boat turn our way. It was a new life, with new and innocent pleasures.

I liked Zurich with its lake and snowcapped mountains. It was cosmopolitan and overall more tolerant of foreigners than bureaucratic Bern. The universities made their impact felt with a diversity of young people, whereas luxurious shops and restaurants catered to wealthy clients and the old part of town hid a motley selection of small theaters, galleries, clubs and crowded cafés.

It was also a city of bells. Besides the blue tramways clanging their way through traffic, church bells chimed every fifteen minutes and, to make sure, they told the hour every hour on the hour. Nowhere else have I been so constantly reminded of time passing, of what I was to do next, when, and where, by bells. One cold winter morning I crossed the Münsterhof square with its old church. The lowering sky was the color of lead, as were the cobblestones and the church walls. The trees were bare and the whole scene had the feeling of a faded print. There was not a breath of wind and in that peculiar Sunday stillness, the first loud clang of a bell was almost like a physical assault. Within seconds, others joined in and suddenly the air was full of sound. These bells, however, were not dutifully counting the hours. Here master ringers were wielding centenarian giants, raising the deep bronze voices in harmony or leaving the high treble soaring above, to create a moment of near perfection. The bells sang in jubilation, they spoke of victory and defeat, of hope and faith, tolled everlasting life and the darkness of death. The few passersby stood like children, wrapped in furs and scarves, awed faces uplifted to the blue spire above. It went on for a long time. When the final trembling echoes faded on the air, the bruised skies released their burden and the first white flakes began their soft, slow descent to earth.

Hubert, running the family business, continued to live in Bern but we spent most weekends together. Successful and kind, this man protected, spoiled and encouraged me. I had always liked him immensely and now it was easy to love him. If at times I felt a soupçon of apprehension about being seduced into the polite world of "that is not really done, you know," I did not despise the bourgeois Swiss way of living. He was patient with my mood swings and my at times flippant remarks, which mostly stemmed from insecurity. I could not yet say, "Yes, please teach me. I don't really think I know everything better, I am just afraid to get hurt." Hubert liked my children, they accepted him, and we spent family-style weekends. We hiked in the mountains with his sister, had dinner with his parents in their pretty castle outside

Bern and visited his brother, a well-known painter who lived in France. Everybody was nice to each other and we were now legitimatized. The two of us also spent a week in Mallorca. Beautiful, still unspoiled Mallorca, where I had no premonition of the important role that island would play in my life. Meanwhile, we talked marriage and went to see an old mansion for sale near Interlaken, where we climbed the steps to the tower, explored the gardens that ran down to the lake and wandered through the empty rooms, deciding who would sleep where. A new life was asking to be lived and I truly believed I was happy.

And then I met a man whom I would love until the end of his life and who would change mine. The meeting was casual and friendly. A delayed Swissair plane and an American journalist who rated VIP care, which made him part of my job. No more than on my visit to Mallorca did guardian angels warn me of things to come or tell me to pass this stranger on to others. Instead, we talked. "Look what I found at the flea market," he said. I had never seen an eighteenth-century Benin warrior statue before and it must have shown, for I received a short lecture on African art. Maybe not love at first sight, but an immediate interest and a fast growing fascination. Fred lived in New York, but was producing a series of children's records in Zurich and spending a fair amount of time there. We met again, talked, went for dinner, made love and it became clear that whatever attracted us to each other was not going away. He went back to New York. Time difference and three-minute midnight overseas phone calls slowed down decisions and at the same time made them inevitable. Filled with guilt, I agonized over my disloyalty, the fate of my children and this new, overwhelming love. I was getting married to Hubert, Fred was living with someone else; it was all wrong. Still, nothing seemed more important than being together. And thus, one day soon, I cried my heart out saying goodbye to my perfect lover-friend, the mansion on the lake and my sheltered Swiss future to follow an American, a man I loved, but barely knew.

NEW YORK AND BEYOND

Fred Grunfeld

My introduction to New York was my new husband's apartment on 79th Street and Fifth Avenue, steps away from Central Park and the Metropolitan Museum. At the time, I had no idea what a privileged location that represented. Actually, I had still to learn whom I had married in New York City Hall on that rainy November morning. Fred Grunfeld was born in Berlin, where the family's business, with its linen mills in Bohemia, had been supplier to the emperor and chancellors for generations. A prominent Jewish family, one of the pillars of the cultural establishment, it had seemed unthinkable that they could be threatened by the up-and-coming Hitler madness. It made of course no difference at all. They stayed on until it was almost too late, while the house on the Tiergartenstrasse, the Kurfürstendam store with its famous staircase published in architectural magazines, all went the Nazi way. (Today, the Berlin Museum shows pictures of the store and the role it played in the city's cultural history.) The family arrived in New York only to find that the person in charge of their security, the person they had trusted, had betrayed them. Their funds were nonexistent.

From the age of ten, Fred grew up in the Kew Garden section of Queens, went to Chicago University and came back to New York. A sort of wunderkind, he ran a music program on WQSR radio and wrote for various magazines. On our first visit, he was working during the day and I ventured out on my own into this incredible, outrageous, beautiful city. I walked, rode buses, ferries and subways, each day bringing new discoveries. In the evenings, we met up with his friends. I had already met Lawrence and Edith Malkin, who had been the witnesses at our marriage and became my lifelong friends as well. Larry, a journalist at *Time* magazine, had gone through high school and college with Fred. We went to Carnegie Hall and Broadway shows, visited the Cloisters, ate hot dogs at a stand in the "village," or dinner on the roof of a skyscraper looking out over myriad lights. The short visit was like a ride on a high-speed merry-go-round and when time came to go back to Europe, I took with me impressions and memories of a world beyond my imagination.

We returned to Zurich and the recording project, renting a 1930s villa in the residential Dolder area. My cousin Akka continued to live with us and looked after Cathy and Marc, who now went to preschool. Giving up my job at Swissair, I joined the production team and turned out to have an unexpected talent for editing tape and inventing sound effects. It had never occurred to me before that a wet chamois cloth on a window might sound like a creaking pump, or a steam iron like an old locomotive. The records taught children through games and folk songs about such things as Great Composers, Wheels and Wings, or the Mississippi. We all enjoyed making them and some of the young American and British artists we discovered went on to make a career in the opera or popular music. To save studio costs we often recorded at home, and several times, when we lacked a singer, I stood in and sang the songs. We led a busy life. Among other things, Fred was correspondent for *Opera News*, which meant we saw just about every performance of the season. We usually left early so he could write the review, leaving me to wonder how the story ended.

Music became part of my life. I had been mostly ignorant of anything beyond some jazz and Mozart, Bach or Beethoven; now there was every kind of music around me and from here on, I would never be without again.

I became part of a large, active Anglo-American community in Zurich and spoke English most of the time. It was a strange sensation to be suddenly regarded as a foreigner, belonging to "them" and therefore not bound to Swiss standards. It had taken me several years to speak Swiss-German fluently, to blend in, and I had sometimes wondered whether I really wanted to become a nice, respectable Swiss citizen. Now I found myself, willy-nilly, continuously translating behavior codes between two groups of people, understanding both, liking both, but not really belonging to either. Be careful what you wish for.

Mallorca

Marc and Foster

Cathy and Laura

Moochen

In the spring of 1961, because it had been raining in Zurich for the last year, or so it seemed, we decided to visit a musician friend in Mallorca. While Akka and the children were visiting family in Holland, Fred and I drove to Spain. We took the overnight ferry from Barcelona to Palma and looked for a village called Deia. The narrow road skirted a coastline broken by rocky headlands and small carpets of beach, more guessed at than seen. When it turned inland we saw, on a hilltop perched between the mountain and the sea, a small medieval Bethlehem crowned by its church. Caught in the late afternoon sun, the houses glowed warm ochre, the mountain wall behind them flamed a deep red, below us the sea stood blue and still. We walked the steep streets, past stone houses shaded with vines, through olive groves dappled with orange trees, under arches of dark carobs and silver-gray fig trees with luminous new leaves shining like small candles. The path led ever down to the rocky *cala*, one of the more inaccessible and beautiful rock-strewn beaches on the coast. Its water was transparent, the green-blue of dreams, a gentle surf grated on the beach, smoothing pebbles into gems. It was early May, the little torrent was still cascading over its stony bed in its rush down to the sea, small birds were singing and somewhere faroff a mule brayed. There was a smell of warm earth, a heady scent of things green and growing that filled the senses. That is how I remember our arrival and I have never wondered how it came about that we simply stayed on, rented a house and sent for our various children from various marriages, leaving our New York and Zurich city-lives behind to be sorted out long distance. We took it together: a crazy, impulsive step that would change our lives.

We decided that Fred's two children should join us. Living with their mother had turned out to be problematic and Fred could hardly learn to love mine while constantly worrying about his own. Soon Foster, aged eight, and Laura, five, arrived from Massachusetts with their grandmother, Fred's mother, whom we all called Moochen. In the beginning, it was not exactly a smooth ride. In Zurich, my children had begun to accept Fred as their new father figure. He had been divorced for several years and had not seen Foster and Laura often. They now reclaimed him as their own, as was natural. They also saw Cathy and Marc as rivals and me as the intruding stranger, which was just as natural. Moochen was an important unifying factor, the grandmother from New York who knew Switzerland well and spoke German. An exceptional woman, she had taken one look at the situation and embraced us all. She and I took one good look at each other and hugged. We would do so for many years to come.

The language barrier was real. All four children could communicate with the grown-ups but not with each other. Foster and Laura spoke only English; Cathy and Marc had grown up speaking German and Swiss-German; our new German au pair (Akka returned to live in Holland) knew five words of English, while the cook was from Galicia and ruled in Spanish. Fred and I spoke those languages well enough to keep our mini Tower of Babel going, but as soon as anyone left the house, the local Mallorquin was thrown in for good measure. (A form of Catalan, it is closer to *langue d'oc* than to

Spanish, somewhat in the way that medieval Swiss-German relates to German proper. It also seemed full of strange piercing sounds many of which can be traced to centuries of Moorish population.) The children learned fast and in an odd way, the confusion helped to draw them together. To the outside world, in school and at play, they were brothers and sisters, belonging to a family. At home—the girls sharing one room, the boys another—the configuration had also shifted. Each child was living with a new parent and a new country; together we went through the process of adaptation and in the large old house with its abandoned garden, we became a family. Hardly a family in the classic mold, but a family just the same.

School started and the children made friends, all the while babbling among themselves in five tongues. It might well have become a handicap for life, but although there were some learning problems, they all ended up fluent in several languages. At times, we worried about our uprooted offspring, but I came to believe with Nathaniel Hawthorne that "[h]uman nature will not flourish, any more than a potato, if it be planted and replanted for too long a series of generations in the same worn-out soil." We watched them grow, each of them a different little person. Foster, dark-haired, and very American, was the best student, but also loved setting out at dawn with the local fishing boats. Marc, the youngest, blond, skinny and solitary, raised silkworms and invented complicated irrigation systems in the backyard. Laura, watching the world with her almond-shaped eyes, loved to draw and followed Moochen around. Pretty Cathy, somewhat fragile because of her asthma, was the child who brought home stray kittens, took cello lessons and learned to make lace. She tried to teach me, but I kept tangling up all the little bobbins and she gave up in disgust. On weekends, we packed picnic baskets and went hiking in the mountains or taught the children to swim in the transparent waters of the *cala*. We were all surprised to find how few local children—and adults for that matter—knew how to swim or came down to the beach for pleasure. On these islands, before tourism changed all that, the sea was regarded mainly as a resource, a way of life and often as a formidable and unforgiving enemy.

On Sundays, we baked pancakes for breakfast or invited friends for big lunches and helped the children finish their homework for next morning's school day. We were all getting used to each other, but I will always remember the day Foster acknowledged me in my role. Pretending to look for something, he shouted "*MOM*, have you seen . . .?" and looked at me with a small hesitant smile. My heart skipped a few beats, I found what had never been lost, and we sealed our victory with a hug. As if they had been waiting for a signal, the others quickly followed and Fred became Dad to all. They would still argue and complain about each other and about us, but they formed a phalanx against the outside world. A rather normal family, after all. As for Moochen, small, silver-haired, elegant and city-bred, she surprised us all by soon being on the best terms with what seemed the entire village, conversing with neighbors and shopkeepers in some sort of Spanish, the inimitable accent all her own. She did have some trouble getting used to the local people putting their heads around the kitchen door, shouting "Hail Mary the Purest!" at the top of their voice, to which one was supposed to holler back "Conceived without Sin." The children loved it, but all through our Deia years, I heard Moochen's polite answer, "Please, do come in."

More remote than the mainland, Mallorca was frugal even by post-war European standards. In the village, most people still cooked on charcoal and drew water from the well. A rundown generator produced our local electricity, which came on for a few hours after dark, after which it would flicker two or three times to give us time to light our candles. Once a day the old bus bumped along the narrow road to Palma, twenty-five kilometers away, where the whole family went to the Saturday market. We treated the children to pizza and ice cream and then took them to the flea market, letting them search for small treasures. The open market offered meat, fresh fish and vegetables, while a small supermarket sold olive oil and lard, but there was no butter, yoghurt or bottled milk.

In Deia, we made do with the services the village offered. In odd places. People had their hair cut at the post office because the Castor de mailman was the only barber in the village. We bought stamps at the grocery store because the owner had bought the rights from the government many years ago. We bought our lamb chops at the telephone office, which was run by the local butcher. Early mornings, at the sound of the fisherman blowing his conch shell, we ran to buy his day's catch. Most of the island relied on the staples it produced, as it had done for centuries. Mallorquin cooking is simple. I fondly remember the foggy winter evenings when a dozen of us would settle around the wood stove in the local *pension*, and the owners would come up with some memorable soups, roast, stews and desserts.

This marriage and this husband's trust in my capacities freed me of self-doubts. For the first time I felt it was all right to ask questions, to make mistakes, to think "that I could do anything" and yes, to be happy. An established writer and journalist, Fred was also a musicologist, an art historian and amateur architect, someone born with that contagious intellectual curiosity that considers nothing too small or too obscure to be worth exploring. His knowledge, linked with a sense of adventure and an innate irreverence for institutions, opened a world of possibilities. Life was again full of challenges and soon we would meet them together, in a way of life I had not dared to imagine since childhood: to live and work with a lover who was a born teacher. I watched his enthusiasm and generosity in dealing with young people. Tall, handsome, erudite and witty, with an easy laugh, he always searched for common ground. His suggestions mostly started with "Why don't you," meaning, let's find a way for you to do what you really want. And many did.

Between us, there was such ease and trust it felt as if we were one person. I always knew when he entered a room and when I looked up his smile would meet me. For the first time in my life, I had the sense of being where I belonged. I had a family who I loved and where I was wanted. It enfolded me like a warm blanket, allaying ugly memories of a disastrous first marriage. Did I ever ask myself whether all this could last? If I saw small signs, the burden of balancing work and home, Fred's occasional impatience with the slow pace and responsibilities of a large family, his attraction to very young women, I disregarded them the way I discounted the scars of my childhood. I needed to believe that from now on this was to be my life and did not allow myself to think that minor flaws might affect the future. Not now. I had taken a leap of faith.

In our small village, everybody knew everybody and people soon made a point of knowing everything about us. They must have had a great time figuring out who was who in our extended family. Moochen, whom I loved dearly and trusted completely, looked after the everyday things together with Antonia, our housekeeper, who was also our key to the village. Our Antonia, who kept her twice-baked zwieback wrapped in clean linen inside a kitchen drawer, who curdled the milk with a twig from the fig tree to make fresh cottage cheese (as was done here since Homer's time), to be served for breakfast with whatever fruit ripened that week in the terraced gardens. Who, as a second mother to the children, checked behind their ears, dried their laundry on rosemary bushes and ironed even their underwear.

At the time, Mallorca was not expensive. I can think of few places as convenient and as beautiful where we could have afforded to live this comfortably on moderate earnings. While living in the rented house we started to look around to buy our own. The local people were not yet interested in a property that had been roofless for the last forty years and where a tree was growing out of the main room. The exchange rate between the peseta and the dollar allowed us to buy a cluster of four small, partly ruined houses for less than it had cost us to rent the house in Zurich for a year. The village watched and decided foreigners were mad. We hired masons from among the neighbors, some of whom became close friends, especially Antonio, who was our housekeeper's brother.

The project became a family experience, where we all learned about building and about each other. The children cleaned the bamboo to cover the roofs, helped to whitewash the walls, the ceilings and wide Mallorcan arches leading from one room to the next. Fred and I went hunting for furniture, old beams, tiles, windows and doors. We all gathered smooth round pebbles on the beach to lay the mosaic floor in the kitchen or carried the terra-cotta tiles up narrow ladders to the roof, where Antonio placed them in regular, beautifully curved rows. We finished the staircases and the stone kitchen bench with flowered tiles baked centuries ago, repaired the old cistern to hold the rainwater, planted the garden and built tables with large stone slabs of abandoned oil presses. When all was done, we moved into our large rabbit warren called the Castillo, where only a few of the thirteen rooms were on the same level. The children chose their own rooms, furnished with objects they had helped find in antique stores and in the Saturday-morning flea market. We had running water and bathrooms, which brought curious neighbors intrigued by the mason's tales. *"Muy bien, muy bien,"* said old Catalina, smiling at me while she trailed her black skirts up and down the dusty stairs through the unfinished house. When she left, I heard her mumble: *"Qué desastre, qué desastre!"* It was mostly fun, as long as we did not count on always getting hot water from the tap or a toilet that actually flushed when instructed.

Mallorca might be affordable, but our income depended on Fred's long-distance relationship with publishers and magazines, which was a continuous effort. When *Time/Life* asked him to do several books on music and art, I found there was room for me to do the research and take pictures. Fred had also accepted a commission for a guidebook on Mallorca and no time to write it, so I did. Actually, we cared little whose name was on the cover; we needed the money and I enjoyed trying my hand at writing. After all, a guidebook was not a historical novel. It mainly meant driving around the island, checking on churches, beaches, restaurants, distances and dates. For other research, we had access to good libraries in Palma and received secondhand book catalogues from New York, London, Paris, Berlin or Amsterdam. Every few weeks the books would arrive, in heavy duffel bags, to the dismay of Castor the old mailman, who finally rebelled and told us to pick them up from the grocery-store-post-office-barber-shop ourselves.

In those early days we explored the island, village by village and road by narrow road, enjoying every moment. A thousand years ago, when Moorish princes still governed most of Spain, Mallorca was known as an isle of pleasure, a cool, green oasis located midway on the journey between the hot Andalusian plain and the arid shores of the Barbary Coast. We still found a truly beautiful island, varied like a miniature continent. In rugged mountains, wild goats scrambled over crags and chasms, while sunny fertile plains were dotted with tiny windmills hauling up water to irrigate the citrus trees. Along the coastline, forbidding red cliffs tumbled hundreds of feet straight into the sea, near bays of blue-green water that whispered on pale sand. On the stone terraces built by Moorish inhabitants stood ancient olive trees, said to bear the name of Allah on every leaf. Medieval farms hid behind fortified walls, prickly pears bloomed in arid regions, and the ripe black pods of carobs leaked their rank gum. There were gardens filled with roses and palm trees, water had been taught to rush down stony steps, and Moorish watchtowers still guarded old Roman roads. Every season worked its spell. Summer winds scorched with the heat of Africa, November brought the blessed rain, and snow covered the high peaks in winter. In the calm of January, eight million almond trees seemed to burst in bloom overnight with the magic of a tree that offered its blossom on a naked branch and grew its leaves as an afterthought.

One spring day Fred and I watched a shepherd guide his flock across a field with a sling and a handful of stones. A gentle nudge with a small pebble for a lamb, a firmer hit for the well-protected backside of its mother. After sharing some wine and dried figs, the old man showed us how to use the frayed piece of rope. He cut a yellow-brown medlar from its branch without even trying and, whipping around, killed a small bird in flight. Watching a simple shepherd using his ancient weapon in that biblical setting of dark-red earth, silver olive trees and crumbling stone walls inevitably brought to mind David and Goliath. However, here it took on a very different meaning. I realized it had not simply been a matter of a big, invincible giant ready to crush the life out of a scared peasant boy. David was also a determined young man with an extremely accurate weapon, facing, yes, a huge, taunting brute, but one that stood still, making a perfect target. The effect of a sharp flinty rock or a small round pebble slung with full force to hit between the eyes cannot be much different from a bullet. David may have been scared, but once his sling was whirring, all he thought of was distance, aim and the desperate need to kill.

ROBERT GRAVES

Robert Graves

In 1878, a Spanish travel guide described the village of Deia as a "favorite haunt of extravagant and rather odd foreigners, many of whom are freethinkers." To Mallorcans, a foreigner meant—and means—anyone who is not a native of the island. Through the years, this included many of the best-known figures in the Spanish arts, from Pablo Picasso and Antonio Gaudi to Manuel de Falla, all found wandering among the olive trees at one time or other. And of course real foreigners: the Archduke Louis Salavador of Habsburg, who made his home here for forty years, writing enormous volumes on "Die Balearen," or Gustave Doré, who found some of his most dramatic ideas for Dante's Inferno in the yawning gorge and thousand-foot cliffs near Valldemosa. Earlier on, George Sand had taken Chopin and her two children to spend an ill-starred winter in that village, bringing it fame that still feeds the local tourist industry today.

When we arrived, few foreigners lived in Deia the year round, a handful of artists, a writer or two for whom cheap houses were a main attraction. Tourists would drive through on the odd bus, but mostly preferred to stay at the other side of the island where they could stretch out on sandy beaches. Along much of our northern coast, you had to be a mountaineer to get to the sea. Still, things were slowly changing. People began to rent houses for the summer season, and several new restaurants opened in their wake. Tourism brought money to the island and it showed. We did not know it then, but it was the beginning of a very different era. In due course Richard Branson would own the luxurious hotel La Residencia, and Michael Douglas, Swarovski and Andrew Lloyd-Weber have well-groomed estates with lush gardens and swimming pools. All in little Deia.

When we settled in Mallorca that spring of 1961, Robert Graves, English poet, author and scholar, was the great white father of Deia. In his mid-sixties, tall and formidable looking, the great pagan face framed by a mass of tangled white hair, the once-classical nose broken on the playing field of Charterhouse, he might be found striding down the path among the ancient olive trees. *Voilà un Dieu!* Instead of thunderbolts, Graves carried an old straw basket stuffed with mail and groceries. Living frugally in a simple stone house he built amid a landscape of silvery olives, citrus trees and asphodels, he enjoyed picking his own olives or making orange marmalade in the kitchen, while testing his youngest son Thomas on his Latin lessons. He called his house *Canellun*, a word that translates to something like "the house further on."

Graves had come to Mallorca soon after having written his autobiography, *Good-Bye to All That*, which dealt with his personal wartime in the trenches and a past he had chosen to leave behind. Robert was close friends with Siegfried Sassoon, and the war left both young poets disillusioned, shell-shocked and suffering from severe neurosis. (Wounded at the age of twenty, an erroneous notice of Robert's death appeared in the *London Times*.) The title *Good-Bye to All That* meant exactly that. "It was my bitter leave-taking of England, where I had been disowned by most of my friends, had been grilled by the police on suspicion of attempted murder, and ceased to care what anyone thought of me." Graves was looking for brighter shores when Gertrude Stein suggested that Mallorca might be a good place to spend some time away from his Apollonian England. "It is paradise," she said, "if you can stand it." (Stein was rather a busybody, for while she was at it she sent Sir Francis Rose and Dorothy Carrington to Corsica, Hemingway to Spain and Paul Bowles to Tangier. Years later Paul Theroux—who would take his own turn on the Mallorca trail—visited Bowles in Tangier. Hearing the stories, he came away saying: "My impression of her was now of a big bossy lesbian, queening it in her salon in Paris, directing literary traffic, sending writers to unlikely destinations in the Mediterranean.")

In October 1929, Graves followed her advice and set out for Deia. It obviously did not deter him that she had also described the Mallorcans as "a foolish host of decayed pirates with an awful language." Thus he came, with the American writer Laura Riding as his goddess-cum-muse and counterpart in a tumultuous affair full of passion, of self-delusion that touched the edge of madness, of jealousy and betrayal that kept the village shocked and entertained for years. By the time we arrived, his life had taken a quieter turn and he was living happily with his second wife, Beryl Pritchard Hodges, and their four children.

Our initial encounter was somewhat of a wrangle. In a local dispute, Graves sided with one of his disciples, who wanted to cover part of the village torrent to make a parking lot. Fred and I opted for the open torrent and signed a petition to the Ministry of Tourism in Madrid. We had barely met the legendary Graves in person when, passing our garden gate one evening he stopped, looked down at me and said querulously, "So how many trees have you planted today?" Taken aback by the big angry man's attack, I blurted out the truth: "We put in eighteen this morning, actually." He huffed-puffed and walked on, followed by his usual entourage, leaving us slightly stunned. The project petered out as such things do, and I don't remember how it came about but we soon became close friends.

Graves had a curious way of accepting newcomers. It might be a book they carried, a stray remark—often misinterpreted—or something else he actually saw as a sign. Once admitted to his circle that person instantly became "the best archeologist in England" or "the best drummer in Spain" or whatever the case. Anyone who did not care to live up to the role he allocated to them had "let him down" and was dismissed. The poet Alastair Reid—Graves's close friend who later on stole his muse of the month and fled with her—said: "He cuts a coat for you, and you have to fit into it."

Brilliant, autocratic, with little or no sense of other people's privacy, he walked in and out of homes, lives and relationships, judging or misjudging them with a self-confidence that swept people along in spite of themselves. I do not think it ever occurred to him that he might not always be welcome. Nor did he take gladly to criticism or even polite disagreement. He was, like his friend Miss Stein, a priori always right, or at least never wrong. Playing scrabble, he would come up with some concoction of his own and I protested: "Robert, that word does not exist." He just looked at me. "It does now, and there are three of my words in the Oxford Dictionary to prove me right." I remember a BBC reporter who found him sitting on a chair in his garden, getting his hair cut. "What beautiful hair, Mr. Graves," cooed she. "And well it should be," he snapped. "It is fed on the best brains in England."

We saw each other socially, our children grew up together, and we would join the Graves Sunday picnics at the beach. I grew close to Beryl and, together with Robert, we traveled to Belgrade for a weeklong seminar on humanism. I saw how, with understanding and cool humor, she managed to keep her husband attached to earthly life, while watching over his mad flights as poet-servant to a succession of muse-goddesses. Fred and I published several articles on Graves and I did the photography for his book on Mallorca. Fred was on good terms with Robert, but had neither time nor interest in taking a place at his court. Robert and I developed a more personal relationship, picking olives, shopping for antiques in Palma, climbing down to swim in the cala and walking home together after picking up our mail, ending up in my kitchen for tea. ("Not a cookie, darling. A biscuit.")

I have seen Graves moody, contradictory, even irrational, and arrogant, but I have never spent any time with him without learning something. His interests were boundless; as tutelary deity of this fair island, he knew where the Iberians once worshipped or why the moonlight in Deia was notorious for derangements of the wits. He would eulogize some girl he had recently elevated to muse level, explain why the green jade stone warmed to the touch, compliment me on a new dress, teach me how many bitter oranges go into a pot of marmalade or simply when to use *such as* instead of *like*. He was part of my life in Deia, and in later years, when I would be alone and troubled he was the friend I often turned to for advice. When I worked in the Amazon jungle, Robert wrote me regularly, care of the main hotel in Manaus, from where the letters were actually passed to me on by plane or canoe.

If today many young readers may know his name only from the television version of *I, Claudius*, he is also regarded as the best-loved poet of his generation. Besides nonfiction works such as the controversial *The White Goddess*, Graves wrote novels and was a superb classicist. In his later years, his mind and memory began failing steadily. I no longer lived in Deia and the last time I photographed him was in February 1984. It was difficult to see him so silent, withdrawn into himself, his own distant world. Still, there would be a sudden gleam of recognition and he was there, back among us, if even for a moment. At the time of his death at the age of ninety, he had produced a staggering diversity of books, written by hand, with a steel-nibbed pen dipped into an inkwell.

He was a dear friend to me.

FAMILY MATTERS AND VILLAGE AFFAIRS

My father-in-law, F. V. Grunfeld, and myself

My father-in-law came to live with us for a while. I had first met Dad in Zurich, where he taught graphology at the university and wrote his books, among them a thesis on Beethoven's handwriting. He shared his age and cultural—if not his religious—background with Robert Graves, whose great-uncle was the German historian Leopold von Ranke, whereas Dad was related to the philosopher Ernst Cassirer. Once they had met in our kitchen—equally suspicious of each other—one would often see them walking down the road together, in deep discussions, and completely oblivious of traffic or people.

I am not sure that at first Dad had been too happy about our marriage. He may have preferred Fred to continue his career in New York and marry someone less burdened. In time, I grew closer to him than I had ever been to my own father. I could talk to him about anything, whether it was the war, graphology or a new marriage with four children. Sometimes he gave me advice, often he just listened.

He made me feel that, beyond the mother and the wife, he saw a real person.

He gave me a wonderful gift: he transformed a large closet into my first darkroom, gave me his own enlarger and taught me how to print. I knew how to develop the film, but being able to print added a completely new dimension. It is an art and although I learned fast, I never became as good as Dad. I now spent hours in my closet, printing small windmills, the baroque organs found in isolated villages, the Palma cathedral, the ancient olive presses, the almond crops or the fishermen. Then, adding long captions or a few pages of text, I sent them to the Swiss magazines, who liked them and paid well.

During one of those 1960s summers Ivan, my first husband, appeared. It was rather a surprise, for he had never paid any child support or showed much interest. Cathy and Marc had not seen him for over two years, which was a long time at their age. Actually, they were a little embarrassed. How were they going to explain him to their village friends? None of them had extra fathers staying in a hotel. All four children came in. "Hello, how you have grown." "Hello, this is Foster, my new brother." This in Swiss-German, while presents changed hands. "Thank you very much. Mom, can we go play now?" Off they ran, shouting to each other in Mallorquin.

I looked at the friendly stranger standing in my Deia home. Handsome he was and intelligent, but a frustrated and suspicious mind had made every little thing a problem. Memories came flooding back. I was of course neither without blame nor ignorant of what had happened to us and his list of grievances probably equaled mine. It took a dead kitten in the trash can and a night with the prostitute next door to make me realize that there was nothing left of the young couple full of hope and good intentions. It had been time to leave and now those images seemed almost unreal. And very long ago.

Some neighbors happened by and we sat down in our large whitewashed kitchen with a glass of wine. Talking about Switzerland, everybody had some nice memories: skiing, hiking, going shopping, good museums. "I went to a meeting in a small Swiss town called Solothurn recently," said one of our friends. "It has an amazingly good opera house." "Yes, I remember that," I heard myself answer. "I lived there for a while and actually was an extra in the opera." Getting up, I saw the friendly stranger looking at me. "IT WAS WITH ME," he said slowly. There was an odd silence. I listened to it, but it only confirmed that I had dealt with that part of my past, had truly left it behind me, somewhat like the mumps, which usually only parents remember. It had nothing to do anymore with the person I had become, and I was able to look back without regret or resentment. Fred crossed the room, touched my shoulder, and changed the subject. Soon, everybody left.

Our days were filled with work and family. Usually Fred and I worked until about four in the afternoon, when the bus from Palma arrived. Stopping at the grocery store, we picked up the mail and went down to the beach. We swam, sat on the rocks and had a drink under the straw mat awning of the café. Walking home in the cool of the evening, we would eat at home or meet with friends. This was the 1960s. We listened to the Beatles, Joan Baez, Bob Dylan and—a favorite to this day—Roberta Flack. I wore long flowing dresses and Indian sandals, silk scarves wound around my head and antique silver bracelets on my upper arm. It was also an important time: the Kennedy assassinations, Vietnam, a man on the moon and a growing awareness of our environment reflected in social revolutions, in Rachel Carson's *The Silent Spring*, Betty Friedan's *The Feminine Mystique* and John Kenneth Galbraith's *The Affluent Society*.

Almost ten years had passed since our arrival. Our quiet island was pasted on the map by tourist agencies that sent a million visitors a year in cheap package deals. Deia attracted a different crowd, but whereas there had always been all-night parties, drinking and gossip, now there were dazed, drugged people wandering around the moon- or sunlit terraces, crying and laughing or staring into nowhere. Even Graves, whose *The White Goddess* had made him a cult symbol to some of the hippies, took off to Mexico with one of his very much lesser muses to try out the benefit of some mushroom and returned the worse for wear. All this coalesced with village life, with local people and the year-round foreign residents following their established routines. For Fred and me it meant watching out for our family and trying to explain to Mallorcan friends that there were still normal people who were just happy to live and work here. Our children led a rather more regular and sheltered family life than most, but they doubtlessly saw and heard far more than we realized at the time.

Still, these were years of an extraordinary creativity. If choosing to be an expatriate spells by definition a certain rejection of accepted social and moral values, it also tends to breed a slight madness capable of pushing mere talent into near-genius. The talent many brought with them. Looking back it amazes me how our at times deranged-looking crowd—freethinkers, indeed—managed to create what they did during those mad summers. Many of the actors in this play have since died, but their books are on the shelves, their plays in the theaters, their art is in the museums and their music is there to hear.

BRITISH COLUMBIA AND ALASKA

For me a new world opened up when I fortuitously replaced a British photographer on an article for the *Daily Telegraph Magazine* about North West American Indians. It was Fred's assignment, but we really wanted to do this trip together and the plan was for me to sell a story to my Swiss magazines to cover the travel expenses. We got as far as New York when our photographer Max Maxwell suddenly decided, "I am staying here. I never understood why you want to go up there in the first place. It's not even a story; there is nothing left but a bunch of dirty Indians." He took a studio job with Richard Avedon, whereas I turned in my old Leica for several brand-new Nikons. For the first time, Fred and I would work as a team. For the first time I faced the challenge to prove that I could hold my own at a professional level.

We took a big risk. We knew the magazine would send another photographer long before accepting the inexperienced wife of the writer. I worried, but Fred looked at me and grinned. "Of course you can do it. It will be fun," he said. In reality, I was so insecure that I left my cameras behind twice: once in a hotel in Toronto on our way to the airport, the second time when a small seaplane picked us up somewhere along the BC coast. I simply flew away, leaving my brand new Nikons sitting on the landing. Twenty-four hours later, a pilot spotted my shiny Halliburton case standing on a nameless wooden dock, somewhere in the middle of nowhere. I realized then how terrified I was by the assignment and all it implied. I had a very long way to go.

Our first working trip together taught me a lot about the risks, frustrations and wonders of a roving life. The first daunting step had been leaving the children behind, and it took time to convince myself. They were in school, I reasoned. Moochen and Antonia were there, as always. Hardly anything would change, as I had never been much involved in the everyday management of our household. The village was small, safe and full of friends. We were not going to remote deserts or scary jungles; we had an itinerary; we passed through cities where we could send and receive mail. We could call and touch base. And so we did set out to share the adventure. I was to have my first taste of the mixture of guilt about leaving home and pride in work achieved and experiences lived.

Neither Fred nor I had ever been to British Columbia or Alaska, and what we were looking for was very different from what most visitors saw. Few travelers, after all, were searching for old Indian cemeteries or a deserted beach where some totem poles might still stand. In 1791, the explorer Allesandro Malaspina led a Spanish naval expedition up the Pacific coast from Mexico to Alaska searching, among other things, for the rumored North-West passage to the Atlantic. On board he carried two artist-correspondents whose drawings had recently been rediscovered in Madrid. We had tracked them down, translated the bulk of Malaspina's journal and now followed in the wake of the *Descubierta* and the *Atrevida* to find out what was left of the great art of the North West American Indians.

Starting out from the Nootka Sound Reservation on Vancouver Island was a sobering experience. I had associated it with Captain Cook, with colorful tribal culture and whale hunts, with bears and cougars haunting virgin forests. Whatever I had expected, it was not this rundown village with its poverty, alcohol and hopelessness. Youngsters and older people lounged about in dirty T-shirts and shorts, showing little interest in their surroundings, each other or in us for that matter. The Indian agent said there was no work for the young and many who might have made a difference were leaving the reservation. He asked an elder to show us some of their artifacts. I was familiar with Fred's small, but impressive collection of Northwest American Indian art. I had seen the photographs of Edward S. Curtis and the art in museums, but it was only when I saw this old man wear a button blanket and the intricately carved mask that I could actually associate these people with a proud tribe. Of old, they hunted, gathered shellfish, caught salmon, halibut and herring, and lived well. More important, there had always been a sense of pride: one of their most daring ventures was the pursuit of the killer whale, himself the greatest hunter of the seas. If such a kill meant food, it was also a demonstration of skill and bravery. The best hunters would jump on the whale and actually ride it bareback, staying with the furious, wounded giant until it submerged. A much-envied name within these tribes was "Stepping-on-the-Whale." It was difficult to associate these feats with the dispirited group of young men we had just met.

Fred sat down with the chiefs, getting the facts, while I photographed my first totem poles on the beach. I did not know then that a pattern was falling into place that would be part of our working life for years to come. It looked easy, Fred sitting there talking, but I was to learn the effort it represented. Meanwhile I wandered off to get the pictures. A handful of children had followed my every step (that, too, would become routine) and took me to see a large wooden bird sculpture standing a ways into the forest. The children had built a primitive shelter nearby, and it looked as if they spent a fair amount of time there. They walked me up to the bird, and I saw traces of red paint where weather had not bleached it the color of driftwood. A little girl repeatedly told me its name, but I did not know enough to make sense of it. Touching its feet, passing their small hands along the carved lines of the beaked bird, they looked up at it with a smile, as if to a protector. The youngest boy, Jimmy, was about six. He was thin and shy, and had a clubfoot. After I gave them some candy and made sure he got his share, he kept close to me for the rest of our stay. Later, when we were getting back on the plane, he held on to my jacket; I looked down at his little face and could not bear to leave that child standing there. I was so new to all this and inevitably identified with our own children. It was my first time, but it would happen again, with different people, in different places. It took me a long time to find an emotional balance, to show I cared without seeming to promise more than I could give.

From Vancouver Island, we headed northward to Yakutat Bay in Alaska, threading our way through the hundreds of wooded islands that dot the Pacific coast. A thousand miles of rugged, jagged coastline, where snowcapped mountains plunged abruptly into the sea. It was like an enormous treasure hunt, with our invaluable sketches as clues. Nudging into inlets and rivers, we compared the pictures to the scenery around us. Much of the landscape remained unchanged, for the white man established only a few ports and lumber camps in this vast territory, leaving the rest as empty as when Cook and Malaspina first set eyes on it. Continuously asking and showing our drawings, it was a small miracle, every time, to retrace a tiny cemetery or a long abandoned settlement with a single bear-faced pole still standing.

One might think that a natural rock formation, which Malaspina's artists recorded as "one of the great scenic wonders of the region" would be easy to find. It was not. While Fred stayed in Victoria, meeting with the museum people and trying to put through a call to Deia, I rode ferry after ferry, scuttling between the Gulf Islands in the Strait of Georgia, showing my pictures, asking and explaining without success. I was ready to give up and return to Victoria when one of the sailors said, "Oh, that! Those are the *Malaspinosi* (sic) rocks. You take the Gabriola Island ferry and when you get off, just follow the road and you'll come to it." For more than an hour, I followed a sandy path through a low wooded area before it turned back to the coast, and there was the fabulous gallery! Carved by tides and frost, the limestone formation looked like a gigantic Hawaiian surfer's wave turned to stone just as it crested, leaving a curved overhang, a sort of half-tunnel with one side open to the sea. Trees had grown along the top, underneath ran a wide platform and the entire breathtaking view was exactly like the centuries-old sketch that had sent me here. Lying flat on my back, I watched sea and sky; even today, I remember the comforting warmth of the smooth, yellow, water-worn stones. In the deep silence that surrounded me, feeling the satisfaction of a task done, I thought of home, wondering whether Fred had reached them by phone. I thought how Foster and Marc would have loved the adventure of riding all the ferries and finding this strange and lonely place. I also began to realize how much I enjoyed the challenges of this roaming life.

Finally, packing up, I trudged back to the dock, where I saw the ferry about a mile away, gaily steaming toward its next island. In my excitement about having found the gallery, I had never thought to ask about itineraries. There were so many islands; I did not even know which ferry would take me where from here. By now, it was late afternoon and it did not look as if I would make it to Victoria that night. I was hungry and tired. My cameras seemed to weigh even more than usual and the idea of wandering off to find a village was only barely more attractive than going to sleep under a tree or on the lonely beach, trying not to think of bears or large crabs or some such things. Where was everybody? The sun was setting and I was still sitting there, undecided, when a jeep drove up to the landing and a young couple called out to me, as surprised to see me as I was glad to see them. The next ferry was not due until the next morning and the village a long walk. They took me home and we spent the evening with friends around the fireplace. Asking about the history of the rock gallery, I was told that local yachtsmen and a few sightseers used it as a place to picnic, but not one person present knew the origin of its name. I read recently (i.e., forty years after my visit), that the Malaspina Gallery was closed to the public, as the limestone was deteriorating and rocks were falling from the overhang. It can now only be seen from the sea.

While I was chatting away with my new friends on Gabriola, Fred trusted in my common sense. He could not reach me. I was not near any phone and cell phones were still very much a thing of the future. He simply left the address of his hotel at the museum, where I found it the next day. I was only taking ferries in British Columbia after all, not lost in a jungle or on the slopes of Mt. Everest. Not yet. Soon these things would become part of our game. Once we were on a story we followed its lead and rarely worried about the way back. Rarely, not never.

The Kwakiutl cemetery's wrought-iron gate in Alert Bay was painted a sad gray, but someone had stuck it with small bunches of wildflowers. Inside, there was no one but the young Indian girl who had shown us the way. It was a lowering day, with threatening dark clouds and rain. Weeds covered some simple white crosses, the totem poles towering above. The thunderbird, whose name, I now knew, was Kwunkwanekulegyi, perched on nearly all these grave-posts, symbolizing the omnipotent ruler of the skies. The raven-beaked giants and carved animal faces were set with pieces of mica that glittered in the fading light and lent them an eerie quality, making them almost look alive. The tall winged poles brought to mind a long forgotten painting I saw as a child, showing the crosses on the hill of Golgotha, looming black against a lighting-rented sky.

Following the expedition's trail, we traveled by ferry, hitched a ride in a helicopter of the Coast Guard and very often walked. I see us waiting for a bus, somewhere in the middle of nowhere (actually it was near Bella Bella), sitting on a broken-down bench and holding a piece of torn tarpaulin over our heads to keep off the pouring rain. Fred was battering the small typewriter on his knees, while I tried to put some order in my films. When the rain showed no sign of letting up and the bus was nowhere in sight, he said, "I guess we walk." Still holding on to the tarpaulin we set out along a narrow path, walking in single file, and trying to keep in step like a Chinese Dragon on New Year's Day. As he was much taller, I hopped behind him, taking two steps to his every one, while he laughed and sang a marching tune to keep me from bumping into him. We came to a small lumber settlement, its roofs silver-gray in the ever-present rain, a totem pole with a tuft of weeds growing out of its head standing in the muddy path. The Indians looked at us, the strange apparition of two white people under a piece of sailcloth, looking for shelter. They offered us a dry blanket and home-brewed liquor.

In Alert Bay, at the northern end of Vancouver Island, a young minister invited us to accompany him on a routine inspection of his far-flung parish. For several days, we chugged in his little motor yacht through channels, inlets and creeks to lumber camps with their solid log cabins, a small one-engine seaplane tied to each dock, much like a car in a driveway. Stocky and red-haired, Richard Futter paid less attention to the religious persuasion of the families he visited than to their immediate needs. He brought mail and medicine to isolated settlements, acted as dentist, married those who wished and baptized children born since his last visit, often as long as a year ago. Knowing every inch of his territory, he showed us where fallen poles lay moldering in the grass or where a single Indian family lived on their tiny island, guarding an ancient cemetery.

Near Kispiox, on the banks of the fast rushing Skeena, stood a group of tall totems in a meadow full of flowers, and a blind old man told us the stories of the carved animal faces he could no longer see. He had a gentle voice as he slipped into the tales he had told many a time, to his grandchildren maybe, giving them a sense of the importance of their clan, their family, and tradition. I had seen children play among the great, still faces, passing their hands along the carved lines of bear, wolf and beaked birds, and saw how reassuring it would be and what a source of pride, to belong to such a tribe. It was a little like my grandfather telling me about the great sailing ships in the harbors of his past; only here was an incomparably greater, far more personal loss, unnecessary and irretrievable.

Until the beginning of the last century, many Indian villages here still had veritable forests of totem poles on their landing beaches. When the missionaries arrived, they wanted them cut down, not knowing or caring that they were heraldic crests and images of memory rather than "heathen idols." It was unforgivable then and incomprehensible today, but after sitting at the feet of those great sculptures, seeing them sway in the wind and feeling the immense power of their stare, I could understand why a missionary could not bear to have them peering over his small shoulder.

The art of the northwestern Indians filled Malaspina and his crew with "wonderment and admiration." It was an art of eyes and faces that went far beyond the imitation of nature and the artists were among the greatest wood sculptors of all time. Once it was part of everyday life and every implement bore witness: weapons, dance rattles and harpoons. Totem designs were cut intaglio into horn spoons, woven into robes and blankets or bent around corners to decorate the four sides of burial boxes. Most of the art along this coast has long been hunted down and sold. Led first by the French surrealist poet André Breton and then by Nelson Rockefeller, the great northwest art rush has been on for years and after more than a century of missionising and souvenir hunting the items are now almost unobtainable at any price.

Just across the Hecate Strait, the Queen Charlotte Islands are home to the Haida, the Tsimshian and the Tlingitt, whose poles still silently watch the wake of dolphins and killer whales. Seafaring nomads, they were constantly on the move, spending nearly as much time in their canoes as in their houses. All tribes roved to eat and roved to fight, but the Haida were the fiercest warriors of them all, thinking nothing of raiding villages hundreds of miles to the south. Their huge canoes were built for war, meant to strike terror in their enemies, and they did. Unlike what we had seen in Nootka's Friendly

Cove, these tribes are still independent fishermen, a far from vanishing race, whose numbers are steadily increasing. Watching them at work, I saw the same strong Tartar-like faces portrayed by Malaspina's artists. The highpoint of the Haida culture was the totem pole, and the British Museum has a two-story marble staircase winding around a Haida masterpiece that is perhaps the finest in existence. "Remember that one?" said Fred. "It was taken from the very place we are standing."

While the elders invited Fred to the inevitable chat, I took a ride in a small seaplane with a local pilot who was very charming, very crazy and very drunk. "What would you like to see, Miss?" I gave the usual answer: cemeteries, poles and settlements, whatever you can find. "Sure, okay, honey, you come with me. I will show you," he said, laughing. We flew up narrow, yellow-colored rivers, between two walls of trees, skimming the muddy water that jabbed at us with half-drowned trunks and branches. We crossed forests and meadows and when I pointed to some long shapes lying in the grass, he landed with a swish and a crunch on a narrow strip of beach. I went off to find what I had seen from the air, hearing him yell not to go too far and something about bears. The Tsimshian pole had been lying there for many years, grass growing from its nostrils, its back partly decayed, but the animal faces still formidable, the bear's teeth ready to bite. The cedar forest began just beyond, gnarled roots and giant trunks rising up a hundred feet; others lay felled by natural infirmities, the broken branches covered with moss bearing an uncanny resemblance to the fallen totem. I sat down and looked around, listening to the utter stillness around me. Where did this art stop and the forest begin? Only a few steps away lay some burial boxes, stacked like so many drawers taken from a dresser, with a single roof to ward off the rain. The roof had long collapsed and the contents of the coffins had spilled out. Pieces of half-mummified limbs lay scattered among clean-picked bones and skulls. Other boxes were so old they contained nothing but humus, new sapling and bushes growing out of them, just as they sprouted from broken totems. Was there a lesson to be learned?

When I came back to the plane, the pilot was kneeling in the water, looking for something: we had lost a wheel. After searching for a while, we realized that it could have fallen off before we landed and that it would soon be getting dark. Half of the plane was hanging in the water, so the plan was for me to climb on the tail, jumping up and down to free it from the weeds. The pilot would start the engine and as soon as the plane could move, he would pull me in through the open door. After I had fallen in the water three times—the weeds not being very accommodating—we managed to flop away and lifted off like a pregnant pelican. By then, we not could stop laughing and I thought we had done really well. Until he told me that in Sandspit we had to land on the tarmac instead of on the water. Which we did, on one wheel, the bare iron bar scraping the runway. Screeching like a barn owl it set off a firework of sparks that brought everybody running.

Malaspina's search for the elusive northern passage to the Atlantic ended in Yakutat Bay. Encountering a solid wall of ice— the immense Hubbard Glacier—the explorer entered it on his maps as Disenchantment Bay. In our drawing, his artists posed the schooner *Atrevida* looking small and forlorn against a romantic backdrop of giant icebergs. We felt just as small, winding our way in a dinghy through the ice-strewn bay. Our Indian guide seemed oblivious to the scenery or the freezing water and steered so close to the huge clumps that we could see the ice shine deep blue in a bottomless ocean. From time to time, an enormous chunk broke away from the glacier wall with a rumbling sound like faraway thunder, the splash sending up a fountain of white spray. The seals stuck their round faces out of the water to look at us and floated away. I remember the first whale I ever saw, the upper part of his head and the rugged, scarred bulk so close I might have touched it, the glorious arrogance of the winged tail rising high before the smooth dive, the keen eye measuring us in passing. It also brought to mind engravings of harpooners and broken-up rowboats, and I realized that it would take but a very small twitch of that tail to dispose of us.

We saw the black bear nosing on the rock-strewn beaches and their brown cousins fishing for salmon in the streams. The villagers took their share and the red filets, strung like laundry on a line, filled the wooden smokehouses. The women showed us how to thread the fish on thin cedar sticks, placing them in a circle around a small fire. Fred and I sat there on the empty beach, looking at each other, as happy as children at a birthday party, and waiting to be served smoked salmon that tasted like no salmon I ever ate before, or since.

We wandered for several thousand miles, met many people, and learned many things. We had taken the ferry from Sitka to Juneau, and climbed the Klondike Gold Rush trail, where a few miners still sluiced the dirt. On a whim, we flew to the Yukon to see Jack London's Whitehorse and Dawson and found two false-front boarded-up towns that looked like the set for a Western movie. For all that, we had barely touched the outer fringe of this immense country. This extraordinary country where the air smelled as if it had never been breathed by any living thing; where skies changed from a star-cluttered black pool to a dome of glowing indigo, and landscapes were lobed and rounded by wind and by snow. A place where we heard the most desolate sound to touch the heart: the wailing call of a black loon over a moon-brushed lake.

We arrived home to find that Dad had died two days earlier in a Zurich hospital. Fred went with Moochen to take the urn to the family plot in Berlin, a journey into the past. She brought me Dad's ring, which I have worn ever since. Our letters to him, mailed in small villages at the other end of the world, telling him that we cared, kept arriving, one by one.

DEIA, WORK, AND HOME

The children showed us the letters and postcards we had sent them, asked about the strange stamps, making us repeat the unpronounceable names. We held a slide show and had them choose their favorites. It would become a family tradition, and when an editor picked their choice for a cover, they were as proud as if they had taken the picture themselves. There was no obvious change in their attitude to us, other than an odd sort of pride displayed to their friends, "Look what our strange parents did." They were sad about their grandfather's death and seemed happy to have us back. In the weeks that followed the boys asked some more questions about Indians, harpoons and killer whales, but the novelty wore off and they returned to their own interests.

The *Daily Telegraph Magazine* liked the American Indian story and gave our pictures double spreads. The rare compliment was the beginning of a new, shared career and a long connection with the magazine. Our trademark, if that is the word, became stories out of the ordinary. People and places regarded as almost legendary—the Spanish Foreign Legion in the Sahara, tribes in Nuristan, black magic in Sri Lanka—all made for unusual tales. I recently found, stuck in an atlas, a list of projects scribbled on a paper napkin. Kilimanjaro, it said, Afghanistan, Lanzarote, sailing up the Nile aboard a felucca, a temple in Sudan where priests worship cats (or maybe it was rats). On the reverse were other ideas, such as "ethnic groups and their tendency to move to places that resemble the landscapes of their origin": Germans to Upper Mississippi, Russians to Great Plains, and Dutch to Michigan. Another list read Einstein/Breuer: MIT; Mies van der Rohe: ITT; Stravinsky: South Cal; Bartok: N.Y.C.; Schoenberg: UCLA; Hindemith: Yale. All scribbled on a crumpled napkin, in Fred's once so familiar handwriting, now long gone.

To sell them to our magazine editors we had to make the stories exiting. We would lie in bed and talk about where we would like to travel next. Having done our research, Fred sent out outlines to the magazines. Once we had the assignment, it was again Fred who dealt with the details, embassies, government tourist offices, airlines, hotels and any other institution that might give us assistance. While at the time, it seemed to me that we shared the work equally. Later, when I would set out alone or worked with other journalists, I realized what effort had gone into the preparations and the importance of developing a relationship with editors and publishers.

Any reporter knows that we are only as good as our latest article. I carried three Nikons and a dozen lenses plus hundreds of films. Expensive, they were developed back home thousands of miles later, and I did not have today's digital possibility of judging the results on the spot. Part of our strength was the sharing of both our small successes and our fall-flat-on-our-face moments. Later, when I worked with other journalists or alone, I never again experienced the joy that came from sharing love and work. Where a look, a smile, a quick intake of breath was all we needed to know that we saw and felt alike. And where, always, the night belonged to us alone. It was a rare privilege.

Our journeys, some of which are bundled together on these pages, spread out over years. In between, we spent quiet times at home, working on books and articles often unrelated to the countries we visited. There were some changes: after a year with us, Fred's young daughter Laura was still homesick. She returned to Massachusetts to live with her mother. The other three soon formed their own little clan and presented a more or less unified front to the world. They missed us during our absences, but also saw us work together, knew that we loved them and would return. Looking back, I wonder if they were sometimes a little puzzled by the odd gifts we brought them. No T-shirts, but an old opium pipe and shadow puppets for one, colored trade beads and embroidered shirts for the other, a handwoven basket or a gold nugget for the third. We bought these gifts with each child in mind. We would try to leave on Monday mornings, when they boarded the bus for school, and return before a weekend. We left contact information about consulates or travel offices with Moochen, although none of that guaranteed contact in emergency. Of course, we did worry, but our work paid for household, education and everything else needed. That we loved what we did was our private bonus.

INDIA

Something in me had answered with joy to the singular pull of discovering countries and cultures unknown to me. A gentle tug, a small beginning, it was to become my life.

For several years, India was our favorite haunt, and every journey there led us to discover a different facet of that country. To me, it had felt like coming home, the very first time I set foot in Delhi. The jostling crowds, the faces and colors, the smell of ghee and curry, urine and garbage, the honking cars, the jingling bicycles, the markets stalls and the beggars, all felt natural, almost familiar. Near the hotel, the small shops, a salesman at the door, calling in the Asian manner, palm forward with a downward movement of the fingers. The sellers of local crafts, with sharp eyes and soft voices, spreading their wares, the multicolored glass bangles, miniature elephants carved in ivory, trays inlaid with mother-of-pearl Taj Mahals. Turbaned Bengalis unfolding piles of silk saris in an explosion of flashing red, deep blue and gold. The *chaat* seller carrying his savories on his portable stall, and the itinerant dry-fruit sellers, usually fair, tall Pathans, *kabuliwalas* from Afghanistan, independent and quick to take offense.

The city was exactly as I had always known it would be. Whereas Fred would probably hear the music and remember the art, I smell the smoke of small cow-dung fires glowing in the Rajasthan desert at dusk. I see peacocks and weather-pocked marble stairs in an overgrown garden, or the stuffed button-eyed rhino thrusting head and horn clear through the stucco wall of a dining room in a Rajah's palace. Once the doors of memory open, there is no end to the flood of images. We climbed the snow-covered Himalayan foothills, walked the desert in Rann of Kutch, saw the gentle beauty of Kashmir and rode the elephants at dawn to trail the tiger through the man-high grass of Kaziranga. We stayed in cities exploding with life and color, watched the sun set in an ocean that washed the steps of a forgotten temple. Since I was a child, I have loved kaleidoscopes, the magic of changing colors, textures, tastes and sounds. How could I not fall in love with India?

Our assignments did not allow us much time in the cities, but the image of poverty, of abject misery in the slums of Bombay or Calcutta, so incongruously close to neatly dressed people on their way to work, marked me deeply. We walked the extent of the rag-roofed shacks and shelters, the tangle of mud alleys where scrawny toddlers defecate at the edge of open sewers turned into rivers of filth and an army of children turned every scrap of paper, plastic, cloth or metal into saleable merchandise. Nor have I forgotten the faces and voices of those to whom we only handed some coins, passing through on our way to other places. Where we moved on, others have stayed and told of it, Mary Ellen Mark among them.

Fred and I made the conscious choice to show another India. An India that was just as real in its pulsating, living presence as the slums in their darkness and despair. Away from the growing industries, five-year plans and universal suffrage, we encountered the country's uniqueness in everyday people. The gentle hospitality of the village elders, the carefully swept yards full of laughing children, the dignity and pride of desert villages where people might not always eat their fill, but women in glowing skirts walked like queens. The enthusiasm of the young teacher who rode for miles on his rickety bicycle along jungle paths and through ploughed fields, to knock at the door of our hut one early evening, saying, "Madam, I have come to have intellectual intercourse with you."

My image of India is mainly tied to the landscapes and faces of Bihar, Rajasthan, the Punjab and the Northwest Frontier. It is Kipling country and it was the writer of a "vision of pure delight" who helped us understand why this land was so passionately loved by Englishman and Indian alike. Carrying our copy of *Kim,* we looked around us and felt that, so far, none had succeeded as well in giving us a sense of the sights, sounds, smells and even the tactile presence of India.

In the 1960s, the India that Fred and I first knew and traveled seemed closer to the Raj than to a modern nation. It was a faraway place where few tourists ventured. There were few hotels of any standard and we considered ourselves lucky whenever we got official permission to stay at the "dak bungalows"—literally the post houses—meant to house traveling administrators. The coveted bungalows usually consisted of one main room, flanked by two bedrooms, complete with rudimentary bathrooms. It was a matter of luck. It could be a clean place, offering *charpoys*—the local wooden bed frame crisscrossed with rope webbing—and simple food. A thatched-roofed cottage, the ceilings of the rooms a Hessian cloth painted with whitewash, or a simple brick bungalow with a wide verandah, sheltered by a banyan tree that offered shade for village meetings and traveling merchants. We might also find a mildewed, colonial bungalow, where we had to argue with the watchman about the validity of our permit, because he did not feel like cooking or making beds.

On one such miserable night, a sulky guardian handed us some dirty, food-stained tablecloths as sheets for greasy charpoys with torn mosquito nets. It made no sense to argue or to bribe. The man was high on local bang, shifty eyes bloodshot and out of focus. We filled the cloths with small rocks to stuff the gaps along the walls to keep out the scurrying rats, and spread our bedrolls on the dining room table, feeling safer a little higher off the floor. We had long learned to carry our *bistra*; a light canvas holdall fitted with straps, it held sheets, a pillow and a sort of mattress filled with kapok. Used by Indian travelers since time out of mind, it was a staple item in the British army and a lifesaver when traveling overnight on wooden benches in a train or finding cots without bedding. Still, they hardly turned the narrow table into a comfortable bed.

Later that night, shining my flashlight into the bathroom to check for a snake or the small bats attracted by the humidity, the beam revealed an undulating, heaving carpet of glistening brown cockroaches, covering the floor and part of the walls. There was a strange smell, a slight whispering sound like paper wings touching and the whole thing was like one of my non-favorite scenes in an Indiana Jones temple movie. I swallowed twice, stood very still and backed out, closing the door as tight as I could. We had been up for most of the night and Fred had fallen asleep at last, so I did not wake him. The next morning, when I tried to explain why a chipped vase had been promoted to chamber pot overnight and warned him not to open the bathroom door, he just looked at me. "Are you all right? Are you sure you didn't have a nightmare? There is nothing in there." Piqued—after all I had let him sleep rather than share my misery—I walked in there to show him some proof. I found bright sunlight warming an empty concrete floor, but no cockroach, not a one.

As our journeys led us into less traveled regions, the government tourist office usually provided us with a car and driver. We set out along roads clogged with cars, scooters, carts, bicycles and above all, with people walking, carrying bales, bags and bundles. I sometimes had the impression that all of India was densely populated and that its entire population was perpetually on the move with all its household goods. Turning into a remote country road, leaving the car for a moment of needed privacy, we would both look around carefully: no one. "Go!" said Fred. By the time I got to the tree, there would be a small, attentive audience of smiling women and giggling children. Small boys would actually lie down on the ground and try to peek underneath my skirts. I took to wearing the local loose string-tied pants and a very long tunic. The first time we took a train, we could hardly believe the view: there were the vast empty spaces, almost devoid of humanity, where "solemn deodars climbed one after another with down-dropped branches, the vista of the Plains rolled out beneath them." The bare and empty India of the desert and the hills did exist! The train itself was another matter.

We packed our lunchbox, or bought chapattis, hard-boiled eggs, curds, pickles and fruit at a market. It was tiring, driving long hours every day in the heat, the car usually old and uncomfortable, air conditioning a world away. The drivers loved to honk, loud and continuously; sometimes an attack of diarrhea, a hornet sting, a night of mosquitoes and sagging bed strings would bring a little extra misery, but the world we drove through made more than up for it. Blue linseed and yellow mustard fields or immense dun-colored plains with the sudden scarlet flame of a golden *mohu*r tree. Tiny shrines along the edges of the fields, a red-daubed lingam with fresh flowers or a wave of parakeets descending on a mango tree. The rivers were wide and shining, the plains melted into blue-hazed hills and snowcapped mountains far away and one felt very small in this immensity, traveling a continent rather than a country. The days might be hot and dusty, but there was always the rapid fall of dusk and the quick cooling off, the mist rising up from fields that released a myriad of scents. The villages, buffaloes plodding home in a pale golden dust cloud, small boys riding on the broad backs. The smell of cow-dung fires mingling with the smell of dust and the scent of cut grass, a smell inseparably part of India. "Even wafting through city streets, it remained a smell born of the empty plains." Paul Scott wrote, "To smell it as the car turns and passes a roadside stall lighted by a naphtha lamp only deepens the sense of pervasiveness, of ubiquity, of vastness, of immensity, of endless, endless acre of earth and stone lying beyond the area of the lamp's light."

Our introduction to Rajasthan was the city of Bikaner, and I have never forgotten my first impression. A walled fortress, rising like a mirage from a sea of sand, it seemed a creation of the desert itself. Accessible by five guarded gates, the ancient temples and palaces inside stood witness to an older and more dangerous era. The claustrophobic feeling of the high walls, of houses blind with closed shutters behind which I felt the observing eyes, the narrow cobbled streets where people covered their face when passing, did not endear this medieval city to me. Beautiful as it was, it felt like a place with a law unto itself, whose residents to this day had neither use nor love for strangers.

We did no more than pass through Bikaner on our way to an army base of the Camel Corps, where we were to spend the night. There, in the desert outside the city walls, the welcome was so warm, the atmosphere so friendly and easy-going, that I dismissed that first, almost menacing impression. Still, I long remembered the holy man standing naked, smeared with ashes, smelling of ghee and sweat, his matted hair reaching to his hips. His eyes staring into mine were yellow, bloodshot and malevolent; a heavy stone was tied with a string to his penis, stretching it almost to his knees. When I looked away, he hissed at me like a snake. We had passed the handprints of suttee widows and a bloodstained, flyblown shrine sheltering a four-armed goddess with glaring red eyes and protruding tongue. A goddess wearing a necklace of human skulls: Kali the Black, the Female aspect of Time and Death, Devourer of all Things. Dancing on the prostrate body of her husband Shiva and representing all the nightmares of the mortal mind. She seemed an appropriate patron for this dark-age city.

THE WALL ART OF INDIA

It is a mostly neglected popular art, a sort of glorified graffiti, but the wall art in towns and villages reflects the culture and life of different peoples, producing a peculiarly poignant form of primitive art. Every region has its own. Large, brightly colored elephants and horses frolic on the walls of Jaipur and Udaipur, while Punjab peasants content themselves with simple white marks like snowflakes. Kashmir sculpts its doors and windows, Orissa draws white flower garlands on ochre huts, Rann of Kutch embeds colored glass in pale cream mud, and the jungle people's drawings tell of hunts, wars and ceremonial dances. If widows are no longer burned, in Jodhpur rows of slender stone hands commemorate the thirty-one suttee maharanis who placed their palm prints on the fortress gate to bless it as they went to immolate themselves on their husband's funeral pyre. In the villages of Bihar, the farewell imprints of small hands on memorial stones standing in a field are still pasted over once a year with silver foil.

Our particular story led us away from where the big temples flaunt the Great Tradition of Indian sculpture. That art, designed to serve the Brahman hierarchy, intended to impress and it does: it is

"The Indian Art," known to the outside world. In remote villages, older and simpler races preserved older and simpler traditions. Art hunting in India is an exercise in serendipity, for some of the best was literally underfoot, drawn in the shifting dust. In a village in North Bihar, near the Nepal border, we could barely move about without stepping on some superb magic diagrams that peasant women drew in front of their reed-thatched huts. A whole universe—earth, sun, moon and stars—was enclosed in their abstract patterns. People crossed the yard, children ran about, but no one seemed too worried about stepping on the *dhuli chitra*, the "dust paintings." The next day someone would simply draw another, equally beautiful in its tracery of transparent whitewash on hard-packed ochre. Draw it with a drip-swing rhythm that Jackson Pollock might have envied.

In nearby Madhubani, the Forest of Honey, we found the mud walls of the houses aglow with paintings. Flat, very strong, very striking pictures in vibrant reds, yellows and blues, of figures playing in the garden of art—dancers, flute players, tigers, horses, trees of life, gods with four arms or goddesses with eight. Here, painting is a woman's prerogative and the husbands of these artistic women are, like many husbands everywhere, not terribly interested in the nonsexual activities of their wives. The widow Parvati, in whose house we were staying, had painted a neighbor's room in preparation of a wedding. Above the bridal bed, the love scenes of Krishna, adored blue avatar, brightened the walls, and Parvati had added fishes of fertility and puffed-up peacocks that looked pure Paul Klee. There was a new government initiative under way to distribute paints, brushes and sheets of paper to the villagers. The widows, who had no income at all, were paid a few rupees for every painted sheet they handed in. The next morning we saw Parvati, crouching on the porch. Wearing a white cotton sari with a deep red border, and holding a paintbrush, she beckoned us with a smile: come and see. On a sheet of paper held down with rocks glowed a tiger in all his innocent glory: a face round as the moon, his body painted in bold red and white lozenges, rows of teeth bared in an idiotic grin, a huge mane framing his face and his tail curved high like that of a purring kitten. "Look, daughter," said Parvati, handing me the painting. "It is for you." The picture hangs in my own daughter Cathy's living room today.

Up in the hills and jungles, art attained a fierce austerity and poignancy unknown to the more comfortable parts of India. Accompanied by a guide, we trekked for several days through the jungle-covered hills of Orissa. Fred—whose idea this was, of course—carried his typewriter, our overnight case and some gifts, the guide was in charge of our provisions, and I staggered behind with my twenty-plus-pound camera bag. The trails were steep and I either pulled myself up holding on to the branches or slid down a slope on my backside. I complained about fatigue, mosquitoes, heat and thirst, I also remember the time when Fred reached to pull me up, the guide tried to help him in turn and we all slid way downhill and ended in a ditch together. Scraped, scuffed, and sore, the three of us sat there, looked each other over and even the guide could not stop laughing.

Toward evening, spreading a tarpaulin under a makeshift shelter, we saw our fire reflected in green who-knew-what animal's eyes and listened to the cries of night birds. Just before making camp, we had come upon a small, silent god standing under a thatched roof. It was not much more than a log—his tubby arms held stiffly to his side, his legs and penis vestigial, his face a study in understatement, but he projected an awesome power. I moved my sleeping bag close to Fred's, but all through that night in this jungly domain, I was aware of a presence.

When we reached the Saori village, the first thing I saw was a near-naked young man sitting on his haunches on a rock. A bow and arrow stuck under his right foot, he was playing a musical instrument, a sort of bent horn that made me think of medieval troubadours. The women, who welcomed us with a bowl of some unidentified mush, wore a simple cotton cloth wrapped around their waist, leaving the breasts free. Isolated, the aboriginal tribes still lead what amounts to Stone Age lives in a hunter's culture and have little contact with the outer world. The orthodox Hindus considered them outcasts; to us they seemed the freest and most lighthearted people in India.

The children had never seen a white person before and were afraid of me. It was my blue eyes, the guide explained. Fred, a white man with dark hair, a suntan and brown eyes they could more or less accept. A woman with white skin might suffer of a disease, but blue eyes definitely spelled a demon. I knew better than to approach them, but it was a strange feeling to see them cringe or run away when I smiled or even just looked at them. Wary as deer, they watched me all that first day, but once a girl sat down not too far from me, others followed, and soon they were laughing and commenting my every move. They never came close enough to touch me.

The Saora decorate their red-mud huts with white chalk drawings: hunters stalking deer, peacocks, monkeys moving through the jungle, a pregnant woman holding a baby or a family feud leaving three casualties spread-eagled on the floor. The paintings were far more journalistic and documentary than the god-and-goddess fantasies of the Madhubani women. They were like the newspaper of the tribe and changed every few weeks, or whenever some newsworthy event occurs. On one wall, I saw an essentially Stone Age drawing of a Saori tribesman riding a bicycle! The most popular subject seemed the tribal dancing scenes, in one of which seventeen women linked arms, dancing shoulder to shoulder, the smallest ones kicking the air because their legs were not long enough to reach the ground.

We watched the real thing that full-moon night, when bowls of home-brewed liquor went around and the drums started calling. The young women formed a long row, their feet rising and falling, their hands flailing, their cries flying up to the brilliant moon, and the drums beat and beat. Their breasts bobbed jauntily as they surged back and forth, bending low with buttocks raised, while the young men pranced in front of them, brandishing spears and letting out bloodcurdling cries. They chanted in short bursts that slowly melted into a chain of throbbing sound, and the whole performance evoked Africa rather than India. They all seemed to have a marvelous time, shouting, laughing and stumping. Early on, an older woman had pulled me into the dancing and giggling crowd, and I had no choice but to stamp and dance with the best of them. I had definitely been declared human by the adults. When everybody had reached a state of near exhaustion, the two groups finally merged. First one couple then another would slip away into the night, the light of the fire glistening on their eyes and teeth. I stood breathless, exhilarated, smelling of sweat, jungle and women. Fred, sitting with the elders who repeatedly offered him the foamy brew, had made some vague attempts to get up and extract me from the throng of gleaming bodies, but a determined poke with a stick told him to stay down and he may have remembered those drawings of spread-eagled figures. Actually, I was never in any danger of being dragged into the forest against my will, but I no longer wondered why these dances figured so prominently in the tribal iconography. Fred said I would probably figure in the next drawing, happily dangling somewhere in the middle of the row, my feet way off the ground.

THE BENGAL LANCERS

It is the story of a very particular army unit that might seem to be more at home in past centuries than our own: the Bengal Lancers of Jaipur. The Maharajah of Jaipur, Saiwan Man Singh, who was Indian Ambassador to Spain at the time, suggested to us that the unit might make a good tale. He was right. His romantic-looking Lancers also made an impressive magazine cover.

They are at home in Jaipur, the capital of Rajasthan. Also walled in and guarded, it is a long way from stark, medieval Bikaner and felt like a much more feminine city. Its Maharanis built palaces of pink sandstone with elegant cupolas and slender pillars, surrounded by lakes and ornamental gardens. In the busy bazaars, women wrapped in tie-dye saris of brilliant red, blue and green chattered gaily to each other and smiled at me. I promised myself I would return one day to this city the color of an autumn sun, but this time we went to meet our formidable hosts: the famous Jaipur Lancers.

The officers of the 61st Cavalry were a group of educated, professional soldiers, a unit straight out of the Raj's picture book. Headquarters offered a large mess hall, a long curved bar and a comfortable clubroom furnished in the proven Victorian tradition of dark wood and mirrored walls. The library had comfortable armchairs, current newspapers, and the books looked used. It could have been a good London club. Sipping drinks among tiger skins and stuffed boar heads, we listened to stories that antedated Kipling by five hundred years. I may have been one of the few European women ever to enter those sacred halls.

Experts in their field, the Lancers are the showpiece of the Indian army. The officers of this elite squadron are India's best polo players and one of the highest-handicapped teams in the world. The polo field lies in the shadow of an impressive fortress that is second home to the team, for both field and fortress belong to the Maharajah, who is a dedicated player. (He died the following year in a polo accident in Cirencester, England.) The CO has one of the finest strings in the country, and players periodically receive extended leave to spend a season in Britain or Australia. Cavaliers all over the world have long adopted their riding breeches, calling them jodhpurs.

As a favorite sport, the officers go pig sticking; a particularly Indian form of horseback hunting that involves chasing a wild boar through the marshlands with a six-foot jobbing spear. It was not the season, but we heard about rushing charges by dark creatures with red eyes, bristling manes and dripping tusks. "One of the sights of dawn is all the chaps standing round sharpening their spears to razor sharp with a small stone. You hold your spear under your arm and depend on the pig charging to drive your spear into the shoulder. There is only one rule: Hold on! It is the most dangerous sport of all."

For all the glamour that surrounds the Royal Polo Team, this is also a no-frills working regiment that spends much of its time in khaki field uniforms, riding up to forty miles a day through the stony hills of Rajasthan. They were great company, intelligent and good-looking, experienced leaders of competent troopers, and nothing could have been more authentic. Still, we wondered just a little about their place in this, our century. Until, one early morning, we stood waiting to photograph one of their maneuvers. The mist still veiled the ground and nothing moved, the only sound the *oop-oop-oop* of a hoopoe bird. Suddenly, they slipped over the horizon and we saw them lined up on the brow of the hill, a line of horsemen standing knee to knee, the sun glinting on the tip of their lances. There were shouts of command, the squadron broke into a brisk trot, then a gallop, sweeping down the hill like a giant scythe. We had seen this scene in Hollywood movies, but nothing had prepared me for the real thing. The final head-on charge at a full gallop was indescribably better, but also a truly terrifying experience. The stinging smell of cavalry wafted across the landscape, dust clouds rose up to choke us, and the earth trembled like a kettledrum. I now understood why a soldier had been standing directly behind me: when the thundering charge came straight at us, I instinctively turned and wanted to run, but the trooper grabbed my elbows and said, "Memsab, do not move." Steadied by the young lancer, who did not let go of me, I took my pictures. The snorting horses with jingling harnesses, the white-teethed turbaned men brandishing six-foot spears, all wheeled in unison, a scanty few feet of empty sand between us, leaving me breathless and shaken.

Later, over a *chota peg* in the officer's club, I owed up to having been scared to death and to my earlier doubts. The commander, middle-aged, mustached and self-confident, laughed, "You are not alone. One of the infantry chaps tried to tell us that we were obsolete. 'You're wrong,' I said, 'and I'll prove it to you.' So the next morning before they knew what was up, I charged their bivouacs with a handful of my lancers, lifted a few tent pegs, and their tents collapsed on top of them. We wheeled off before riding them down, of course, but you should have seen them scrambling up the trees!"

Rann of Kutch

In a village in a remote corner of India, somewhere in the Rann of Kutch, I was bitten by a dog. The Rann is a vast salt marsh on the eastern shore of the Arabian Sea, inhabited by foxes, wolves, chinkara gazelles and wild asses, besides migrating flamingoes and a multitude of other birds. We knew all about the rare wild asses, but very little about the people living in this inhospitable land. Some eke out a living by mining salt, and seminomadic pastors wander the flat expanse of salty clay until the monsoon turns it into a brackish inland sea and the shepherds into fishermen. When the sun once again bakes the mudflats into a dazzling crust of white, they abandon their boats, tied to a tree, until the next rains. It creates a rather Daliesk image.

Their village looked like just any group of ordinary, thatched-roofed houses, but up close, the walls of the low mud houses turned the color of pale cream, were smooth as silk to the touch and decorated with small pieces of colored glass. The doors and windows had wide, elaborately sculptured mud frames of various colors, similarly inlaid. Inside, oil lamps lit up objects of painted wood; the clay jars in the corner showed designs of fish and other animals. Offered tea, we sat on pillows along the wall. The men had hennaed beards and wore simple peasant shirts topped by turbans in unusual dark red, green and black designs. The women were tall, their robes embroidered with pieces of mica and mirror reflecting the light. They seemed on equal standing with the men, laughing and talking freely without any sign of servility or subservience.

It was late afternoon, the sinking sun slanted through the thin trees and bushes of the nearby desert. I had wandered outside, watching the changing light, when several women in deep-red saris walked past on their way to the well, carrying large copper pots on their heads. The sun glinted on the robes, turned the copper into gold, lit up the pale sand and the soft feathery green of the trees behind them. It was incredibly beautiful and I started shooting. I remember feeling a sharp pain in my left leg and looking down: a small, mangy yellow pye-dog was holding on to my ankle for dear life, snarling and tearing. I tried to shake the thing off, but the picture in front of me was so perfect, the sunlight a matter of minutes, if not seconds, I could not possibly have stopped. There was a hollow sound, followed by a shrill yapping and a lot of shouting in Sindhi. One of the men had hit the dog with a stick; it had let go and was running away across the plain.

I had taken my pictures, the sun was losing its perfect hue, and the moment had passed. People now crowded around me and took me to the old headman. Adviser in troubles and healer of wounds, he sat me down and took my foot in both hands. It was a nasty bite, ripped and bleeding, and I began to feel the pain. A basket produced a clay pot, the pot a cloth, the cloth a small jar with strong-smelling black paste, which the old man carefully daubed into the open wound, filling it completely. It stung like fire and I pulled my foot back, but he held it firmly and pushed the two ragged edges of the wound together until they touched. Covering it with a large, fresh leaf, he signaled me to sit quietly, all the while humming under his breath. The women had followed us in the hut and were murmuring and shaking their heads. I remember thinking how lovely a group they made in the lamplight, their strong-boned faces framed by blood-red cotton scarves, their mirror-embroidered dresses, their arms covered from slender wrist to near shoulder with ivory bracelets. It had all taken minutes. Fred and our driver, who had been visiting a house nearby, came running, and a heated discussion began. Some of the inhabitants of the village were untouchables and among their jobs was the curing of hides and discarding of bones of slaughtered animals. The small bitch had puppies and lived off scraps of meat and hide buried in large pits. The question now raised was *rabies*: did she attack me because I had gotten close to her pups or was there a real danger? Then we were in our rickety car, driving through the desert night to Bhuj, the nearest town, about forty miles away. The young doctor's waiting room was lit up and full of people, but when he heard the dog and rabies tale, he took me straight into his office. I held out my foot to show him the ankle and he took off the rough bandage and the leaf. "You said this happened just now?" "About an hour and a half ago," we confirmed. He pointed at my leg, almost accusingly and we all looked. The wound was virtually closed!

He asked me what the old man had done, and I told him about the black, strong-smelling paste that now conjured up visions of magic healing. The young man bent over, sniffed and started to laugh: "They are wonderful! He filled it up with tobacco paste! Of course! A very strong disinfectant, it constricts and is a great painkiller! But rabies? No, you'll still have to have the shot." In those days, *the shot* meant several long needles stuck in a neat circle all around my navel. It was almost worse than the bite.

Next morning we returned to the village to finish our work. Bringing gifts to the headman, we were in turn welcomed with the bowl of sacred buttermilk offered to friends and a special meal of rice and mutton speckled with cardamom pods, a feast to which most of the village must have contributed. Some of the women stood behind my pillowed seat and chanted. The driver said: "It is about you! They are singing about a white woman who walked out into the desert in the evening sun. A ferocious animal attacked her, but she kept on walking, dragging it along and did not let go of the shiny box she was carrying. You will become part of the local folklore!"

We left with regrets. I would have liked to stay a little longer among a people who filled their hard lives with such joyous art. My ankle was swollen and painful and I limped for a while, but there was no infection and it healed without any further complications. Tobacco paste indeed.

FRIENDS

Jahanara Jaipal Singh was a very large, very dark-skinned and very impressive woman who carried her power well. Minister of Tourism and Aviation at the time of Indira Gandhi's Government, she invited me to meet Mrs. Gandhi in Delhi. I was excited, but when I actually met her, I stood in a long line with other people. She looked at me without seeing me, rather cold eyes, rather bored and barely a nod. No pictures allowed. When she left in the car a few minutes later, she did manage a dazzling smile and a hand wave through the open window for the crowd.

While Fred was interviewing people in Delhi, I spent a weekend in Jahanara's home in Ranchi, where her cook taught me that Indian food is not just curry powder. The kitchen, a separate hut in the courtyard, was where I learned the basics. When picking herbs, first beat the long grasses for snakes, then chase away the waves of parakeets that descended on the mango trees, so you can pick the fruit without being splotched with bird droppings. He taught me how to choose specific spices for different dishes, how to knead chapattis, and gave me his recipes for sweets like *barfis* and *jallebis*, the chewy confection with almonds and pistachios. I had my first close look at a tandoor, the ubiquitous clay oven shaped like a huge jar. The charcoal fire on the bottom heated the sides of the oven to scorching point about half way up, the chickens— marinated in curds and spices—were spitted on an iron spike and placed upright in the oven. The heated clay itself released a mellow fragrance and the marinade dripping on to the hot coals created a particular kind of smoke. Half a dozen unpromising, scrawny birds emerged crisp, golden red in color and, thanks to the curd marinade, were actually tender.

Jahanara invited local politicians to dinners flavored with whisperings and small intrigues. The majority of her guests seemed convinced that I was a member of the CIA. Working with *Time/Life*, a single woman reporter, met the prime minister; I simply had to be linked to that outfit. Not that it bothered anybody, people just wanted to bribe me and get on the payroll. They would corner me, explaining that they would like to "be of service to me in my work as an American reporter." The fact that I was neither American, nor on assignment for *Time/Life* did not faze them at all. I asked Jahanara what it was all about, but she just shrugged her shoulders and said I could do what I liked!

The party was good, musicians played the flute and the small drums while the guests ate, drank and talked. The *barfis*—chewy, marzipan-like confection with almonds and pistachios—were set out on small tables together with the *pan* and the candied ginger. I drink, but have never taken drugs. I react strongly to even a simple sleeping pill and have always been afraid drugs might drag up memories it took me a long time to bury. Unaware that Jahanara customarily served *bhang* or the stronger, more expensive *ganja* in some form at dinner, I happily nibbled the sweets. I woke, lying fully dressed on a daybed, covered with a sheet. I remembered having dreamt that I was sleeping in a large room, where people in flowing white dresses walked in and out without taking any notice of me, also of hearing strange music and at one time, chanting. I was not far wrong. I had been sleeping for more than twenty-four hours, during which life in the large house went on as usual and people dressed in white were indeed passing by my bed. There had been a student demonstration in front of the house, which explained the chanting, but nothing had brought me back to the world. Jahanara had returned to her ministry in Delhi, while I had missed the small plane that was to take me to Patna. If the guests still thought I was a CIA agent, my performance must have left something to be desired. (Years later, when I lived on Long Island and had Betty Friedan as a neighbor and friend, we found out that we had been in Delhi at the same time. We had met Mrs. Gandhi during the same week and, yes, Betty had been approached for her contacts with the CIA, which explained Jahanara's indifference. Corruption was par for the course.)

Jaharana had two sons, the youngest a prince, his father the head of a large and influential tribe. The older brother, Ranjit, was a tall and handsome playboy, complete with expensive clothes and a red sports car. Both came to spend a summer with us in Deia, where young Veri quickly became Moochen's favorite page. The slender white-haired woman and her elegant princeling wandered down to the *cala* for a swim, they took the old bus to go shopping in Palma and cooked up strange, delicious meals. When autumn came, Veri went up to Oxford. Ranjit, who rather disliked the fact that tribal elders back home knelt to wash his younger brother's feet, moved to France and became a successful engineer with Airbus. He had also fallen in love with Cathy, saying, "I don't know how I am going to tell my mother that I am marrying a white girl, but we will have such beautiful children!" Cathy liked him well enough, but she did not marry him.

TIGER IN THE NIGHT

Standing in a sort of parkland with rose beds, ornamental trees and mowed lawns the medieval temples of Khajuraho are now a popular tourist destination. In the 1960s, when Fred and I traveled the four hundred miles from New Delhi to the state of Madhya Pradesh in the mid-1960s, the carved sandstone temples were barely visible in a setting of scrub and jungle. Their architecture and erotic sculptures were not yet widely known and attracted few visitors, most of whom were scholars. Once or twice a week, late mornings, a small plane touched down in a clearing, unloaded a handful of passengers and flew them out the same afternoon. Fred had an appointment the next day, but needing more time to photograph the sculptures, we decided that I would stay until the plane came around again. I found a room with an elderly couple in the only small farmhouse close to the temples. The husband made a little money explaining the sculptures to the tourists.

The next morning, a skinny ten-year-old boy kept following me around and once shyly handed me my camera bag when I reached for it. By the end of the day Kisha, the farmer's grandson, was my full-fledged, proud assistant. When I offered to share my room—a rope-webbed *charpoy* and a small table with a tin washbowl the only furniture—he gave me a big smile and shook his head. "I am *chowkidar*; I am night watchman!" The jungle crept right up to the temples and yellow-flowered vines invaded the porch of our shack, but he wrapped himself in his blanket and slept in front of my door. That evening he took me to the nearby village to see a wedding. Walking along the dark path skirting the jungle I shone my flashlight and we sang and shouted to frighten off snakes and whatever else might be lurking. It may not have helped but it made us feel better.

On my third and last night, I was woken by a crash and a shout, "Tiger, Memsab, Tiger!" Kisha flew inside, blanket and all, frantically trying to close the door and shaking with fright. Tiger?? I got up and pulled the shaking boy inside. What tiger? "There, there!" The brave night watchman had turned back into a frightened ten-year-old. I stood listening and suddenly heard it. A large animal, snarling, the deep-throated coughs coming closer, and I suddenly realized that this was real and murderous. We crouched on the floor, arms around each other and listened, our eyes riveted on the flimsy screen door that would not have kept out a housecat. We smelled the rank, menacing odor and heard the raspy breathing right outside the hut. I had wild visions of blinding it with my flash, but the cameras were sitting on the other side of the room and I did not dare to move a muscle. Actually, I don't think I could have, for I was paralyzed with terror. If we could smell whatever was so close, out there, it would certainly smell us, dripping with fear. I did not see my whole life pass in front of me, but I asked myself whether this was really to be the end of my wanderings, of my life, to be torn apart by a tiger in a shack in the jungle? Kisha whimpered and I pressed his face against my shoulder to smother the little squawks. The snarling coughs had stopped in front of the door, as if hesitating. That moment, waiting for the thing to come through the door, I fully believed I would never see my family again. There came a sudden noise, something like a *wooofff*, then something heavy breaking through bushes, followed by a half bark, half squeal. After that, silence, while we waited for what seemed an eternity. The next thing was the farmer calling, "*Kisha, koi-hai?*" and the old man entered our room. Taking the boy in his arms, he kept repeating, "Oh, how good the Gods were to us. The jaguar came and looked for you. Then he leapt the fence and took the dog!"

When I tried to get up, I nearly fell. I started to shake and was soaking wet. I looked down and saw the pitiful little puddle of pee. I knew it was Kisha's, but it might as well have been mine. We went next door where the wife made us tea and I sat until morning, watching them offer grains of rice, a cup of milk and a chaplet of flowers to the small lingam in the house shrine. We talked little, but I thought back to the long walk through the jungle night I had taken with a child who wanted to be my protector and realized that I had risked both our lives with my ignorance. I left on the afternoon plane, worrying whether the jaguar might be back this or another night. I had seen the prints of his pugs within a yard of our shelter.

WHY DON'T YOU WRITE ABOUT THE MAN

Manuel de Falla and Leonid Massine in the Alhambra, Granada

I met Fred in Delhi, where he finished his interviews and a week later, we flew home to Deia. Having outgrown the Deia village teachers, Foster, Marc and Cathy now went to school in Palma. Franciscan Friars ran the boys' school, housed in a beautiful monastery complete with a thirteenth-century cloister. It had an excellent reputation and both our boys boarded with a respectable widow who had taken in students for years. They were five altogether, sharing meals and doing their homework under the watchful eye of their black-shawled keeper. Cathy was in a small boarding school run by the Sisters of the Immaculate Conception. We were not catholic but both schools accepted them without hesitation. Fred and I had permission to pick them up on Wednesday afternoon; we would take them to a movie and for dinner, bringing them back by nine o'clock. On Friday, they all climbed in the bus together, rumbling back to Deia and home.

In those months of quiescence, putting short texts to pictures for my Swiss women's magazines, I realized that I enjoyed writing.

Not that I thought of myself as a writer, by any means. I loved being a photographer and we were a team, our roles self-evident. Then, one day, while doing research for Fred, who was writing his *Time/Life* volume on Spanish music, I could not find any decent material on Manuel de Falla. Who was after all the country's most famous composer! Fred heard me complain and shouted: "Then why don't *you* write about the man. You certainly know enough about him." So I did. In German, as it was still very much part of my culture and I was not that sure of my English. Writing that slim volume was important to me on several levels. It was the first book I published under my own name, a small milestone in my life; I had felt sufficiently sure of myself to write it, and it confirmed to me that Fred, capable of declaring war over the wrong use of a semicolon, believed that I could do it.

Falla was indeed the most important Spanish composer of the twentieth century. The only one in whose work the dark bloodline of Spain ran true. Iberian to the core, he arrived at an inimitable mixture of bitterness and languor. Where others wove Spanish melodies into folklorism, he wrote *Love, the Magician, Nights in the Gardens of Spain* or the *Atlántida.* One of the central figures of what would be known as the "New Music," Falla spanned the turn of the century and in his Paris years counted Ravel, Debussy and Dukas among his friends. Stravinsky called him the "most loyal of my musician friends." The Princess de Polignac was his sponsor, Leon Bakst created the costumes for his ballets, Picasso designed the stage sets, and Diaghilev performed them with the famous Ballets Russes of Monte Carlo. Together with Federico Garcia Lorca, he organized the first "Cante Jondo" contest in Granada and brought flamenco to the attention of the musical world. (My book was published in Switzerland. It sold steadily for years and established me as an author. I remember the thrill, years later, showing my children a copy, shelved in the Library of Congress.)

In 1939, Falla left Spain for Argentina, together with his sister. She had since returned and now lived in a convent near Jerez de la

Frontera. When she agreed to meet with me, we took the children on a trip through Andalusia and I visited Maria del Carmen. She was very kind to me and spoke about her brother as if he was still a young man and alive, stressing that he had always hoped to return to Spain. It was not to be. Falla died in Alta Gracia in 1946. What caused a composer whose music was so closely interwoven with his country's culture to go into exile? She answered that after the victory of the Franco regime and the assassination of Garcia Lorca, he could not bear to stay in Spain. The Franco government offered him a large pension if he would return, but he refused. Maria gave me a note for one of Falla's closest friends, Segismundo Romero. The old gentleman lived in Seville and received me warmly, but was reluctant to answer my questions. I had expected this and could fully understand it. Franco's regime might have aged, but even in the 1960s all civil war issues, and certainly Lorca's death, were still very much taboo and often dangerous for those who talked too freely. He said he needed some time to think it over. We had dinner and talked about gypsies and flamenco and about the *Harpsichord Concerto* that Falla wrote for the great harpsichordist Wanda Landowska, the piece that would mark the revival of the harpsichord in European music. He made me a present of some documents and a postcard handwritten by Falla. We said goodbye and agreed to stay in touch. The next morning a letter was delivered to my hotel.

"After the outbreak of the civil war on July 18, 1936, all contact with Falla was interrupted for several months. On the second train that left Seville, I went to see him in Granada. I found him at home, ill and deeply afflicted by the murder of our friend Federico Garcia Lorca. He told me how he had news one evening that Lorca had been arrested. Falla assumed that the arrest had to do with Lorca's religious views and did not believe it would have serious consequences. Just a few days before, Falla had fallen and hurt his knee so badly that he could hardly walk. He therefore decided to wait until the next day before finding out more details. Early morning he drove to the

Comandancia and asked to see the commanding officer, with whom he was on friendly terms. The officer accompanied him immediately to the Guardia Civil. Falla, with his hurt leg, could not climb the steep stairs of the building and waited downstairs in the car. When he returned shortly, Falla could see by the expression on his face that they had arrived too late. Lorca had been arrested around three o'clock in the afternoon and shot in the back a few hours later, together with other prisoners, in the hills along the road to Viznar. Lorca had not died immediately, whereupon they had smashed his skull. All were thrown into a mass grave. This is the truth about Lorca's death, as Falla told it to me at the time. He never recovered from the events of that war."

Segismundo Romero.

Romero gave me permission to include his letter in my book, which was published in Zurich, and I have no reason to think it has ever harmed him.

When Manuel de Falla died in Argentina in 1946, Franco had his remains brought back in a battleship and ordered a state burial in the crypt of the cathedral of Cadiz. The gesture shocked those friends who were aware that Falla, in spite of his deep love for his country, had left it because of his total refusal to accept Franco's reign.

Given our own past, did Fred and I ever wonder about living in a country ruled by a dictator? Certainly. In 1936 the Mallorcan military command had sided with Franco at once. The new regime demanded that village mayors have a clean, non-republican record. In Deia such problems were solved over a game of dominoes in the café, where elders agreed on the names to be submitted to the authorities. On the island the Civil War more often brought out long-standing jealousies and personal vendettas related to inheritance, mistresses and water rights than arguments over politics. When we arrived there was little left of Falangist influence. Once again the Mallorcans had begun to regard mainland Spain as a separate country, a distant government associated with unemployment compensation, medical insurance and a friendly visit of Manuel Fraga Iribarne, Minister of Tourism, to Robert Graves. Occasionally an issue of *Time* or *Newsweek* was held up at the border for a cover that displeased Madrid. The local authorities were far more interested in developing the island's economical infrastructure and the tourist industry.

THE INSTITUTE

Robert Graves and Julian Huxley

In the summer of 1969, the Deia Mediterranean Institute was established by Dowling College in New York. The Institute offered a two-semester, fully academic program with professors and counselors in residence. A group of about forty students and some well-known literary figures and scholars were to spend September until May in our village.

John Cheever enjoyed Deia, but did not humor Graves and kept mostly to himself. Beyond my first impression of the New England gentleman with a Yankee face and a clipped accent, complete with crewneck sweater and khakis, I found a delightful friend, a man as witty, sad, and complicated as his Wapshot stories. He was also unpredictable. Over dinner, he could suddenly turn bitter, even cruel about friends and family. Or, facing his private demons, he might choose to feel sorry for himself.

His daughter Susan and her husband, Rob Cowley, were old friends of Fred, who during an earlier visit had brought our children a bright orange inflatable dinghy that was the sensation of the summer.

Cheever wrote to a friend, "Susie and Rob met us in Palma and we drove over the mountains to the other coast. Deya is a cluster of stone houses between the sea and a steep range of mountains. The prices are incredible. Wine is nine cents a bottle and full pension is less than three dollars a day. In the morning I worked and then walked a mile or so through olive and lemon groves to the sea. The coast is rocky and the water as transparent as air. Above the sea is a small café in a cave where you can play chess and drink gin and tonic. (. . .) This is a mixed bag of Europeans and American expatriates. One man is famous for having spent five nights with Christine Keeler."

Anthony Burgess, arriving fresh from his success with *Clockwork Orange*, loved his audience. His students adored both the man and his lectures. Offering these young Americans a glimpse of his dark and violent vision of the future was like exposing them to a whirlwind or an open furnace. Burgess also loved the nightly parties, where he chose to drink, sing and argue with not always the best. One late evening, or rather early morning, he tumbled down a ten-foot stone terrace, together with his opponent, and twisted his ankle. His wife, the Contessa Pasi, belabored both parties and everyone else in sight with a stick until they stopped laughing and carried him home. I am not sure how he remembered Deia, but when we met again in Paris, it did not seem to have left any strong impressions. He would later write, "Deia had little to recommend save Graves's magic. A literal magic, apparently, since the hills were said to be full of iron of a highly magnetic type, which drew at the metal deposits of the brain and made people mad. Graves himself was said to go around sputtering exorcisms while waving an olive branch."

For me, it was the first time that I had come in such close contact with American students. Standing in for Fred, who was away on an assignment, I gave some lectures on Falla and Spanish music. Fascinated by their generosity and self-assurance, I was also shocked by their innocence, bordering on appalling ignorance, in matters of world history, World War II, drug problems or just plain human behavior.

I could not have imagined at the time how much sorrow the Institute and its encounters were to bring me, how much my life would change.

READY FOR THE WONDERFUL

There's a race of men that don't fit in,
A race that can't stay still;
So they break the hearts of kith and kin,
And they roam the world at will.

—Robert William Service

Some people are born with genes that draw them to foreign and faraway places. I was always attracted to explorers like Mungo Park, Richard Burton, or Darwin, Mary Kingsley or Ida Pfeiffer—who out of scientific curiosity or some Romantic passion set out on voyages that were both internal and external. They "pushed out towards the unknown in obedience to an inward voice, to an impulse beating in the blood," Joseph Conrad wrote in *Lord Jim*. "They were wonderful; and it must be owned that they were ready for the wonderful." In our own, imaginatively circumscribed century, Fred and I inevitably felt some sense of diminution. Straying into remote regions, meeting people of the jungle, the snows or the desert, I never was under the illusion that we were *discovering* them. They might be new to *us*, but we knew they had been living their lives well before we passed by to tell their story to the world. What I did share was the obedience to that inward voice and a pure delight in finding the wonderful. The intense pleasure in the promises of a new morning and the deep satisfaction in our work as the day unfolded. Even in later years, working alone, it was never mere romanticism, ennui with the "perfection" of home life or even the love for my profession that made me set out. It felt like a spring that needed to be filled from deep inside the earth. A part of me, a part that feels whole and content, has its roots in my travels; the person I am today was shaped as much by my journeys answering the unspoken summons and pursuing the unexplored, as by the family I love and the men I married.

When I first started to travel to out-of-the-way places, I wanted to bring back an objective story. I realized that my personal impressions were as valid as any literal accuracy. Few people see the same thing or the same truth, even through the eye of a camera. The pictures I know as my own are those that took my breath away in the split second before I clicked the shutter; looking through the camera I had actually *recognized* something I had never seen before. They show things that gave me joy or made me cry, images I remember because I always wanted to and some that I did not manage to forget no matter how hard I tried. Those moments and those images are mine alone.

I also learned from others. Early on, the English writer Dame Rose Macaulay showed me that her *Fabled Shore* belonged to a different Spain from that of Murray or Baedeker. Where a rather dour Richard Ford dismissed Valencia's famous rococo portal as grotesque, a fricassee of palm trees, Indians, serpents and absurd forms, Macaulay asked "Why absurd?" To her it was one of the loveliest things in Valencia. (She was of course also a person who happily rode to High Mass in her English village church on a camel.)

I therefore dared to embrace Gaudi's fantasy of fun-fair towers made into a cathedral, even though Evelyn Waugh declared that it was unlikely ever to be finished, unless by "a millionaire a little wrong in the head." Personally, I often tend to associate places with writers who first made them come alive to me. Sometimes I found what I thought they promised me; sometimes I walked my own very different path. And while I crossed or followed the song lines of those that had gone before, I was also happily spinning my own. For although this is not meant to be a travel book, a large part of my life was defined by my wanderings and these are the tales.

Was it all glorious, easy and harmonious as *The Sound of Music*? Would I actually enjoy being shoved into the stinking mud by an aggressive black pig, while trying to squat over an open latrine? Worrying about jumping spiders and fire ants? Russian soldiers arresting us at gunpoint in the Danube Delta, where people in striped pajamas labored in malarial marshes? Being kicked by a bad-tempered horse in Mongolia? Sleeping with a gun under my pillow because drunken miners in Brazilian gold camps tend to have funny ideas? Not to mention ordinary travel fatigue, the Englishman's bugger's muddle of missed, canceled or nonexistent transportation, of being freezing cold or sweaty hot, of dealing with rejection, insults and sometimes just no-story-at-all? Hardly. But what I remember above all else is enchantment and deep gratitude. The crazy, joyous happiness that floods you when you are in the one place on earth you want to be at that moment, doing the one thing you want to do most of all—and doing it well. And an overwhelming feeling of awe, because you walk a planet so beautiful it breaks your heart.

AFGHANISTAN AND NURISTAN

In the late 1960s, attending a dinner in Delhi in honor of one of King Nadir Shah of Afghanistan' relatives, Fred and I were introduced to his French wife. We shared a more intimate lunch and soon after we arrived back home, a formal invitation arrived: we were to visit Afghanistan, with special permission to enter a little known region called Nuristan. It was long before the Russian invasion, the Taliban, Al Qaeda and Bin Laden, and Afghanistan was not much talked about in the Western world. Even our Indian friends gave us that "Why *ever* would you want to go *there* for" look. Few had read Robert Byron's *Road to Oxiana*, and Kipling's wild Afghans conformed far more to the image they shared. Fred was editor of *Queen Magazine* at the time and could not wander too far too long, so we decided that I would first set out alone to explore. I would go and see Kabul and Bamian before we would travel to Nuristan together. It was another first, another step to an independence that would slowly change our relationship. Landing in Kabul, I found a dusty, mud-rutted, bewildering and delightful Central Asian city and wandering rather aimlessly through the crowded streets, I felt pure joy. The heat on the mud walls, the young men walking hand-in-hand, the quick turn of veiled heads when I passed, followed by a rapid chatter and muffled giggles. Children touched me with shy fingers, but rarely did they beg and never in front of adults. I felt some old men's disdainful looks, proud illiterate patriarchs affronted by the sight of a foreign female's naked face. In the center of town, I crossed large avenues with public buildings and mosques, the ornate Foreign Ministry, some hotels, shops and apartment buildings. The "new" town, Char-I-Nao, was obvious reserved for foreigners, Russian and American engineers in charge of road construction, Chinese and German agricultural specialists and French biologists. Most of the local inhabitants lived in the mare's nest of narrow streets climbing the hills, walled alleyways lined with low mud houses without electricity or running water. Nearer to the congeries of bazaars, the streets were crowded with horsemen, heavily loaded camels and mules carrying crates, barrels or bundles of firewood. Felt-booted nomads struggled to cross the street at a traffic light, despairing to get past drivers who in turn yelled and honked their horns at their ignorance. I saw tall Pathans, bearded Sikhs and Hazarath with flat Mongol features. Men wore long shirts over loose pants tied at the ankles, one end of their turban flopping down over their shoulder. Many women wore the *chador*, leaving their face unveiled, others moved like shrouded ghosts in their covering *burqa*, but among them walked uniformed schoolgirls in amazingly short skirts. It happened to be a religious holiday and a festive crowd had gathered on the lawns behind the great mosque. The wrestlers held a fascinated audience, striped robes of Sunday silk shining in the slanted sunlight. People carried small birdcages with even smaller birds, but far from wanting to sell them, they were simply taking their feathered friends for a stroll. Stalls sold bottles of soft drinks in the most unlikely bright greens, purples and reds; flat slabs of *naan* were dug out of blackened ovens and the smell of frying mutton hung over it all. Rice with grated carrots and raisins—a little meat buried way underneath and the whole topped with thick creamy curd—was served in earthenware bowls and eaten while comfortably lying on the grass in a circle of friends, chatting and passing the time of day. Tonight, the holiday over, the peasants would squeeze into overcrowded buses or squat in the back of a gaily painted truck, shuttling back to their villages and everyday problems.

A perfect day? While I was watching the wrestling in the square, men had pushed me aside, pinched my backside and laughed when an old mullah first covered his eyes with one hand and then actually spat at me. I should probably have felt somewhat intimidated, worried about being here without Fred, about the coming weeks traveling alone. Instead, it was here that I first began to understand the significance of being a single foreign woman in a crowd. A couple forms a unit and is recognized as such by others, moving within a sort of shell. Alone, I was definitely more vulnerable, but also more approachable. I was involved and my impressions were my own; I was the person women smiled at, who was offered apricots and spat at by a bad-tempered old man. Did I prefer this to sharing with Fred? Definitely not, but wandering alone through bustling Kabul, I felt as if I touched my childhood dreams, come alive.

Later that evening, demonstrators wearing the small white turbans of religious leaders, passed in front of my hotel, carrying banners reading "death or victory." It was a counter demonstration to the one staged earlier that week by Sunni orthodox priests who protested against the celebration of Lenin's birthday, unveiled women, short skirts, alcohol being sold in public places and other signs of progress or loss of dignity. Police and army lined the streets, protecting public buildings and the royal palace, nudging the parade along pre-chosen routes. The arguing, the shouting and pushing lasted a very long time. I went to bed in my small room on the ground floor, close to the noisy street, the blowing horns, the blaring transistor radios, the arguing men and clattering hoofs. Somewhere far off, tribal drums pounded the beat of the wild *attan*, the ancient dance of the Pathans. Finally, it all died away and the night became so still that I could hear the creaking of new sandals when a straggler walked past. The last sound I heard before falling asleep in bustling Kabul was a donkey braying.

The next day I was assigned a guide and a driver who had their instructions and would not let me set foot in the street or the market by myself. I realized that the invitation had been for a journalist/ photographer team and that the Afghan government tourist office had not expected a woman to show up alone. They probably also thought I would be grateful for a protection that to me felt more like a restriction. I was not grateful and said so, politely, whereupon I was advised, politely, that I was leaving Kabul the next day for Bamian. Short measures for unruly female photographers?

BAMIAN

I woke early and returned to the tourist office to convince them that I needed to call Fred, who was still in London, and explain my change of plans. They did not even hear me out. All they wanted was for me to go away and become somebody else's problem. When I said I would complain "higher up," they suddenly remembered that I was here on a very Personal Royal Invitation and promised they would let Fred know I was on the move.

Outside the car was waiting. Two bearded, turbaned young men—the driver and my guide—put my luggage in the trunk and me on the back seat. Without a word, we set out for a long day's ride on the rough country roads. A few miles out of the city, the desert wind blew and people had their own problems. Water. Because although clouds had formed, no rain had fallen for over two years and the fields were dusty with a fine powder that seeped into everything. At ten thousand feet, the Unai Pass, crossed under a yellow moon, was eerily quiet but for a high whistling wind. When we arrived in Bamian on its high plateau, thin clouds were veiling the sky and it was starting to rain. Our driver took off his jacket, stood bare-chested and lifting his head, he sang. Or maybe he prayed.

The guest yurt was clean and comfortable, the dish with flat bread, curds and pickles most welcome. I went to sleep listening to the rain and, expecting a wet and maybe dismal morning, woke to a perfect sunrise. Below me, between the plateau and the village, a small river bordered by green and silver poplars ran alongside the familiar red dust road. Goats tinkled their bells and from the town a faint hammering and singing floated up to me. Across the valley, carved into a pale pink cliff face riddled with thousands of caves, stood two giant Buddhas, the taller figure measuring no less than 175 feet in height. Generations of monks carved a honeycomb of rooms, cells, libraries and refectories as well as hundreds of sculptures in the cliff face, culminating in the two largest Buddhas in the world. The statues dated back to the third century AD, their niches once painted in bright colors, their faces and pleated robes covered with gold leaf and studded with precious stones. For centuries, this was a place of pilgrimage, a sacred valley filled with monasteries and *stupas,* seen glittering from afar with gilded statues and domes. Age, earthquakes, invasions and iconoclastic depredation did their work, but the Buddhas survived from the knees upward albeit without adornment other than dignity and the respect they inspired. From closer up, I saw the enigmatic smile on the mutilated face, the broken hand raised in a gesture of blessing. Robert Byron writes in *Road to Oxiana* that "neither of the Buddhas have any artistic values. But one could bear that; it is their negation of sense, the lack of any pride in their monstrous flaccid bulk that sickens." I loved his book, but as I failed to understand this total rejection, I squatted happily on my rock and left with a feeling of peace. Never mind Robert Byron.

The statues survived until in the spring of 2001, when the Taliban government sent its minions of the Ministry for the Prevention of Vice and the Promotion of Virtue to finish with bombs what time, Genghis Khan and earlier religious fanaticism had not achieved: the willful and total destruction of the great Buddhas of Bamian. The Minister of Information then actually issued the following apologetic declaration: "This destruction was not as easy as people may think. You cannot simply blow up these statues with a few canon shots, for both are carved out of the sedimentary rock and are a solid part of the mountain." That was what sickened *me*, dear Byron.

THE SAPPHIRE LAKES OF BAND-E-AMIR

The whole situation was rather odd. Usually, Fred and I would start out with a theme, fitting pictures to the text or vice versa. This time the story was neither ordered nor sold, our travel dates had been decided by the royal invitation. We were badly prepared. Fred would be arriving soon and expect that I had some idea of what was going on. The best thing I could do was make notes and take pictures, hoping some story would take shape. It might be right for *Queen Magazine* or turn out to be something entirely different. So far, it had been more a "let's see what we can make of this" experience.

I was getting to know my two companions a little better, but they were still wary of letting me out of their sight. The driver did not speak any English and my guide kept pointing ahead, repeating, "Lakes very good," while we were bumping along narrow roads, wading across rivers, and climbing a high pass. Suddenly a large valley opened up on the breathtaking sight of several lakes, strung like a jeweled chaplet of emerald, turquoise and lapis lazuli in a landscape of pale sand

and honey-colored rocks. Waterfalls cascaded down white travertine walls; the pinnacled plateaus seemed crowned with imaginary castles and behind them rose the snow-covered ridges of the Hindu Kush. The lakes had magical names like Zulfeqar, Gholaman, and Qambar. Finding our way down to a white beach, we brewed tea in the shade of a small, abandoned mosque. There was no one in sight, no traveler on land, no small boat ruffling the still, transparent water. I was very tempted to go for a swim, but both guide and driver threw up their hands: "No, no, no bath here! Lake is very, very deep, very dangerous, on the bottom live very big fish, very bad fish!" The two men soon fell asleep in the afternoon heat. Short of bathing, I lay listening to the gently lapping wavelets, seduced and awed by this enchanted shore worthy of any oriental fairy tale and thinking how much I liked this country. Never have I seen a deeper color blue than that of the sapphire lakes of Band-e-Amir.

Years later, in 2011, browsing through Wikipedia I learned that, together with Bamian, the lakes have become the heart of Afghanistan's tourism, attracting thousands of tourists every year. Band-e-Amir was declared Afghanistan's first national park, but that did not save it. The absence of maintenance authority, lack of attention and funding resulted in unregulated grazing and uprooting of shrubs, causing soil erosion and landslides. Human waste, trash, boats with gasoline engines and fishing with explosives have led to severe pollution. Another small paradise lost.

HEADING NORTH

We turned north, following the ancient caravan route. Nomad tents showed like black dots on the mountain slopes and down the road came camels, head to tail, plod, plod, plod, led by small boys on donkeys. It struck me again how different the dark, double-humped camels of Central Asia were from their sleek, haughty-faced cousins of the Arabian Desert. Bulky, born at the wayside and walking from calfhood with the even progress of the caravan, the slow, lumbering pace has become part of the Bactrian's nature. With their scruffy look created by the thick, continuously shedding fur, they have been part of this rugged landscape for thousands of years, and the sight of them grazing among the tamarinds, a near biblical scene, added to my sense of displacement, of being in an ancient and distant land.

One late afternoon we crossed a swollen river, when the car stalled and we were stuck. Simply stuck, stranded on a bank separating us from a group of nomad's tents. Surrounded by mountains, we were about an hour's drive from the next village. Never having ventured off the road, neither my guide nor the driver knew the area and were terrified of the Kuchi nomads, whose number we could only guess by their small fires. My innocent suggestion that we might ask them for help met with horrified refusal, the inevitable throwing up of hands and cutting-of-throat gestures. Soon it was pitch dark and my companions refused to leave the safety of the locked car. Wrapped in our blankets, listening to the roar of the water and the howling of the nomad's dogs, we waited for dawn. The old truck that came rumbling along made it across and helped us pull the car up the slope, albeit to small avail, as the ignition coil had burned. Someone had to go to the next town and get help or buy a spare part. We decided I would ride with the truck driver and my guide to the next small town to get help. It being daylight and our presence now known to others, our driver was less afraid to wait alone. As we passed the Kuchi tents three huge dogs attacked the truck, jumping straight up to my window, snarling and slavering in my frightened face. Truly ferocious animals, they answer only to one master, will take on wolves or bears and of course any thieves that might covet the flocks. Turbaned men, knives stuck in their belts, did nothing to call them off and watched us leave without a move. The driver swore and stepped on the gas, while I slid down in my seat, hoping the brutes would give up when they no longer saw me. Straightening up a little self-consciously once we had passed the camp, I saw my window was streaked with slobber and blood. It made me feel rather more sympathetic to my companions' terrified refusal to approach the tents on foot in the middle of the night. The truck driver said he would not like to pass a night near their camp, alone, stranded with a broken truck. Through that dark night on the riverbank we had stayed awake. None of us saw nor heard the soft-footed men who most certainly *did* take a good look at us. The official car and the presence of a foreign woman with cameras probably dissuaded them.

I have since been invited into Kuchi homes on various occasions, sitting on worn rugs under the wide-slung black tent, sharing the family's meal of flat bread, goat cheese and tea spiced with cardamom. This time the dogs stayed quiet, heads resting on paws, but their eyes watched my every move. In general, the Kuchi were hospitable, they asked about the countries I had been and sometimes allowed me to take pictures. I was also expected to treat infected eyes and suppurating wounds. Like most journalists who travel these areas I carried a small first-aid kit and did the best I could, having little medicine and less experience. Led to an old man who had an eye scooped out, no explanation forthcoming and no refusal on my part excepted, all I could do was fill the cavity with antibiotic ointment and cover it with a patch. I had candies and vitamin C for the children; I confess to once giving a shiny silver-blue package of Alka Seltzer tablets to a young woman who was desperately trying to get pregnant. She tied it on a string of beads and hung it around her neck. For all I know it worked. We continued through the fertile valleys of the Hindu Kusch. Climbing and descending, we passed fields of wild tulips, orchards with apricots and peaches, vineyards with raisin-drying sheds, fields green with rice or rippling with golden wheat. Here the walls in a village teahouse—where I was the only woman among a dozen men in striped gowns noisily slurping green Uzbek tea from China bowls— showed images of gardens with nightingales among fruiting trees. At the end of the road was Mazar-e-Sharif, the holy city of Afghanistan with its great blue-domed mosque holding the tomb of Caliph Ali, son-in-law of the Prophet. When the muezzin's call invoked the name of Allah, hundreds of pilgrims, Afghans from faraway provinces, Bedouins from Iraq and travelers from Iran, kneeled in unison, their foreheads touching the floor. All reciting the same prayers with the same precise gestures and the same fervor. It was a powerful image of Islam. Outside, there was room for gentleness. In courtyards full of blooming roses the blue domes shone reflected in still pools, the people of Mazar walked with their children in the shade of the poplar trees and vendors proffered their ware. Above, flights of white pigeons brightened the sky with bursts of silver wings.

About twelve miles outside Mazar lay the place I really wanted to see: Balkh, site of ancient Bactria. Said to be the oldest city in the world, it dates back to 2,500 BC; here Zoroaster preached and Alexander married Roxanne, daughter of a Sogdian king. The citadels and fortresses built by his generals flourished for nearly fifteen centuries, until the tide of Genghis Kahn's Mongol army swept up to the gates. The city resisted longer than expected and he ordered its total destruction. One would think that this would have been the end of it. However, when the army returned, it found a number of fugitives. Then, wrote his young chronicler, Ata-Malik Juvaini-Ali, "Wherever a wall was left standing, the Mongols pulled it down and fulfilled upon them the verse: *Twice shall we chastise them*. And Chingiz-Khan thus disposed of Balkh." All along the old silk routes, that deathly refrain became familiar reading. (Today's historians estimate that the Mongol ruler killed 11 percent of the world's population living in his time.)

Modern Balkh offered little more than a bazaar, a few shops and stucco-block sheds. A mere track led us to the remains of ancient Bactria. Spindly trees begrudgingly lent shade to a small, unimpressive mosque and only the pure Persian style of its glazed tiles and twisted columns told me that here once stood a city equal in splendor to Herat and Samarkand. We bumped up a steep slope and met with a most unexpected sight. I stood at the edge of a vast empty dust bowl enclosed by a continuous, jagged and crumbled wall, about seven miles in circumference. Inside were no marble ruins, no great standing arches or broken gravestones. The wind sighed among rough, sun-bleached mounds, creating eddies of brown dust, moving, changing, dissolving and building new hillocks; several thousand years of living, a past beyond historic measure, vanished forever. Walking down the slope my feet touched small bones and bits of pottery, relics of civilizations that flourished for thousands of years until the city's final decay. The only person I met was an old man dressed in rags, searching for small objects to sell in the bazaar. He offered me a worn silver coin in return for some food, insisting it was ancient. (On my return to Deia, I gave it to Robert Graves and we talked about having it examined in the British Museum, but we never did. It seemed enough that it came from the soil of Bactria.)

Sitting near my small fire that night, I was intensely aware of the dark plain below me, aware of centuries past, having left but the shadows of history. The smells of earth and dry grasses had remained the same, but ghosts crowded this emptiness where rocks and pebbles remembered the glory and the shame. I did not look up dates or reread the tales of battles to see who won or lost. Here time, having brought bleakness and desolation, had long settled the score. Nights like these, and there would be others, left their mark. I am not a melancholy person. I love my life, my children, my work and my friends; I love to be in love, I love light, laughter, music and beautiful things. I do not engage in morbid soul searching nor do I seek to be absolved of sins in the hereafter. I am a woman, curious about life and eager to enjoy what it offers. Why then should a sleepless night, spent in a place filled with echoes of past violence and death, leave me with such a feeling of peace? Why would the star-mantled sky smooth my doubts about being a good parent, when the very fact that I so enjoyed being here, halfway across the world, should be evidence to the contrary? Looking down on barrenness and destitution, why was I not afraid of that "shadow at evening rising to meet you; I will show you fear in a handful of dust"? Why was I less afraid, even if only for a moment, to face my own fear: that one day I would awaken with my hands holding broken shards?

The Game of Men

In these northern regions of Afghanistan, a foreign woman amidst a crowd of turbaned Pathans, stocky Uzbeks and Turcoman with slanted eyes, I watched men play *bouzkashi*. It is the Afghan's favorite sport and seemed to me an accurate reflection of their character. The carcass of a beheaded, disemboweled goat, its legs cut off to minimize a hold, serves as the "*bouz*." Soaked overnight in cold water to make it stiff, it is placed in a shallow hole. Two wooden poles stand at each end of the field and a "circle of justice" is traced with chalk in the dirt. The players have to grab the bouz from the hollow, ride around the poles and deposit it in the circle. If the rules seem simple, the game is anything but. The men are chosen among the best horsemen of the region. The horses raised on these steppes are wild and beautiful; their riders have the courage, the strength and the cruelty necessary for the game. Man and horse train together until the horse becomes an active participant in the game.

Men sat on the grass, wandered around, stood in the back of a truck or perched on top of a bus. In a rodeo ambiance, vendors offered candied almonds and fruit to the chattering crowd. Smoking charcoal braziers offered kebabs, and an ancient cart sold drinking water where we would look for a beer or soft drinks. Old men wore striped Joseph's coats of silk in many colors and small boys rode by, three to a horse, or stood on their saddles better to watch the game. I saw a few veiled women preparing food, but none in the audience, and I realized my presence was tolerated because of my guide and driver, while the cameras marked me as a foreigner. (Today the bouzkashis are as popular as football games in other countries; they are spectacles where all visitors are expected and welcome.) The team's banners flew at the end of the field, there was laughter, bets were laid and men shouted and gesticulated, cracking their whips to make a point.

Horns sounded and the players appeared. Dressed in tunics, loose pants tucked into high-heeled black boots, they eased their horses across the field. They did not deign to look at the crowd. On this day, reins in one hand, leaving the other free to lift the bouz, clutching the braided Mongolian whip between their teeth, they were the lords of the steppes. Big men, averaging six feet and 240 pounds, I guessed their age around thirty: this is a game for men in the full strength of their lives. Thin drooping moustaches and curly astrakhan caps recalled the arrogant, feral look Joseph Kessel attributed to his hero Ouroz, entering the arena on his mad horse Jehol.

We were all waiting for a gray-bearded official to give the sign; when he fired his gun, bedlam followed. For several minutes, I could hardly see anything through the dust clouds covering the scene. Everybody pushed and shoved, whips lashed out, a rider fell and vaulted back in the saddle. The horses were snorting, stamping and roaring. The group spread out to pursue a rider who held on to the bouz for dear life but finally had to let go of it. A well-trained horse was busy pounding its forelegs on the carcass to keep others from grabbing it when a player, hanging alongside the flank of his horse, pushed through the melee. In one fluent movement, his head almost brushing the ground, he grabbed the eighty-pound sand-filled carcass with one hand, hoisted it on his saddle, and tore away. Another horse tried to cut him off, colliding at full speed, and a rider-less horse ran on, trampling a body on the ground. The first horseman, still pursued by several others, now streaked toward the finishing line. A big white horse actually grabbed the carcass with its teeth and tried to tear it from the rider's hands, bringing a screaming crowd to their feet. The leading horse, exhausted and foaming at the nostrils, made the last turn and the winner, with a shout born of rage and triumph, hurled the bouz into the circle. It was over.

Everybody shouted and argued, but an older man standing near said to us: "Bah, it is all right, but not as good as it used to be. Men were not afraid to die in this game and some usually did. Nowadays we have teams and even *rules!*" He must have been doubly disappointed on hearing that the thrown man got away with no more than broken bones.

A few days later, I happened on another, much smaller bouzkashi played by some merchants at a cattle fair nearby. Hoping to photograph some faces this time, I moved too close and caught a vicious lash on my right shoulder. In spite of my heavy jacket, it left a nasty welt and I realized that it might have cost me an eye or disfigured me forever. People around me showed no sympathy whatsoever; some laughed and others made it quite clear that I had no business being there, a woman yet. Not at all sure that the blow had been unintentional, I watched the rest of the game from a somewhat safer distance.

Nuristan

Kipling set his short story "The Man who would be King" in a distant land called Kafiristan. Now known as Nuristan, it remained a legendary place. A land of mountains, gorges and rushing rivers, of small emerald-green valleys hemmed in by the snow-covered peaks of the Hindu Kush. Our twenty-first century knows Nuristan as an international combat zone where Western armies seek to destroy the Taliban and Al Qaeda hiding in the caves and clefts of craggy, treeless mountains. In the late 1960s, Fred and I learned about it as a remote region, dangerous for different reasons. One needed a special permit from Kabul to enter the province of Nuristan, where the inhabitants paid no taxes because the government could not make them pay, where men were exempt from military service because no one could compel them to comply. Where, rumor had it, they were as likely to shoot you as talk to you.

For us it was a rare opportunity to visit a people of mysterious antecedents, who built sculptured houses on the dizzying heights of the Hindu Kush, the extension of the Himalayas that for centuries deterred the tribes of Central Asia of entering India. We knew that few Westerners had actually set foot in Nuristan, but learned later that Eric Newby was on his "Short Walk in the Hindu Kush" at about the same time we were there. Bruce Chatwin was also wandering around—boots strung around his neck—traveling with Peter Levi, who wrote, "I had a lip sore, a septic hand and a bruised toe, Bruce had mild heat exhaustion and a sunstroke temperature. He sat dazed on his bed, dressed in a long Arab gown, reading fearsome sentences from The Royal Geographical Society's Travelers' Guide to Health, such as *'after collapse, death soon ensues.'*

As comfortable as I was traveling alone, a hundred times a day I turned to my head to share something with Fred, who was not there. He met me in Kabul; that night his arms held me close and I was home. He brought news, notes and pictures from the children and all was well. The next day, we turned eastward together, following the Kunar River to where the Basghal flows into it from the west. We traveled past irrigated farmland, fields of wild marijuana and small rock-walled meadows; there were apricot trees, mulberries, walnuts, wild almond, honeysuckle, roses and gooseberries. It was beautiful country and looked like a trekker's paradise. Our driver let us off in a valley where the clear, trout-filled stream surged down over its rapids, supplying power to a flourmill. Some cattle grazed near a farmhouse and high above us a glacier spilled down the mountainside.

Our goal was the village of Kamdesh, at over six thousand feet altitude. It was a long, hot climb and for once, I gladly handed my camera bag to a boy who skipped up the trail like one of his skinny goats. Fred and I did not speak, we wheezed, sweated and gratefully rested several times under the critical eyes of the two local men who had come down to meet us. Nuristanis think nothing of climbing thousands of feet to bring home a handful of wheat, cultivated on handkerchief-sized terraces, each one carefully protected by low dry walls. The path led through lush forests of cedars, wild olives and green oak, crossed narrow wooden bridges made of slippery tree trunks guarded by miniature mud fortresses, and continued over steep steps and slopes. We passed a small mosque, two bearded men in loose white pants conversing while lounging against scrolled column capitals on the verandah. All I wanted was to lie down next to them, drink the cool water and stay a while.

When at last we reached Kamdesh village, the elders welcomed us with green tea and showed us to a hut, where the *charpoy* beds—the wooden frames strung with rope—stood ready. We rested till the sun had lost some of its heat and a light breeze was flowing down from the snow-covered peaks above, giving us just enough courage to take a first look around. The village clung to the mountainside like a swallow's nest, the flat-roofed houses spread over several levels, their hold on the steep slope looking precarious. Most were built of flat gray stones interspersed with cedar beams in the traditional timber-laced stone masonry. The older houses were made of carved cedar, with balconies that projected over the steep streets below. A narrow staircase carved from a single trunk ran along the outside wall to the upper story and the flat roof, where wheat, apricots, mulberries and dung patties lay to dry. Every available inch of wooden space was carved with the most intricate floral arabesques and geometrical designs, interspersed with abstract repetitions. Some lintels showed the long backward curving horns of a wild ibex, and once I saw the stylized and *upside-down* face of a person, supposedly the owner of the house.

When evening fell and lamps were lit, our hosts invited us to share their dinner of flatbread with melted ghee and fresh goat cheese. The food was served on a table, we sat on low chairs, and a wooden bench was fixed to the wall, all reminders that Himalayan people used furniture. Our guide, a young man from the Kabul tourist office, far from admiring the beautifully carved chairs and utensils, stared at his bowl in horror: the goat cheese was streaked with coarse black hairs and some other odd, unidentifiable ingredients. He had been sent to accompany us to Nuristan, wherever that might be, but not in his nastiest dreams had he expected to toil up steep mountains, sleep on a bare string bed under a smelly blanket and eat questionable stews tasting of rancid goat fat and worse. All through our stay he sulked and kept looking at us sideways, hoping we would feel the same way and that, maybe, we would leave soonest. Our hosts ignored him, as they did me, and when he knelt in prayer they watched, but did not join him. He was city and I was a woman.

Nuristan. It means the land of the enlightened, land of those who have seen the light of Islam. It was not always so. The people of Kafiristan were pagan, they prayed to gods and goddesses and made effigies of their ancestors that were set out to be present at all important family occasions. Known for their brigandry, cupidity and love of fighting, they were also generous, loyal and hospitable. They appreciated music and dance, drank wine pressed from their own grapes. The beams of their houses, the furniture and utensils were carved with motives of horses and wild goats, flowers or vine leaves. The graves, now often abandoned, were marked with carved cedar boards or statuettes of helmeted warriors on horseback. When did all this change? The old headman explained, at first rather reluctantly, then with great passion, how around 1890 Afghan troops invaded their territory, destroying the villages, burning the wooden houses and the effigies, killing the men, taking women and children as slaves. The priests of Islam followed the soldiers. The inhabitants fought back, fleeing ever higher up into the mountains, but finally chose conversion over constant persecution. The Kafir people accepted defeat, the mullahs built mosques and watched patiently, knowing that time was on their side. It was then that the region was renamed Nuristan. In a telling last gesture, sometime before the official, enforced ceremony of conversion, the Kafir headmen of several villages invited a group of imams to a grand parley over a meal, where they killed them all. After that, Islam reigned, erasing the personality, art and traditions of a people that had kept their independence for over a thousand years. Muslims by force, they no longer tended their vine, embellished their houses or sculpted statues of their ancestors.

Tall, fair-skinned, often with light hair and eyes, our hosts looked different from the other peoples of Central Asia. I saw red-haired boys with freckles I would have placed in Scotland. A popular legend traces their origins to Alexander's soldiers, others to the Greek colonies of Bactria, driven out by the Muslims around the seventh century. After reading about a warlike, fiercely independent people, we now found them to be mostly farmers and herders. The men wore long drab cotton shirts, embroidered waistcoats without buttons and soft hats of light-colored wool with rolled brims resembling those of Henry III. A big knife stuck in their belt or a rifle draped over one shoulder gave some a raffish look, but they did not show the innate arrogant and warlike demeanor of the Pathans in the border regions. It is true that our visit fell in a time of peace. A decade or so later, with Russian armies and government troops invading their isolated region, these men were the first to pick up their arms and fight with the innate passion for independence and the love for revenge they had always been known for.

To me the Kamdesh women seemed distant rather than shy. Fine-boned, with narrow elongated faces, they wore long robes with red borders, woolen leggings, shoes made of goatskin and heavy silver pendants in their ears or a pin in the nostril. They did not approach us other than to serve the meal, but for all their slightly timid airs, they did most of the heavy farmwork in the fields. The men provided by hunting and herding. Making butter and curds, they stored it in the cold river before carrying loads of sixty pounds, stuffed inside a goatskin, for several days up and down mountains of unimaginable heights to exchange it for grain or woolen hats and leather boots. The goat was one of the essentials of everyday life. It furnished milk, butter, cheese, meat, and clothing. The hides also served to make the seats of chairs, or the ancient looking musical instruments.

Our hosts accompanied us to neighboring villages, where the welcome was just as courteous. We brought small gifts, shared meals, and listened to older men sing sad ballads about snow and roses, while others danced to the peculiar, monotonous music of the four-stringed harp. We watched the fighting cock partridges. They were only small gamecocks but the darting heads and slashing beaks were the same and so was the bloody, ragged end. The screaming turbaned men, betting money in hand, evoked a far earlier age. But nothing is permanent, for on the wood fire stood an enameled kettle imported from China, and one man proudly showed us a Russian transistor radio, lovingly wrapped in an embroidered and tasseled cloth. We spent our last night in Kamu, a region that teems with wildlife, from ibex to deer, brown bear and wolf. The narrow road led along the river, the mountain wall high on one side, the rushing water far below. We were to stay at the hunting lodge of King Mohamed Zahir Shah, but had no idea what to expect. It turned out to be a mud building with a square tower, similar to structures we had seen all through this region, where most villagers had reason to fortify their homes against enemies who were often their close neighbors. The property was well kept—the gate and a small lawn looking a little outlandish—but the word "royal" did not immediately spring to mind. Here beauty lived in the gardens lush with roses and white mulberry trees, in the sight of mountains and stream-filled valleys. Once inside it was clear that this was a khan's lodge. The walls were hung with trophies, the rooms had fireplaces and there were sculpted beds and animal skins on the floor. We were told that when the king came or lent this house to friends, all kinds of linen, tableware and special food and drink were brought in. To us, people of little importance, the servants were friendly and helpful. As in other village homes, we were offered fresh cheese and flat breads with ghee, but here the goat stew was delicious and expertly cooked with herbs and vegetables.

Nuristan had been an enigma to us; we had been allowed a glimpse of this ancient, untamed land and its people. When time came to leave, we filed down the mountain with our new friends carrying two wooden chairs sculpted with small, delicate horse heads, the seats strung with strips of goat hide. I had also bought a heavy sculpted pot used for storing goat fat; buying its contents—which I left with our hosts—had paid for all. It has stood in my studio now for decades, cleaned, scrubbed and oiled, but it never lost its smell. Fred brought home his own treasure, a *wadja*, the ancient four-stringed harp, its slender neck carved with the head of an ibex. We left this country with the feeling that it would continue to exist more or less unchanged, no matter what was happening in the rest of the world. We were wrong. For years now, once unknown names like Kamu or Kamdesh appear with terrifying regularity in the news bulletins:

November 5, 2008, the *New York Times* published an article about GIs in a remote Nuristan outpost, drawing Taliban fire. "They are ensconced in a small stone castle. Once a hunting lodge of Mohamed Zahir Shah, Afghanistan's last king, the castle is home for a year to an American cavalry troop, an Afghan infantry company, a Navy corpsman and two American marines." A picture showed "our" castle in Kamu, barely recognizable, all the windows nailed shut, the walls bristling with weapons and heavily fortified with corrugated metal sheets, barbed wire and sandbags. Where we walked in well-kept gardens, the slopes are strewn with splintered trees and shattered boulders. Petty Officer Ramon Gavan was quoted, "This is where you realize not to take every breath for granted."

October 3, 2009: CBS News: "The Battle of Kamdesh was the bloodiest battle for US forces since 2008, with 8 Americans killed and 22 wounded. The insurgents forced the inhabitants to leave the village; then a force of 300 Taliban assaulted the American outpost."

March 10, 2010: "Kamdesh district. A convoy of US military vehicles comes to a halt on a rocky, winding road. Any advance will bring guaranteed rocket and gun attacks from the insurgents. 'It takes an act of God to get us to go any further,' says Captain Mathew Frye."

And it continues.

It has become a place that reflects such terrifying changes that it is almost impossible to recall those emerald valleys hemmed in by the snow-covered peaks of the Hindu Kush. A place that for many years belonged to one of my happiest memories.

SPAIN

It took us on short ferry ride from home, to the mainland of Spain. The story of Don Quichotte was not about faraway places and strange adventures, but it would remain one of my favorite journeys. As the trail of the errant knight led us into a world often untouched by time, castles stood watch over wide empty plains, monks chanted behind closed portals, shepherds told tales, and history lay like a palimpsest on the sun-baked land.

Al Mansha, the dry land, the wilderness, the Arabs called it. Neither a province nor a territorial stage, it stretches from the mountains of Toledo to the Sierra Morena. There are no cities here, just villages, and a scattering of small market towns. The summer heat, shimmering over an ocean of yellow grain, is as fierce as noon in the Sahara. I don't think anyone would come here just to see it, other than maybe Théophile Gautier, who believed in visiting *"les pays dans ses saisons violentes,"* including Spain in the height of the summer. Esteban Frances, our Catalan friend who designed the sets for Balanchine's *Man of La Mancha,* wandered about for days looking for inspiration and went home deeply puzzled, saying it was impossible to do anything with it. He did, of course, and very beautifully so.

"Her name is Dulcinea, her country El Toboso." Sleepy, boasting a single windmill, El Toboso is one of the loveliest villages in the Mancha. A village forgotten by everything but literary fame, a double-edged and peculiar sort of fame, which has turned its very name into an inside joke. The inhabitants of El Toboso, however, fail to see anything to laugh at and took pride in showing us the "Casa de Dulcinea," despite the fact that fictional Dulcinea passes through the book as the eternal feminine mirage. Of Dulcinea, Cervantes tells us her hair is gold and there were indeed a striking number of fair-haired, blue-eyed girls in Toboso. In June 1968, the time of our story, the wall-to-wall streets were unpaved and water was drawn from the well. Yesterday grew into today, flowing gently toward tomorrow, with few events to mark the passage of time. In the spring of 2011, Pedro Almodovar set his film *The Return* in such a village of his native province. They are all there, the cobbled streets, windows encased in black ironwork, devoid of potted plants and lacking in any kind of decoration, the women in long black skirts sitting outside their houses, making bobbin lace. Unchanged, they remain the very essence of La Mancha.

On our journey, Fred soon found a shepherd, an old man with a weather-beaten face, time on his hands and a wealth of local stories. He was wearing a modern cap against the sun, but at trouser level shone a magnificent silver belt buckle—seventeenth century from the looks of it—and his feet were shod in the traditional leather sandals worn by Manchegans long before Quixote. Asked if he had ever wanted to leave here, to see the flowering gardens of Granada or the sea at the shores of Malaga, he made a curiously embracing gesture toward the distant horizon. "When I was young, I once traveled to the Canaries," he said, smiling. "Pero *este* es mi tierra, y es bonito." (But *this* is my country, and it is beautiful.)

In the ancient castle of Alarcon with its Moorish battlements and huge Gothic dining hall, we climbed the winding stairs to our round room in the tower. Kneeling on the worn stone sill of the narrow medieval widow, I watched the sun set over the immense empty plain below. It was as if nothing had changed since the knight roamed this very land and to him every inn appeared a castle. The sun slipped away. In the green sky, the stars began to candle, while for a moment time itself appeared to hesitate and anything seemed possible. The magic and a promise of tales veiled by time and light; an atmosphere so mysterious, I did not know how to capture it. And it was beautiful.

In travel stories, food can be both important and not at all. If there is no time to eat, or not much available, you make do and it really does not seem to matter much. In La Mancha, the barrel-shaped *manchego* sheep cheese with its distinctive zigzag patterned rind and the unleavened, unsalted bread are part of the red peasant earth since remembrance. There were strong dark-red wines and bottles of light *Blanco*, chilled by being hung in the well; pies stuffed with partridge and wild hare, or stews of minced chicken and forcemeat balls. Our problem was finding a place that served them. The splendid old wayside *posadas* that once catered to muleteers and George Borrow seemed mostly have come down in the world, having turned into truck stops. We finally found an old inn, inhabited by a troupe of itinerant sheep-castrators from Galicia, who played music and sang ballads in return for a plate of stew and a straw mattress in the stable. Two farm boys arrived on mule back, singing a clear high-pitched melody that floated above the trees, an intensely jubilant chant that filled the evening air. Fred was of course delighted and invited them all. We ate together and drank the local wines until I went to bed and fell asleep hearing Fred happily arguing with the musicians. Early morning found him still sitting in the courtyard, playing the panpipes with two shepherds. He pulled me down next to him, put his arm around me, and played a ditty, while a third young herder slowly danced to the tune.

Of the hundreds of windmills once dotting La Mancha, only a handful are still standing. Since they have stopped turning, creakingly, around the beginning of the twentieth century, they serve purely decorative purposes. However, at the hour of dawn— the time specified by Cervantes for the fierce, unequal battle—it is quite possible to see them as hulking black giants against the dark red sky. *"Take care, your lordship," said Sancho: "these things are not giants, but windmills." "It is quite clear," replied Don Quixote, "that you are inexperienced in the matter of adventures. They are giants, and if you are afraid, go away and say your prayers."*

At sunrise, as the peasants of Campo de Criptana ride past them on their way to work, the mills come to life. Hoping to get some pictures in the early light, I had asked a farmer to meet me on the hill just before dawn. While sitting in the car watching the black night lift, we heard on our radio that Robert Kennedy had been assassinated. I remember how difficult it was to grasp that devastating news reaching us from so far away. We continued to sit in the dark, listening to those disembodied voices from across the ocean, and only slowly comprehending what they told us. Waiting for our Manchegan peasant, in a different age and a different world.

He arrived just before the sun rose, his dog trotting behind the donkey, small paper-cut silhouettes against the dark red sky with the mills looming black in the background.

"Please, pass just once more?" I would ask and he duly did, saying, "Si, maestro." I shot until the sky turned to pink and then to blue and yellow. Walking over to thank him, I suddenly realized I had never seen this man before in my life! Here was a farmer on his way to work who without hesitation had passed and re-passed the mills, simply because a total stranger asked him to do so. I tried to explain, but he just smiled, said, "Con Dios, Señora." and cloppety-clopped down the hill, his donkeys' hoofs raising little puffs of dust on the trail.

THE SPANISH FOREIGN LEGION

If we had been surprised at the popular appeal of armies (since the Bengal Lancers we had spent a week with a German Mountain Brigade that also rated a magazine cover), we were very pleased to receive permission from the Spanish military authorities to visit their Foreign Legion in the Sahara Desert. The legendary French Foreign Legion had mostly passed from the scene, but Spain would still let one dream of patrolling the desert on camelback in the old Beau Geste manner. I say "dream," because the reality was somewhat less romantic. We arrived in El Aaiun, where a young officer accompanied us to headquarters. The whitewashed town built round the legion camp seemed deserted, a hot wind blowing through the empty streets; there were a few bars, music twanging behind doors half ajar. Seeing me look, the officer turned to my husband. "There used to be a brothel here. Five women for eight hundred men. But a priest came and wrote a letter to the Minister and the Minister didn't like that, so they sent them away last year." To me: "Excuse me, Madam. We do have a cinema now."

In the cantina that evening, the food was decent, sufficient and the same for all ranks. I looked around at the legionnaires' faces.

I had expected the hard types from the movies, but most of them looked more like farm boys from Jaen or store clerks from Bilbao with a tattoo. "We don't get that many toughs, not as we used to," lamented a veteran officer. "They don't come and face the desert; they stay home and make trouble pissing on street corners." Still, the Legion attracts just enough old-style desperados to uphold the best traditions of a service that prides itself on toughness, *sangre y gloria* and teaches its soldiers to consider themselves *novios de la muerte*, the bridegrooms of death.

What kind of person decides to join the Foreign Legion, I had often wondered. The strongarm types who come to the legion for sanctuary do not always wish to discuss their reasons, but at one isolated outpost in the desert, an amiable, soft-spoken Frenchman admitted to Fred that he was a retired terrorist. As an ex-OAS commando, having attempted to assassinate General de Gaulle, he now found all borders closed to him. For some, it represents an escape from poverty, a step up the economic ladder, like the young Sudanese who walked all the way to the Spanish frontier—a matter of two thousand miles—in order to join up. Germans were considered reliable. An ex-bricklayer from Hamburg enlisted when he ran out of money on vacation in Andalusia. "I like everything about the Legion—the food, the company, the climate and the training." A few Americans stayed on to become sergeants, because they liked the lizard life in the sun. The English did not seem to do so well. "They have mostly been unable to adapt to the hard life and often try to escape or feign illness. When one actually succeeds, he goes home and writes those exaggerated stories about the horrors of the Legion." Tales of horror? Maybe something like the story an officer told us of a legionnaire and his mistress who murdered her old lover and buried him under the new favorite's bed? The dead man's dog sniffed out the body and gave away the show. Or about the night, not long ago, when Mauritanian raiders slipped past the sentries, cut the throats of half a dozen legionnaires and made off with their rifles? We listened and lingered a while in the bar—the only place one could get a beer—but soon a trumpet sounded the long drawn-out notes that signaled "lights out and douse the fires."

In the area around El Aaiun, the legionnaires performed long-distance maneuvers, but also patrolled on foot for signs of trouble. We drove for an hour or so, left the car and started walking. It was tough going. Even the bearded veterans griped about the sand: the hot *sirocco* wind drove it into our eyes, ears, teeth, noses and throats, into the lenses of my camera and the transmission of the waiting Land Rover. I could see why the field uniform calls for heavy goggles, a *siroquera* cloth that protects the neck, and open-toed sandals that allow the sand to run out just as quickly as it pours in. With nothing special to report, we soon returned to camp, where we found the bugle and drum corps conducting rehearsals in the noonday sun. The men, dressed in shorts and sandals, stood lined up in the exercise ground in front of the barracks. We watched and listened and nothing seemed out of the ordinary, until a sergeant suddenly marched up to a legionnaire and smashed his fist with full force in the man's face. The bugle fell clattering on the pavement, blood streamed from nose and mouth, but the soldier did not utter a sound and the rest went on tooting without missing a beat. It happened very fast and the sergeant, who was screaming insults in Spanish, had not seen us arrive. Fred instinctively took a step forward, but the officer with us held his arm and said, "No, do nothing, they are tough. The men prefer a beating to digging holes in the sand for a day with a hundred-pound pack on their back." I never found out what the poor bastard had done. Played a wrong note, most likely.

At dawn, we set out in three Land Rovers to Smara, about three hundred kilometers inland from El Aaiun. Every patrol here leaves in twos and threes, for no one takes the desert for granted. Smara is not a favorite outpost of the legionnaires. The fortress lies in a lunar landscape of rocks and sand so arid and impenetrable, it makes the simple pleasures of El Aaiun seem like the lights of Paris. A legionnaire planning to escape would do better to try in the coastal town, for as one of the officers remarked: "Anyone running away here is welcome to it. There is no way a deserter could survive. The nomad patrols would find him, but if they would look for him at all, it would only be to save his life. If the temperature can soar to over 50C in the shade, at night frost is quite common in the mountainous area. There is probably no place else outside the polar regions so hostile to most forms of life. The Tuareg say that God created the Sahara to teach men humility."

Here, in a region that was unmapped and unclaimed until the beginning of the twentieth century, the Spanish have constructed a series of desert forts with watchtowers and crenellated walls. The difficult job of patrolling the immense stretch of border with Mauritania falls to the Tuareg camel corps. The sight of their patrol padding across the horizon made me glance at Fred to share the joy of it, and he grinned back: yes, I know! The officer in front, his lance corporal behind with fluttering pennant and then, in single file, a dozen troopers with sharpshooter's rifles pointing straight up to the sky, sabers ready at their pommels. All men wear the dark turban, the veil wrapped around their faces leaving just a space for the eyes; their bright red capes, filling with the desert wind, show a glimpse of white and soft blue robes. If I loved the sight, it was a lost cause. I had been prepared for a certain attitude from tough legionnaires toward a woman photographer, but both the soldiers and their officers were friendly and polite. If anything, they tried to flatter me. The glamorous-looking Tuareg rode past on their sleek camels, glancing down from their high-backed saddle, the gray eyes above the *tagelmoust* dismissing me like something very unpleasant lying in their path. Even under the best of circumstances, black-veiled men can be somewhat unnerving, but here the contempt was almost tangible. I have rarely felt such disdain in a stare and their camels were not much better. I had to stand quite close to where they passed to get a decent picture, and they usually managed to drool some of their nasty green gob on me. If their masters did not actually order it, they were certainly not displeased with the slobbering performance.

The nomad troops were well paid for doing what they like best: policing oases and caravan routes and bringing aid to isolated families. Our scout seemed to think that this was the living fulfillment of a nomad's dream. He had a strong and well-fed camel, a rifle, a khaki uniform, a steady supply of imported groceries for himself and his several wives, and a chance to educate his children in an oasis school. There had not been any real fighting for a long time and renegade sheiks were becoming rare, but before the regular controls, rival tribes raided each other's camel herds and killed over the water holes in the best Lawrence of Arabia tradition. The small family groups in the low black tents we passed lived mainly on milk and dried meat from their herds. The men dressed in voluminous robes, some carried long straight swords in leather scabbards. The women wore dark blue or red dresses and embroidered scarves, jewelry of beaten silver and often showed the blue Agadez cross tattooed on their forehead. They wore no veil. They watched us and some called out a greeting, but did not ask us to come in, nor did we stop.

Many miles before Smara we crossed two boys and a young girl, dressed in simple strips of black cloth with a hole to put their head through, and left open at the sides. "Tuareg children on their way to fetch water," said one officer. "The next well is quite far from here." He told the driver to stop. In the trunk, we carried a metal tub filled with ice and beverages. The idea was to pour off the water of the long since melted ice and fill the children's water bags, saving them the long walk. The oldest boy, about twelve years old, was the only one who spoke. The driver produced some sort of funnel and together they started to fill the bag. Suddenly, the boy flew into a rage, screaming at the top of his voice and throwing the bag on the ground. No one understood why, or what he was saying. Until a soldier tried the water and realized what had happened. On the rough ride, a bottle of white wine had broken and the contents spilled into the melted ice: the boy had smelled the alcohol. It was a nightmare. They could not drink the water or even use the bag to fill it at the well, as it was now contaminated. The younger children moved away and sat in the sand, watching us without a word. The older boy ran around in a circle, hooting rhythmically in high thin screams, a throat-scraping squawk like an angry blue jay. When our scout tried to calm him down, he met with a hail of rocks. Finally, he grabbed the boy by the shoulders and brought him back to the car. Explaining got us nowhere and in the end, the scout gave the children his own goatskin water bag and a new jerry can. He tried adding some bottles of soda, but they would not go near them, nor would they let us drive them to the well. Shouting curses, they continued on their way. And so, after a while, did we, embarrassed and ashamed, although we had meant well.

Arriving at the fort, turbaned, black-veiled sentries manned the high, whitewashed walls, while a group of legionnaires near the gate stood ready to leave on patrol. The bugler on the crenulated tower sounded our arrival, and we were home for the night. The officer's quarters had the basic regulation army furniture, but many rooms showed Berber carpets, wall hangings, saddlebags, pottery or other native objects. Most of the camel corps officers had spent their entire army life in North Africa and were often intensely proud of their role in this latest installment of the centuries old love-hate relationship between Spaniard and Moor. They loved the desert with the passion of a man for a demanding and dangerous mistress. "I have been here for over twenty years and they have been the best years of my life," one said. "I could not go back to Madrid again. Outside the desert, I would not know how to behave."

We accompanied the officers and their nomad troops on patrol. Once again, the camel under me straightened its hind legs, jolting me forward and threatening to impale me on the saddle pommel. And once again, yielding to its swaying motion, I felt fine. We left at dawn, following unmarked trails, passing a cluster of black tents or children herding a few goats. The red and yellow sand shone like rippled silk. In this land of dunes and sand the play of light creates the magic. Even heavily loaded camels barely leave a track, make no sound and pass like ghosts. In the increasing heat we all fell silent, the creaking of saddles and the soft tinkling of small bells the only sounds. We came to the rough, gravely terrain the nomads call *reg*. The hot wind came from the south and the sun looked like a tarnished silver plate. I never experienced a full sandstorm, but here we were caught in the path of a dust devil. A huge, red-brown column rising about two hundred meters in the air and whirling like some ghostly dervish, headed straight for us. The camels stopped in their tracks, turned their backs to it, and lay down. We all followed suit, face in the sand. The dust enveloped us, buffeted us with hot air followed by a hail of small pebbles carried on the wind. It was over in minutes and the troopers took it all matter-of-fact. Fred had half covered me and held on as if I would fly away; now we looked at each other and he grinned: "Well, it's something to remember?"

There was no visible trail, but the guide never wavered. The commander told me that among the Tuareg there is a tradition of blind guides, who smell the sands. "To us, sand may be scentless and dead, the blind guide lifts it to his face and knows where he is." We were probably following a well-travelled route, but nothing was obvious to me. Bushes seemed to float uneasily above the grayish pebbles, heat blurring the images; a huge tree appeared until the mirage evaporated and turned it into a small shrub. A silver-blue lake glittered in the distance or hills floated upside down in the sky. I saw a caravan approach, with camels and riders in long robes; they passed and turned into a young girl riding a donkey. The lake had disappeared, leaving a few puddles, but they too melted away. Sometimes a caravan would turn out to be real. First I would see a dark line floating above the horizon, next I began to make out small dots, the heads of the camels. Until they were actually next to us, it looked as if they were wading belly-deep in a white fog. The scorching sun raised boiling white vapours from the red sand, creating a landscape full of illusions, full of deceptions, where herds stilled their thirst at chimerical lakes. *The lying waters of the Sahara*, our scout called them. We talked about the salt flats of the *chot* that lie to the east, a lifeless, forgotten dead sea, where bitter salt and infertile clay have created a world without vegetation, without fish or bird, worse than the driest dunes. "You have seen the *chot*," he said. "Then you know. In the dunes life may be reduced to the barest minimum, but men live. In the *chot*, death is *mektoub*, inevitable."

The sun fell with unlikely speed into the *reg*, giving way to a sky tinseled with stars. We made camp and fires were lit, reducing the terrifying vastness of the desert to a human scale, a pool of light, people, animals, food and bedrolls. A legionnaire dug a hollow in the centre of the embers, poured bread dough into the hot sand, covering the flat loaf with ashes and glowing embers. We ate it with canned meat and readied our sleeping bags close to the comforting fire. On this trip Fred and I had little privacy and that night I would have wished for more. The starred sky seemed so near I felt as if I were floating upward, higher and higher, finally to be lost in space. I looked at Fred and saw the same need in his eyes, the need to love. He reached for me and we lay close, sharing. For a few seconds, a shower of shooting stars lit up the night-gray sand. Then the glittering dome, unimpressionable and infinitely peaceful, once again covered the world.

In the morning, the commander led us to what may well be one of the world's most extraordinary galleries of prehistoric art: a series of rock outcroppings, half buried in the sand, on which were engraved hundreds of superb pictures of animals and men. They belonged to an epoch when the Sahara had water, for they showed river animals like crocodiles and hippos. Today's buff or sand-colored animals are mostly inconspicuous or come out mainly at night, but six or seven thousand years ago our journey would have been like a safari in Serengeti, complete with giraffes, antelope, lions and leopards, buffalos, elephants and rhinoceros. There were also signs of human activity: tombs made of piles of rock, or Stone Age axes and fish harpoons lying among fossilized fish bones in the middle of sand wastes where now no rain may fall for ten years. We had the impression of an inhabited landscape that, one strange afternoon thousands of years ago, had suddenly been abandoned, leaving a desert the size of America and the only water a scattering of pools. Fred was mesmerized and would have thrown over everything for a few weeks of exploring right there. Having seen his fascination and his reluctance to leave the site, the commander surprised him on our last day with the gift of a sliver of carved prehistoric rock.

We spent the night in an oasis bowered in date palms, with its familiar musty smell of standing saltpetre water and the sound of the endlessly repeated single note of small desert frogs. We were welcomed in tents where tea, poured from high in an amber arc, splashed frothing in each glass. The food we brought was gladly accepted but not served, for that evening we were honoured guests. Women rolled cleaned, un skinned hares into a ball and buried them into a pit, covered it with a thin layer of sand and built a fire of dry brush on top of it. The meat was succulent and tender. In the trooper's pit camel feet were simmering under hot embers until they turned into a gelatinous mass that is considered a great delicacy.

The officers sat cross-legged, talking to the elders of the tribe. Fragments of song ending on odd native quavers floated back to us from the soldier's fire. Later, things shuffled and rustled in the dark and the dogs growled deep in the throat. The night was bitter cold, the sand glowed silver under a myriad of blazing stars so brilliant, so close they seemed to crackle, to hiss. Galileo said that when he looked through his telescope at the spinning planets, he could hear God's voice in the music of the spheres. At dawn we woke to a drawn-out, insistent voice calling the faithful to prayer, "*Allaah-uou-akhbaar, la-ill'la.*" God is alone. Theodore Monod, one of the greatest Saharan travelers, thought it "the most mysterious, most beautiful, most perfect desert in the world."

THE WAY OF SAINT JAMES

The city of Santiago de Compostela celebrated a Holy Year, and thousands of pilgrims answered the summons to make the sacred journey. A journey imbided with medieval history that Fred and I had often discussed, but could not afford to make just for our own pleasure. Now that it was a potential story, we decided to follow the Royal Road to the city of Saint James, leading from the Pyrenees to the far coast of Galicia. It would take us about two weeks by car and we were tempted to take the children, but also remembered earlier trips where they counted every step to castle or cathedral before deciding whether to follow us or continue to play cards in the back of the car. (Grown up, raising children of their own, they recalled those days and asked how we could let them get away with that. "You should have made us!" Truth is they absorbed far more of the lessons stuffed into them than they realized; many of their adult interests are closely linked to their early exposure to this multicolored world.) This time, having to produce the story, we settled for meeting them afterwards for a long weekend in Malaga and hopping on a ferry to show them the kashba of Tangier.

For a thousand years, pilgrims have entered Spain via the Pass of Roncesvalles, the crossroad in history where Roland's horn once sounded over Charlemagne's rearguard. Led by their bishops and princes they came, rich and poor, old and young, from England, Germany, Italy, from the Lowlands and the Balkans. Some walked barefoot, some carried chains or a switch for self-flagellation, others a picture of the saint and all considered the pilgrimage an act of reparation. Along the road, miracles and visions were at the order of the day: one met angels, beggars, kings and wayfarers. King Edward I cantered along on his high horse, Francis of Assisi wore out his sandals in the dust and a Flemish traveler carried along a mermaid in a tub. It would take them several months to reach the shrine of the saint, assuming they survived the very real dangers lurking around each bend. The journey ahead was not for timid souls; it was perilous and fraught with danger, and pilgrims were well aware that they might meet death before the end. Travelers faced hunger and exposure, attacks by wolves and bears; they drowned in fast rivers, while robbery and murder by innkeepers and ferrymen, or even by fellow pilgrims, was commonplace. Arrived, they would kneel at the tomb of Saint James and pray for remission of their sins or a wondrous cure of whatever might ail them. Something usually did.

Among the various roads that led to Santiago, we chose the Camino Frances, the heart line in the hand of Spain. It crosses the northern regions hardly touched by tourism, where winters are harsh and towns still wear the scars of medieval sieges. From the French border, it descends to Pamplona, crosses Navarra and La Rioja, winds past Burgos through arid plains of Castile to Leon, and climbs the craggy heights of Cebrero to finally, approximately eight hundred arduous kilometers later, arrive in the city of Santiago de Compostela, at the Atlantic shore of Galicia.

Fred and I set out from a small village in the Pyrenees on a foggy, rain-swept morning, the sort of day that would have dampened any pilgrim's zeal. The last person I saw before the mist swallowed her was a woman herding a flock of goats. She wore a bright red sweater and stood on her mountain slope, busily knitting something with large wooden needles. I waved to her but she simply watched us go by. It was not exactly "Have a safe journey," but at least we did not need to pray for protection from "the perils of thieves, wild beasts, murderous innkeepers, jugglers, or actors." Reading about the mishaps of the medieval pilgrims I asked myself what on earth made all these people wake up one morning and face such a journey.

The answer was the legend of Saint James. The apostle is said to have brought the Gospel to Spain before returning to Jerusalem, where the Romans executed him in 44 AD. His remains were brought to Galicia in a stone tomb, the site of which was revealed to a peasant nearly nine centuries later, when King Alfonso II erected a small church on the site. At the time, the Christian crusaders were not very successful in their holy wars and desperately needed an apostolic figure that would give heart to their soldiers in the way Mohammed inspired the Moors. Under the red-crossed banner, the Christians advanced, all the while turning gentle James, Fisher of Man, into Santiago Matamoros, Saint James the Moorslayer. The saint's tomb became a popular shrine, and, through time, a majestic cathedral grew on the site of the modest church. Traditionally, European pilgrims had gone to Rome or slowly plodded through Byzantine Anatolia to Jerusalem, but after the Turks occupied the region that route was no longer safe. Now there was Compostela, Field of Stars, easier and safer than Jerusalem but more difficult and therefore more meritorious than Rome. The Santiago pilgrimage was secured; it would soon come under royal protection and become a lucrative source of revenue.

Our own climb across the Pyrenees was grim and nearly finished off our loyal little MG convertible that was far too low-slung for the rocks, holes and ruts in the narrow mountain trails. Arrived on the other side, we faced wild and rugged country. The road climbed the low, dry, boulder-strewn hills, borrowed beauty from slender dark cypresses or ran dusty across the empty plains. The landscapes were often breathtaking, the silence more powerful than any sound. It had lain upon this land since the beginning of time and did not heed our passing. We were never far from cities and civilization, but ours was a journey along a path that seemed to avoid the living. Strangely lacking in direct human contact, it was full of symbols instead, offering its lessons along the way. The castles, hermitages, crosses and hospices where pilgrims once prayed, rested or were cruelly set upon were ancient, beautiful and too many too recount. Here a gilded and bejeweled Saint James, set on magnificent altars, often outshone the wooden crucifixes where a thorn-crowned Christ agonized with broken limbs. Small hamlets remembered the saint by adding "del Camino" to their name and the spirit of his era was alive in their stories and their music. Floating through a barred window of the Cistercian convent of Las Huelgas near Burgos, we heard the purest Gregorian chant, sung by a choir of nuns as if with one voice. In the remote valley of Santo Domingo de Silos, young monks had revived the Mozarabic chants of the eleventh century and were recording them. Somewhere in the dusty, chalk-dry plain of Castile, where we shared our lunch of bread, cheese and wine, a seventy-year-old farmer sang us a song that may have dated back to the time of Columbus. His daughter said, "Father, the country is poor, the harvest is bad, we have no reason to sing," but the old man continued his endless ballad about saints and sinners, seafarers and kings. About miracles, and the knightly James, wielding his sword and carrying his lobed, grooved shell.

Early on, it had become customary to bring home a Galician scallop shell as proof of the completion of the journey" and it remains the pilgrim's badge, the leitmotiv of the *camino* until our days. Fred and I sheltered in simple inns where *le coquille de St. Jacques* was carved in ancient lintels above the door. A twelfth-century hospice housed a statue of the saint dressed as a pilgrim holding a shell and modern travelers found their way on "shell maps" offered by tourist offices.

Medieval manuscripts referred to Burgos, the home of El Cid, as a "town rich in gold and very strong horses, but poor in trees and full of evil and godless people." I do not know about the people, but here we saw one of Spain's most astonishing cathedrals, which seemed built mainly to glorify the power of Church Militant. Our main impression was of an enormous structure in the French Gothic style, topped by with German spires, bristling with pointed octagonal pinnacles, and covered with statues of saints and gargoyles. Standing in the square, Fred calculated we would probably need a week just to take in the exterior. Not to mention the plethora of incredible art, altars, balconies, ornamentations, sculptures and *retablos*, of knights, angels and heraldry and even crouching lions, that cluttered the interior of church and chapels. I did have a glimpse of a beautiful cloister, but the whole effect of this vast cathedral was that of such amazing overabundance that it bordered on the fantastic.

We left a little stunned and continued across the monotonous, sun-baked plain, passing a village or two and crossing a small river, to emerge in a different landscape. More rivers followed, forests stood on a distant hill, and Leon waited nearby. The city was crowded, humming with life and friendly people. We took our poor abused car to a garage to be revived, had dinner in a very good restaurant and checked into a modern, comfortable hotel. (The *albergos* provided for pilgrims had always been clean, but rather resembled youth hostels with bunk beds in dormitories and long lines for the two showers somewhere down the hallway.) Early next morning, in spite of undigested Burgos, we set out to see the Leon cathedral and received a wonderful gift. In the large, still empty square stood the "House of Light," a pure Gothic jewel with some 1,800 square meters of stained glass. Closely modeled on the Flamboyant Gothic style of the royal cathedrals in France, it drew its own lightness from pale yellow stone. Rays of sunlight, filtering through some 125 windows in glorious shades of yellow and orange with vermillion echoes of cinnabar tinged everything with a soft, luminous glow. Someone was playing the organ. Eyes drawn upward with the rising pillars to the wide, unadorned vaults of pale stone, I had a feeling of joyous levity. We sat close together on a bench and received beauty.

The adventure of the *camino* is by definition a religious experience, but the stones tell a story of their own and the Romanesque architecture I discovered on this journey had a lasting impact on me. I was deeply moved by these solid medieval constructions, pierced here and there by a single blinding shaft of light. They grew out of the ground like stone mushrooms, sprang from the earth without reaching for the sky and contented themselves with humble surroundings. In the village of Fromista, we stumbled on the small church of San Martin. The interior was empty; here mass was said but once a year. A sign, handwritten in German, said, "You stand here before one of the purest Romanesque monuments in the entire world." The year inscribed on the lintel was 1035.

We had taken a good two weeks to make the journey. Arriving in the green valleys of Galicia, the city of Santiago offered a climax of dynamic dissonances: a twelfth-century Romanesque cathedral of monumental dimensions with Plateresque facades and medieval towers. A Renaissance city where the walls of the narrow streets almost touched, where late Gothic cloisters stood cheek to jowl with Baroque hospices and churches in every imaginable Christian style. The western facade of the cathedral formed part of the popular Praca da Obradeiro, the Workshop Square. The ground rose to meet the church and the statue of Saint James watched us as we walked up the magnificent quadruple flight of steps. Above him shone the star that led to his discovery.

It was a sunny morning, the crowded square was full of light and color, people laughed and called, clapping each other on the back. The carved shell in the cobbled square was point zero, the meeting point where everybody arrived. It was a motley crowd. Exhausted after weeks on the road, pilgrims dressed in rough robes and sandals put down their rucksack on the stairs. Many wore wooden crucifixes, one man actually dragged a large cross, another carried chains around his neck, but most of them just looked like tourists wearing sensible shoes. Some knelt in prayer, others burst into song, while staunch local politicians with briefcases crossed the square to the seat of the city council and students entered the offices of the university. Real tourists with real luggage checked into the Hotel de los Reyes Catolicos, once the Royal Hospice and founded in 1492. Children ran between stalls that sold brightly painted shells, gourds for drinking from the wells, pilgrim's staffs, and other paraphernalia. We bought sandwiches and mingled with the crowd. The whole scene was much like a country fair, allowing for some slight differences. Bells were tolling and voices chanted behind wooden doors. Visitors entered the portal, passing the central pillar known as the Tree of Jesse, and placed their right hand into indentations worn into the marble by pilgrims making that same gesture for a thousand years. mixing with the crowd were priests selling small scrolls with a text of absolution signed by the archbishop. I had not realized that selling indulgence (instituted in 1095 to allow crusaders to buy remission of sins committed in harrowing feats of barbarism and idealism) was still an officially accepted practice. Fred approached a young priest who showed him a list of sins to choose from like a menu, each with the penalty added in pesetas, to square the account. There was an extra charge for a carved wooden box. I looked with slight unease on these black-frocked vendors of salvation, recalling a Dutch saying from my childhood: When a coin clinks in the box, a sinner's soul jumps into heaven. Fred bought a small scroll for our Antonia, just in case, although we doubted that she had ever had a bad thought in her head.

Arrival at the cathedral spelled the completion of the journey, but some walked the few extra miles to Finisterre, the edge of Europe. There our road too would end, at a wild and rocky shore where the Roman Legions watched in "religious horror" as the sun sank into the Sea of Darkness, the Mare Tenebroso. Long before Christianity, the Celts believed that on these cloud-hung cliffs erring souls gathered to follow the sun across the sea. By following the *camino*, we had walked in the steps of events that took place when the Western world was young. Medieval Europe believed in sorcery and miracles, but it was also growing in wealth and confidence. Soon it would accept that maybe not everything was beyond human understanding, that not all knowledge came from God, and that mysteries might be explained. (In Spain, this development would take far longer than in some other European countries, as the murderous persecutions by the Inquisition helped paralyze thought and led to the breakdown of intellectual life on the brink of modern age.) The pilgrim's trail bore witness to the people who walked it, to their achievements, their sacrifices, their dreams and hopes. The popular Spanish name for the star-filled heavens of the Milky Way is "The Way of Saint James," and people said it was made of the dust raised by the pilgrim's feet. My own small miracle was that, a thousand years later, it had remained one of the most beautiful journeys through history.

DEIA ENDING

Fred and me in Deia

During these years, it seemed as if the Gods smelted only gold in their crucible. We traveled, enjoyed the challenges and gratifications of work, were glad to return home, turning to each other with need and love. Waking up in the morning, watching the sun touch the dark beams on the whitewashed ceiling, I sometimes silently prayed that no lesser godlings would glance our way and envy my happiness. Still, the heartbreak came. Had I been willfully blind to warning signs? Or had those deities always known that one day the very source of that happiness would look around him and say, "I cannot stand perfection"?

The perfection—or should I call it predictability, even boredom—slowly set in. A short year before the Institute and its influx of young students, we had bought a fortified farmhouse on the coast to Valldemossa. It was to be our new home, our new adventure. Set high on the hill, Son Rullan looked down on the brown terraces and the rugged rock of the Foradada standing in the sea below. One of the oldest *fincas* in Deia, the parchment deeds went back to 1355, but a Moorish bowl and knife handle found buried in the walls dated our new home even before that. It was a big job and very exciting, restoring so old a house. We discovered roof beams painted with the eight-pointed Maltese crosses of the Knights of Saint John. One of their most powerful commanders at the time was a Mallorcan knight named Fuster, and it was very likely that the Knights Hospitallers used the small fortress as one of their hospices on the island. (My daughter Cathy has since married Juan Antonio Fuster, and it intrigues me that my grandsons may be the descendants of the healer/warriors who once occupied this very house.) Renovations had started when Fred received a grant to continue his studies at Columbia University. He left for New York and I carried on with the work, once again with Antonio as our foreman assisted by Mito, a gifted young Swiss/Mallorcan friend whom we called *manitas*, little hands, because he could restore an antique painting, mend a broken pot or build a harpsichord with the same effortless ease. Together we searched the island for old beams, windows, doors, tiles, and furniture that would bring this house back to life.

Having gone up and down the hill almost every day, I stayed up above one evening to sleep on a stone bench still warm from the sun. I wanted to spend some time there without workers and the noise of building. All through that silent night, I felt the empty, half-ruined house watching me, it's tangible past present in the stones. I had expected to be somewhat uneasy, but it did not seem to mind my presence. The moon slipped over the mountain, its light so bright I could have reread the letters I was holding. There was no need; I knew by then that my husband had not left for New York alone, taking instead one of his girl students from the Institute. Rumors flying between New York and Deia had found their mark swiftly enough and when I called New York that morning, a female voice answered.

Life in the village being what it was, I pretended all was as usual. I continued dining with friends, shopped in Palma, swam at the *cala*, went on a trip with the Graves, and politely agreed with those who assured me that all would be right once Fred came back. By the time he did get back to Deia, his degree achieved, while I had almost finished restoring the house, nothing was right and our life together seriously endangered. We held out until after the summer, when in his state of current madness he announced that he would move up to the big house alone. Well, more or less alone. The family, meaning me, was to stay in our village house. Foster and Cathy went off to college and high school in Bloomington, Indiana, where they would be living with Fred's sister Inge, whose husband was dean of a department of the university. They therefore saw little of the unfolding nightmare, while Marc stayed with me and took the brunt of his friends' sympathy—and ridicule—over Fred's adolescent behavior in full view of the village. The girls were young and he flaunted them. Few of our friends could believe that this was happening to us, the solid family; even fewer thought that it was more than a phase. The student from the Institute had been a passing infatuation and so were the others, they said; it is a typical midlife crisis, just wait it out. As for me, I knew that if it could happen to us at all, there was but a chance in hell it would pass. This was not a case of casual, however humiliating infidelity or the age-old protest against the bonds of marriage. It was the rejection of a rare gift, of a love that had embraced each other's past, built the present, and recognized that the future was ours to share because we could imagine it no other way.

At one point, this man dared to ask me, "Is this killing you?" Was this love, pity, condescension? I stared at him and thought, "You are an idiot. Don't you realize it is killing *us?* That if I survive this, I will be a different person? I will not look back then to see whether you have come to your senses." Meanwhile, I *did* flounder badly, drank too much, smoked too much and in an empty gesture of defiance took a lover, mainly because he was there. I shied away from friends, my cameras stood ignored. The full moon watched me sitting on the stone-stepped terrace, tightly curled hands clenched between knees, waiting for dawn. The voices of oboe and clarinet in a sonata that once spelled light and love now mocked my heartache. There were also times when, full of rage, all I wanted was to go up that hill just one more time, and blow the house sky-high. What of the meetings, the bitter words, the tears, and the halfway reconciliations? All the king's horses and all the king's men.

Robert Musil wrote, "There is a time in life when everything perceptively slows down, as though one's life were hesitating to go on." So it felt to me. I seemed to exist in limbo, incapable of making any decision, threatened in my whole being. Feeling sorry for myself; what had I overlooked? Had I closed my eyes to cracks in the wall because I could not bear my shrine to crumble? I did not realize, even then, how much our relationship had shifted through the years, that from being a student, I had grown into an equal, a wife and partner. I had not seen the difference, because my love had remained the same; for Fred time had frayed and chafed until the future seemed the mere continuation of a well-trodden path. He told me later that for the first ten years he never even looked at another woman. Then the magic, the excitement of teaching, of creating, was fading. I had become grown-up. New ventures beckoned him, this time without me.

Long after the breakup, when I was making new decisions in a new life, I received a cable. In German, from Fred. "After leaving the Countess D'Agoult, Liszt wrote to her: Here unfolds the painful martyrdom of two beings who were everything to each other and who will now search incessantly, like two blind people, without ever finding each other again. MUST THAT BE?"

It was too late.

While time may not always heal, it still goes by. One either survives or shrivels to a sorry life or even a sorry death, neither of which I had in mind. One day I realized that if nothing else, I was now responsible for my children. It meant stepping up to the real world, teaming up with journalists or writing the stories as well as taking the pictures. Foster and Cathy were in safe hands across the ocean. I entered Marc in the British School in Palma from where he would come home on weekends to Antonia and our Moochen, who had stayed with me rather than with her son and some girl she referred to as "that person."

Friends had put me in contact with *Life* magazine, and I left for New York. After an interview and a show of my work, the magazine gave me a first assignment: covering a women's football game in Shea Stadium. I could hardly believe it. The glowing feeling that if *Life* liked my work, I had passed the test. I had not been at all sure that I would be able to make it on my own, and *Life* was the best any photographer could do. It restored my wobbly confidence, but now I began to worry about the assignment. I had never seen an American football game and did not have the vaguest idea of what was supposed to happen. I met the New York team, went to see them practice in Central Park and took some shots of good-looking girls with their kids, who had come to watch mom play. The night of the game, they were unrecognizable. Giants with helmets and shoulder pads kept running past me at great speed, screaming "kill, kill," and one of them nearly broke my nose when her elbow hit my camera. I felt totally inadequate, but kept shooting. When *Life* liked the story and gave me another assignment, I walked on air! I arranged to pick up my films, only to walk into a room of shocked and crying people: that very Monday morning, without any previous notice, the staff had been told that *Life* magazine was closing down!

How could that happen? *Life* was not just a magazine; it was an institution. I know how special even I had felt entering the building minutes ago, feeling that I actually belonged there, just a little, a sort of reflected glory. To the very privileged and often arrogant journalists and staff of *Life*, it was incomprehensible. The closure cut my personal career with the sacred magazine very short indeed, but I was proud to have worked with them at all.

Around that time, *Magnum* published one of my pictures giving credit to one of their photographers. I went to see them in Paris, thinking they might accept me as a member and I might branch out with my photography work in France. The French tend to be a cliquish lot and rally around their little clubs like female elephants around a threatened newborn. I would become friends with William Klein and Marc Riboud, but nothing further came of it. Using my *Life* magazine article as a new introduction, I called on other contacts. I set out to build a career of my own. Soon after, I left for Rio to cover the carnival for *Queen Magazine*.

BRAZIL

It was not a country I ever shared with Fred. As editor of *Queen Magazine* he once sent me to cover the Rio carnival. Then I had done a story on the beginning of the new capital called Brasilia. I had stood at the Iguaçu Falls, where rivers from three countries come together, thundering down over steep cliffs in glorious cascades festooned with spume and rainbows. I visited the German-speaking southern towns of New Hamburg and Blumenau, where blond, blue-eyed children wish you "Guten Tag." Each time I had promised myself that next time, Fred and I would travel this fascinating country together. Here I was again; on my own.

Brazil and its people radiated a particular energy and a fierce love of life that touched me. The two were not always perfectly aligned, and if the delicate balance between sweetness and danger approached something close to poetry, it could as easily turn to grief. In Bahia, the oldest and most African of the Brazilian cities, I was the guest of Jorge Amado and of the artist Carybé. Introduced by a mutual friend, Antonio Olinto, the culture attaché at the London embassy, I could not have been welcomed more generously. Amado took time to lead me on a search for old votive figures, while Olinto's wife, Zora, a sorceress, invited me to a ceremony of Candomblé. A form of voodoo, it worships a Supreme Being called Olorun, or Zambi, who rules through subsidiary divinities, to whom people appeal in hardship, sickness or love. As at the time the government still officially banned the ceremonies, I was allowed to accompany my new friends, but not to take any pictures. Both Carybé and Jorge Amado held high honorary positions in the Candomblé congregation. (Carybé died in 1997 of a heart failure during a session in a Candomblé yard.)

We found a mixed crowd of people waiting outside a white wooden house. From the open windows came the sound of voices chanting in Yoruba. Bahia thrived long before there was a country called Brazil, and African slaves nurtured a heritage of a religion and a language very much alive after four hundred years. As we advanced to the entrance of the barn-like room, a young man splashed us with perfumed water to cleanse our bodies. My companions answered some ritual questions I did not understand, some incense sticks were waved around and we were admitted.

An odd mixture of candles and harsh neon lights lit a room decorated with banners and paper streamers. From the ceiling hung shiny fish cut from silver and green metallic foil in honor of Yemanjah, goddess of the sea. On the walls, I saw more cutouts: a harp, a trident and the Star of David—all symbols of Candomblé. There were small baskets filled with cowrie shells used for divining, and I smelled the spicy food prepared for the banquet after the ceremony. Dressed in white, flanked by two matriarchal aides, the head priestess sat on a throne-like chair under a gold cloth canopy. Old, fat, dark, wearing large white turbans and shiny pink blouses trailing strings of colored beads, these women exuded a silent power all their own. Behind them hung a gilded crucifix and to one side stood a life-size figure of a mounted Saint George, here veneered as Oxossi, god of hunting and patron saint of the Candomblé. Through time, divinities have conflated with Roman Catholic saints and some people present here tonight would attend church next Sunday.

The room was filling fast and we took our seats on the wooden benches. The drums started to throb, the priestess rattled a gourd, and a procession of women emerged from a back room. Young and old, black, mulatto, and Afro-Indian, they wore long full skirts, white petticoats and lacey blouses. Some of them had shaven heads, sign of novices to be initiated. They circled the room to the uneven beat of the drums, moving their hips and arms in a curious rocking motion, as if they were swimming. The crowd, led by a man wearing a black top hat and a garland of flowers, continued to chant in Yoruba. When the rattle slowed its rhythm, the dancers fluttered facedown on the floor, and lay still. One novice now took the floor alone, whirling and approaching the priestess. Holding out her hands, she started to shake. Gyrating wildly back to the middle of the room she let out a piercing shriek, the white of her eyes showing in the dark face, her hair falling loose and her dress slipping off one shoulder. The other novices joined her, holding her up and uttering a series of bird-like squawks. Two women approached the dancers, untied their sashes and retied them as veils over their heads, a sign that the spirit of Candomblé had accepted them. A boy entered through the back door, wearing a beaded basket upside down on his head. The drums beat faster, the chanting mounted. The boy kneeled in front of the priestess while an older man, dressed in a silver tuxedo, cut the throat of a black cock, tied the feathers in a bundle and sprinkled the blood on the floor. The priestess rose and blessed the offering, the drums stilled, the chanting died down. The mass was over. As soon as the priestess and her aides left through the back door, the dancers mingled with the crowd, embracing family and friends. People got up from the benches, chatting and laughing, children ran in an out of the room, heaped platters of *acarajé* with its deep-fried bean bread, shrimps and rice, appeared. It was time for the celebration dinner.

Carybé and I left before the banquet started. "You do understand why you could not take pictures?" he asked on our way home. I knew that usually only initiated members were admitted to ceremonies where animal sacrifices were performed. I had also heard a rumor about recent trouble in the cult house when a white man had tried to interfere with the ceremony. "What actually happened there? I heard they threw someone out?" I asked. "I heard someone ended up with a knife in his belly," was the answer.

I had missed the carnival with its rhythms of samba reggae and glimpses of Orfeu Negro's ghost on his fatal search in the Mardi Gras crowd. Even so, Bahia was easy to love. I was seduced by the beauty of the bay, by the blue, pink and yellow houses, the extraordinary mixture of this city's population and the history of miscegenation that is at the root of its culture. I made new friends, among them the artist Iracema, who gave me one of her paintings of the Amazon River that remains among my most favorite possessions. There was the easy-going, lifestyle the language, the food and the multifarious magic of its music. Sergio Mendes was the new king of jazz; we danced through the night, and sometimes a singer's voice in a backstreet café would draw me into the singular world of *saudade*. At first, I understood the word simply to mean nostalgia, regret for something you once knew, like childhood memories or songs from times past, but *saudade* is far more. It is a Byzantine desire to go back to a time that never was, a bittersweet memory that is no memory at all. The sound of a shepherd's flute in a distant valley, silent tears in the dark of night.

Bahia was nicknamed the Capital of Happiness. It was also the place where I was mugged. One early morning, walking down a narrow winding street in the lower city, my way was barred by a young man with a knife. Which he put at my throat. Of course, I thought, *my cameras*. But no, he reached for a thin golden necklace, the only jewelry I wore, and yanked hard. The knife nicked my skin, although I don't think he meant it to. It was just that within seconds of his attack, several women appeared out of nowhere and pounced on the boy. They screamed at him, grabbed his arms, hit him on the head and shoulders, and pushed him down the road. Two of them took me between them and away from the struggle. They steered me to a nearby courtyard and plunked me down in an old wicker chair. Soon the rest of them returned, one holding my broken necklace. They made me take off my bloodstained T-shirt and washed it on the spot, leaving me sitting there in my bra. Their voices went on for a long time. If I did not understand everything they were saying, we did understand each other very well: they reproached me for walking alone, for wearing jewelry, finally, for being in this area at all. I in turn tried to explain that I was very grateful, that I was not hurt, that I was sorry, also that in my work I did this kind of thing and, finally, that I would not wander around by myself in their neighborhood ever again. They patted me on the back, and fed me mango juice and sweet cakes fried in palm oil. When I left several hours later, wearing my dried T-shirt and a bright orange band aid under my chin, two young women accompanied me to the main square where we parted, embracing like old friends. Of the young man, I saw no more.

BRADESCO

Amador Aguiar

The assignment was simple and straightforward: pictures for the *Daily Telegraph* on an extraordinary man who lived in Sao Paolo. Amador Aguiar, owner of Bradesco bank and multimillionaire, believed in lending young pioneers small sums of money while offering 10 percent on the smallest deposits. It was the kind of daredevil banking suited to the time and it worked, for largely thanks to it, Parana grew into the one of the richest coffee states in the world. His bank was more than a bank; it was a way of life. Mr. Aguiar, in a Victorian way, believed that "nothing is as important as character and hard work." He therefore created a "City of God," after his own idea of how his employees needed to live to enable them to function best as human beings and workers. I wandered around enjoying his city, which was more like a village, with multicolored houses, flower-lined streets, swimming pools and modern schools, all on the tatty outskirts of Sao Paolo. It was a sort of utopian community, but also faced harsh criticism for isolating people behind high walls and gates, guarded by private police. Actually, as soon as employees saved enough money, they had the choice of leaving their low-rental housing and buying a home "outside." I liked Mr. Aguiar and his wife, who invited me to their home. A prime target for political terrorists, he had two personal bodyguards and carried a pistol wherever he went. He put it down on the car seat between us as he drove. "Senhor Aguiar can make and break politicians, industrialists and financiers, but maybe more important, he has given the chance of a decent life to hundreds of thousands of small men, all of whom know him or of him," said an official in San Paolo. "That, to me, is what makes him a formidably powerful man."

The Bradesco story had paid for my trip, but all along, I had been aiming for the Amazon. I knew that the Brazilian government was building a vast highway through the Amazonian rain forest, one of the most impenetrable and pitiless jungles in the world. A legendary place, it promised a story along the lines that Fred and I had been covering for years. This time I had to try it on my own. I was as always curious to explore a world unknown to me, but I also knew that if I succeeded it would establish me as an independent photojournalist. It was not easy, but Senhor Aguiar of course knew all about it and was willing to help. We called in a mutual close friend, Sergio Correa da Costa—Brazilian Ambassador to London at the time—and between them, they produced permits, letters of introduction and a ride in a military plane flying north.

THE AMAZON

It does not matter how often you have seen pictures of a rain forest or read about the Amazon, none of it prepares you for the actual sight. Droning for hours in a small plane over a dense carpet of greenery, I saw, for hundreds of miles around me, the weather being shaped. Small fluffy clouds touched with pink and golden light floated nearby, a fiery orange-red bar marked a far horizon, while beyond clear skies stood dark pillars of rain under purple thunderclouds streaked with lightning. It was like watching the twilight of the gods. We were moving slowly enough and the plane was small enough to give me a sense of immense space, of infinity. Below us, the forest continued to flow by, showing an occasional glint of silver rivers but no sign of human habitation. I could not but wonder what would happen if we fell into that sea of broccoli. What was down there? Who lived there? Who was looking up to see us sail by? The pilot saw me watching and grinned, "Believe me, it would be a long walk home." He told me of the Catalina flying boats—small freight planes used in many armies at the time—returning to base, their bellies stuck with arrows like porcupines. I suddenly had a vivid image of Peter Matthiessen's

Lewis Moon playing in the Fields of the Lord, naked and painted, stamping his foot, peering up at Wolf's plane and releasing the arrow from his black bow.

The Transamazon Highway was to be the backbone of five thousand miles of roads, connecting the Pacific Ocean to the Atlantic. After little more than a year of backbreaking work, the road builders had managed to extend the red mud road through nearly 1,500 miles of jungle. It ran roughly 200 miles south of the river and construction had started on both ends, working toward the middle. I had no idea when, where or how I would be able to join one of the work crews. Armed with Sergio da Costa's ambassadorial letters, I contacted the governor's office in Manaus, whose staff kindly put me in the old Amazonia Hotel and promised to ship me to "The Road" with the next batch of materials, "maybe in a week." I wandered around the city, looking my fill at the turn-of-the-century extravagances of the rubber boom. No roads lead to Manaus, yet it is a town of crowded streets and hurrying traffic, its handsome old buildings lining wide avenues like European transplants, and pretty fin-de-siècle kiosks sheltering small orchestras playing Strauss waltzes. The gold-domed opera house opened on New Year's Eve of 1896 to the voice of Enrico Caruso. Its curved roof came from Alsace, its stairways from Italy and the boxes from France. Fantastic Manaus, situated one thousand miles from the ocean, in the middle of the world's largest forest, is also the chief port of Amazonas. The tide in this river city can reach as much as forty feet, and most of the huts along the bank are built on stilts. I watched great dark balls of crude rubber being loaded by cable car to a unique floating quay and from there to the ships. The heat was tropical and the pungent smell of rubber hung over everything. In this town of contrasts, near-naked Indians in dugout canoes paddled past freighters from Hamburg and New York, vultures searched through the garbage of luxurious restaurants and, at the very edge of the jungle, well-dressed hosts invited me to formal afternoon tea in lush gardens alive with tame *pacas*, peeping tree frogs, squawking parrots and pet monkeys.

There was much to see in the city, but I began to feel a little jingly and hired a boat to go up river. It was a rickety affair with a small square cabin on deck, a boat such as a child would draw. On board were the captain and a young boy, who cooked whatever we fished or hunted. They treated me a little guardedly, like the eccentric woman I must have seemed to them, travelling alone instead of with other tourists. Near Manaus, the Amazon meets a tributary, the Rio Negro, flowing down from Venezuela. Stained with tanning from rotting vegetation, it is as black as the Amazon is sandy and, a curious phenomenon, never the twain do mingle: they simply smack into each other. The line of demarcation is so clearly defined that for a while our boat floated half in the inky waters of the Negro, half in the yellow muddy Amazon. For several miles, the two ran side by side; then the mighty river swallowed its dark tributary.

Chugging along the Amazon River for the very first time: the heat, the silence, the sounds, the smells and the distances. The muddy water hides piranhas, electric eels and tiny fish called *candiru* that insinuates itself into body orifices. The huge *pirarucu* leaves its swirls and eddies; the grayish-pink porpoises trace silver arches in slow motion. Many local legends surround these river dolphins called *botos,* and no one here kills them for either sport or food. They bustle about on the river bottom looking for shrimps, hunt fish, (including piranhas) and stick together in muddy water by touching flippers as they swim. A small group played around our boat, blowing bubbles. The skies were gray, it rained a lot, and I did not ask where we were going or what I was supposed to look for. The captain told me the nearest Indian tribes lived thirty days travel from here, combining canoeing and walking through the jungle. I had no way of knowing the truth, for here distance had a different meaning. Besides, the men usually answered my questions with "okay" even if they had no idea what I was talking about. In our little cockleshell, I did not fret about time. I felt very close to what I came for, not just the highway story, but also this, the river and the jungle. We meandered, we kept getting soaked, the sun dried us, nights were rather chilly, and I could not believe that I was really here.

We skirted the jungle wall, which looked impenetrable, a tightly woven curtain. I saw palm trees at the edge of the water and further in huge trunks soared out of a tangle of hanging vines and lianas. I saw flowers high up, and realized that here the parasites were orchids. I heard the piping of tree frogs, the rhythmic sawing of cicadas, which stopped whenever the rain started. The smell coming off the jungle was sweetish, slightly foul, like fungus on rotten wood. It seemed an ornithologist's paradise. I recognized flights of parakeets and various kinds of parrots, flaming red macaws, always in pairs, and fat short-tailed green birds with red spots. Some screeched, some whistled, some made a booming sound. One kind of parrot clucked and babbled in fruit trees, others hurried by in swift and trembling flights, barking like exited puppies. The flocks of white egrets were loud and gave off an intense smell. They hunched on their perches halfway up the taller trees, preening their feathers after the rain and taking off they trailed their long black legs. I caught a glimpse of a hoatzin, a large, very strange-looking bird with a bright blue face and a spiky crest as it scrounged among the shrubbery, hissing and grunting. We saw vultures, the ubiquitous *urubus*, wheeling above before descending in sweeping corkscrew spirals.

As for the trees, I was really at a loss. Some were aflame with blossoms; others bore pods, their tops resembled tufts, sprays, bursts, feathers or open fans. The captain showed me rubber trees, pointed out a purply-looking tree with nasty-looking spines, another with large silvery leaves, also a silk-cotton tree and a wild fig tree. I felt less ignorant remembering that here botanists have identified over a hundred different kinds of wood within a half-mile square area.

The few local people living along these shores fish, hunt, and gather wild fruit. Some grow a small plot of plantains, jute and manioc or tap the rubber trees. They are the *caboclos*, the river people, a cross of Indians, loggers and rubber tappers. Copper-colored, undernourished, suffering from tuberculosis, black water fever and malaria, they live in small sheds often washed away when the water rises. We talked to some of them. They looked gaunt; the men wore torn T-shirts and shorts, the women calico dresses, and most had straw sombreros. On the wall of one shed hung a gaudy calendar, but I saw no trace of art or artifacts among them other than some crudely decorated paddles. A family showed us a pet boa constrictor, the children kept piranhas tied to a string or baby caimans in a mud hole. No more than five inches long, the creatures were perfect miniatures, complete with long fingers and toes. Picked up by the tail, a tiny crocodile made angry clacking noises and snapped at the child's hand.

A variety of animals shared these people's world, among them the *paca* (a tailless orange-brown furry rodent with white dots like a bambi), the sloth, the capybara (the world's largest rodent) and monkeys as well as all those. birds There are snakes, among them the poisonous coral snake, the fer-de-lance and the bushmaster, but most are nocturnal animals and do not tend to lie in wait for people. The anaconda, largest of the boa family, seems to be the only snake likely to attack without provocation. The hornets, ants, scorpions and spiders would seem to be more of an everyday menace, while the mosquitoes and tiny biting flies called *pium*, that cause raised blood dots, are a real pest.

The crew shot at anything they saw moving along the riverbank. They tried to wade ashore to retrieve whatever it was, but sometimes it was just a total loss and we could only hope someone or something behind that green curtain profited by the killing. We did get two plump brownish birds that tasted like chicken. At one point, something strange and frightening happened. I joined them with a revolver, which was no good at all. I then borrowed a rifle and a bird did fall out of the tree into the water, but I kept trying. Only when I found myself aiming at a heron, shattering the pole it sat on, did I wake up out of this frenzy. I have never hunted for sport, never had any interest in guns. Now I had actually tried to kill a heron. One of the most beautiful creatures on earth, a bird I watched every time with joy! It was incomprehensible.

Humaita Camp

About a week later, the small plane landed on a dirt patch near Humaita on the Madeira River. "Biiig, ye-ell-oow, you like caterpillar!" Shouting with laughter a young Indian boy pointed first at a fat yellow bug sitting on my bare arm and then at the line of mud-streaked bulldozers behind us. We had only walked a few yards from the plane to the waiting jeep, but already my hair felt damp and my shirt stuck to my back. For a moment, I just stood watching the cargo being unloaded and tried to imagine how it would feel if I had come here with a signed contract to work from dawn to dusk for endless months to come—which is exactly what eleven thousand men had done.

The first to move in were the topographers and engineers, who reached their appointed area by canoes along some of the Amazon's many tributaries, hacked their way up the embankment with machetes and set up a basic work camp. Once sufficient space was cleared, bulldozers were floated down the river on rafts, thrashed their way up the banks and forged into the forest. Planes dropped canned food and bags of rice, brought in men and small equipment to build more permanent quarters with tents and cooking facilities. I lived with those pioneers, well inside the eerie world I had so wondered about while looking down on it from the plane. From here on, my contact with the outer world would be through the construction company, via the governor's office in Manaus to the London embassy, where Sergio had promised to keep an eye out for news about my whereabouts and get in touch with my house in Deia and Moochen if need be. Moochen and I had talked about everything together and in spite of the absences and dangers my decision might involve, she fully backed it. I had spoken to her again from Manaus and all was well at home. Knowing that she was there was a great source of strength. I had told her I was still in Brazil, without adding too many details of what I was doing, or where and why. I was now truly on my own and if in the following weeks I sometimes asked myself what the consequences would be if something happened to me, I also felt the quietness that comes from having made a decision. My life had changed completely. Fred had left me, had left our marriage and our family. He was living in our village with a new lover, in the very house we had planned and built together. I had to accept that and the darkness and despair it brought. But I had made sure the children were safe, and although I was alone, I was working. I now had to prove that I could do it. And I would.

The group of engineers I joined had been here for months. They had not provided for a female guest, but a curtain was put up to create a separate corner for me. I had little or no privacy, but the men whose space I shared never intruded on mine. They installed a latch on the inside of the outhouse and always sent someone with me to the river to stand guard when I bathed. I spent the days following people around, sharing and learning. The jungle provided a diet of fish, turtle, caiman, monkey and snake as well as a small rodent called cavy and some birds, to go with our cassava and rice. I remember turtle meat in a broth, cavy roasted like suckling pig and, my very favorite, a fish soup made of *pirarucu*—the largest sweet water fish in the world—flavored with some strong-tasting, sorrel-like herb. I ate most things without questioning their origin, with the exception of monkeys roasted on a spit: with their round little skulls left on, they looked too much like a small child.

Unlike what I expected, the jungle seemed very silent. Darwin, on first entering a Brazilian forest, wrote, "A most paradoxical mixture of sound and silence pervades the shady parts of the wood. The noise from the insects is so loud that in the evening it can be heard even in a vessel anchored several yards from the shore: yet within the forest a universal stillness appears to reign." Enormous trees soared up for one hundred feet or more, closing in around me and roofing the jungle like a great glorious cathedral. Sometimes a ray of sunshine slipped through the green canopy, but mostly the jungle floor was immersed in a soft twilight. The ground underfoot was spongy, the air heavy with a sweetish smell of decay. It seemed I only heard the sounds once I had accepted the silence. Slowly I would begin to hear small, unidentified noises filtering from above, monkeys and birds chattering and chirping unseen, the twittering and fluttering, the high, faint, shrill calls. I had never experienced a world as mysterious as this before. Henry Tomlinson, in *The Sea and the Jungle*, wrote: "It's something that has been here since the beginning, and it's too big and too strong for us. It waits its time, I can feel it now." I did feel it and if I was not afraid, it was because the people with me knew and loved the jungle and made me see its beauty. The Amazonian forest is different from an Asian jungle, where one feels the presence of animals on a closer level. There I might worry about tigers, jaguars, snakes or a mad elephant; here it was not a sense of any tangible danger that made me look over my shoulder. It was the jungle itself and I never lost this awe of a world in which, left alone, I would not survive for long. Standing there, I suddenly felt weak, dizzy, with the terrible ache of Fred's absence. How could I hope to live this kind of life alone, when such a great part of it had been the joy of sharing, the building of memories? I needed him more than ever, I wanted to go home and make everything whole again. And knew that it would never happen.

The days were hot and humid, but almost chilly during the night. The men hunted in black and silent water, flashlights searching through the brushwood and the swamp, lighting up the animal's eyes like red stars for the few seconds needed to aim and shoot. I accompanied them, but was grateful that wading into the swamp to grab a maybe dead, maybe wounded caiman was something they spared me from doing. The crocodilians showed beady eyes just above the waterline and seemed paralyzed by the flashlight for short seconds, but then moved very fast, thrashing their tail like a whip.

I saw rodents, a snake or two and monkeys, but never a jaguar, although I did meet its smaller cousin the *onca* fleetingly. Buzzing clouds of mosquitoes and nasty small black gnats were still the most aggressive thing encountered so far. I learned not to lean against tree trunks, not to touch plants or to sit down just anywhere. I had no mirror, but I knew every bite, bump, and scratch. I tried everything from commercial repellents to Vicks VapoRub and rancid diesel oil, until a local woman took pity on me and smeared some greenish ointment on my face. It burned and smelled awful and I never found out what it was, but it reduced the swelling and I was so grateful I did not wash for days.

There were isolated groups of Indians living not too far inside the forest, some of whom had made contact with the workers. It was not always like that: in a camp about a hundred miles down the road, gifts put out had been smashed, a doll pierced with arrows. I heard that the doll had long blond hair and blue eyes, while one of the other gifts had been a small transistor radio, left blaring under a tree. Here some of the men now spoke a few words of Portuguese, learned while bartering fish for rice. One day, when I was watching them getting their canoes ready, they invited me to go fishing with them. Their dugouts were light and narrow, usually paddled by one person sitting up way up front. The engineers were reluctant to let me go and one of them, a big man, first insisted on accompanying me. The Indians watched him step down into the canoe and shouted with laughter when it promptly capsized. I felt bad, but in the end, I went anyway, cameras on my lap, looking back to the camp and wondering what I was getting into. We were two canoes, the small man sitting in front of me chattering away to the Indian paddling alongside us, blades knifing the water. I suddenly heard the word *gramafono*, repeated several times, as he was obviously trying to explain this phenomenon to his friend and I realized that, at this very moment, I was witnessing our world flowing over into a very different one. Turning to me, he said, "You cook?" As I nodded, he went on. "You work?" And then, "You have man?" I thought about that for a moment, the truth being, *no I do not, he has just left me*, but that did not seem the right answer somehow, so I said enthusiastically Sí, sí, man, also niños!" He looked me over, grunted and continued to paddle. An hour or more had passed, when I asked, "Fish?" For an answer, he pointed downriver. Sometime later, about half a dozen more canoes appeared from small hidden streams. We paddled on together, the newcomers totally ignoring my presence, although it cannot have been an everyday occurrence to see a white woman with cameras sitting in their friend's canoe.

Night falls quickly in the Amazon. That night there had been no sunset or warning; it was as if someone had simply drawn a curtain. The sky was a star-filled ribbon between the black trees that lined the river. The men had fallen silent and there were just the smoothly gliding canoes and the soft swish of a paddle. We were still moving away from our camp. I was beginning to wonder how long this would continue, when someone barked an order and the small flotilla veered toward the bank. Instead of preparing nets or poles, they all jumped out of the boats and simply disappeared into the jungle, some carrying their paddles.

Suddenly, the night was full of unfamiliar sounds. Something large touched the side of the canoe with a thump, there were flapping noises and thin high sounds in the air, a continuous whispering, murmuring and calling. I could not always place the croaks and squeaks for here fish grunted like pigs and frogs could do almost anything; they whistled, peeped, quaked and cawed like birds. Inside the jungle, the trees were alight with fireflies, clouds of insects were singing and branches were constantly cracking, breaking, falling. The river lapped and gurgled, unseen night birds called high above and once the hair-raising call of a howling monkey echoed from the forest. Alone in that small canoe somewhere in the middle of the Amazon, listening to the cacophony, I realized I was a long way from anywhere, not just from the camp. Alone, but a miniscule part of the night, part of these black trees, of the river, the star-filled sky and the very jungle. I also realized I was enjoying this immensely, that what I felt was simply a deep and true happiness. I was healing and I loved my life.

The men returned as quietly as they had gone, without any explanation, but carrying a cavy—a sort of guinea pig—they had chased and probably beaten to death. Judging by the happy chatter that broke out once they were all back in the boats, it was more than they had expected to bring home that night. We set out again and they signaled to me as before: soon, soon. Or maybe it was "Why don't you just shut up?" Finally, in a bend of the river, we tied the canoes to overhanging boughs and fished by the light of a single torch. They obviously had meant to go there all along, because their movements were casual and spoke of long habit. These Indians usually spear fish or shoot it with bow and arrow while standing in the canoe, but here they fished with lines in what seemed a deep hole. We caught mainly piranhas, one of which lived up to its reputation by hooking its teeth in the bare heel of my guide. Yelping, he cut it loose and the other men laughed like children, still hauling in those blue and silver fish with red-ringed eyes and a set of triangular teeth as sharp as a razor. When pulled up, they made a strange half-hissing, half-screaming noise that made me shrink as far back as possible from the growing pile in our canoe.

Now and then, I had still pointed vaguely to the sky and backwards to the camp but no one paid attention and I no longer insisted. When we finally did set out for home, I had lost all track of time and could not read my watch in the dark. The Indians were right: they had gone fishing and I had come along, so why was I fretting? I also realized that my worry had not been for myself, but for my friends back in the camp and that I could not do anything about it. We paddled until the sound of a motorboat and the bright lights coming up the river proved me right about the worried engineers. They scolded me like a child lost and found, telling me how differently it might have turned out. I did appreciate their worries; they were right, this was their world, not mine. I apologized. The night on the river, I kept to myself, hoarding its spell like a treasure. "The most beautiful and deepest experience a man can have is the sense of mystery," said Einstein. That night I came close.

THE GOLD OF CREPURI

I had first heard about the gold miners of Crepuri from the engineers in Maici camp, but did not have time to follow up on it. When I returned the year after and said I wanted to do a story on it, my friends first refused to help me. Hundreds of miles south of here, way far in the jungle, dangerous, drunken miners, diseases, planes can't land for days because of the rain, anything could happen, etc. I insisted. They gave in. But not before they taught me how to handle a gun. The pilot who brought our staples also supplied Crepuri camp and was willing to take me, but he agreed with the engineers that I was crazy to go there by myself.

I arrived late in the afternoon, the only passenger in the Cessna. Before boarding, the pilot said, "How much do you weigh? I have a load of one thousand pounds of merchandise and cannot take another ounce." He put me and my cameras on the scale, unloaded the weight in rice and we took off. After nearly three hours of flight I saw the camp, a tiny cluster of shiny wet roofs embedded in a tightly knitted carpet of green. When we descended on a narrow clearing of red mud that served as a landing strip, people stared at me. A woman loaded down with cameras? What is she doing here?

Crepuri had no main street or square. Its forty-odd houses huddled together at the end of the short runway. Weeds with bright red flowers grew high on the muddy paths between the huts, covering up blackened tree stumps where the jungle had been cleared and burned. No roads lead out of here, for the simple reason that there was nowhere to go. The nearest town was Itaituba, two hundred miles away. The only transport out if here a canoe or the small single-engine plane they called teco-teco. A speck of humanity in a vast green void: several hundred men, fifteen prostitutes, a group of ramshackle huts and three bars, which claimed to serve food. Malaria, fever and heat. With only one reason for it all: gold.

The current gold rush started in the town of Santarem, when a stocky man called Nilçon emerged from the jungle carrying several jerry cans filled with nuggets and gold dust. He distributed his treasure generously among the local girls and the stories of his riches and orgies spread like wildfire. Santarem lies in the State of Para, nearly 1,500 miles north of Rio and 500 miles inland from the Atlantic, at a junction where the blue Tapajos River flows into the muddy Amazon. The area was Indian territory, practically unknown, dangerous and unhealthy, but soon hundreds of men were paddling their canoes upstream. Settlements sprung up along the tributaries, but the search for gold remained a one-man operation for the freelance adventurer, the black market dealer, the individual prospector. The mining camps are so far removed from civilization, that even today very few Brazilians are aware of their existence.

That day, arriving in Crepuri, I was offered the choice between the lodging for miners in transit or an empty shack. The guesthouse was an open affair, a palm-thatched roof supported by a row of beams with hammocks slung between them. I chose the shack, which was built like all the others—wooden frames plastered with honey-colored mud, roughly shingled roofs, bamboo screens for doors and windows. From the outside the restaurant, the shop, and the brothels looked exactly alike. Kauby's restaurant served dinner at seven. The walls were bare, there was one long table with benches on both sides, cases were stacked in the corner and a screen divided the dining room from the only other room in the house, where Kauby lived with his mistress. Waiting to be served the worst dinner I can remember having anywhere, I listened to the conversation. "Pedazo shot his girl this morning. He then tried to rape her, but saw she was dead and left her lying in the road," said the skinny man behind the stove. Kauby, a Creole from Guyana, paid no attention and stared indifferently out into the rain. The cook turned to me. "A man can't wash his gold in peace anymore. Last week Jose Mao came back to camp at night, stopped to piss and got stabbed in the back. For a lousy three ounces." For the first time, Kauby showed signs of interest. "He owed more to the *patrao*," he said, handing me a plate of sticky cold rice, garnished with pieces of pork fat and gristle. Price: two grams of gold. A beer? Another gram and a half. The place was filling up and I watched the people, who in turn had come to watch me. Soon we began to talk and everyone had a story. Most were Brazilian and spoke Portuguese. My Spanish was fluent, my French and Italian good, I had spent time with my engineers and now spoke enough Portuguese to have a conversation. Cuyabana, with his gaunt malaria face, missing front teeth and quick furtive eyes, walked for two months through the jungle to get here. I remembered looking down for hours from the plane without seeing a single break in the monotonous green world below. "Did you always know where you were going? Did you have a compass?" He grinned: "*Noao, puton,* I walked by the sun. When it rained I did not know which way, but I walked, because if you stop you go around in circles and die mad." "What did you live on?" "I carried twenty pounds of farina and hunted. There are always monkeys and birds; at one time I shot a young boar."

Dona Maria sat next to me. A small woman, with the face of an Andalusian gypsy and the voice of a drill sergeant. When she arrived here three years ago, having left her husband because he "was no good," she did not have enough money to pay for a meal. Now she owned one of the restaurants. (The next day, she proudly showed me an enormous refrigerator that ran on kerosene and brought out her gold jewelry weighing several pounds.) "What made you choose this place?" "It was new to me," she said, "and had plenty of gold. The bars were full every night and when the men were drunk, they would pay as much as a handful of gold for a girl. There is still enough gold here now, but few people are rich. *Garimpeiros* don't usually hold on to anything. They find gold, they spend it, they don't find any, they live on credit. Ei, last year one *moco* struck it rich, washed out about four pounds of gold. So what did he do? He chartered several planes and took anybody who wanted to come to Santarem, to see a football game, five hundred miles away! They drank until the gold was gone and all they brought back was a dozen red football shirts. Now he is back in a pit; it's all or nothing with them."

The room was quite full now. It smelled of beer and frying oil; people sat relaxed, elbows on the table, recalling crimes and anecdotes. "Remember Bodinho, who was clearing a patch of jungle when the *teco* dropped food and he was killed by a sack of flour that fell on his head?' They roared with laughter. Voices mingled, overlapped, leaving me to concentrate on the stories of my immediate neighbors.

"Elizeu, tell me what you think. On Sunday a two-headed snake come in my house. Sebastao say is a warning that somebody want to kill me, but other people say a double-headed snake a good spirit."

"Napoleon at last found the man who killed his brother eight years ago. He found him in the camp of San Domingo and shot him at the bar."

They ran down the list of killers and victims, but gold rarely seemed the first motive, and most of the killing was over liquor and women. Crepuri has no cemetery. The jungle is deep and the river takes care of the dead. Besides, here a man is rarely known by his

Afghan nomads on the way.

Afghan woman.

Afghan nomad woman cooking in tent.

Afghan tribesman.

Sculptured schoolhouse in Kamdesh, Nuristan, Afghanistan.

Mosque in Kabul.

Nuristan tribesman.

Pathan tribesmen.

Afghan women, Herat.

Afghanistan, Hindu Kush.

Road north of Kabul.

Nomads, Afghanistan.

Bengal Lancers, Jaipur. Indian Army Elite troops.

Bikaner desert: Indian Army Camel Corps.

Bikaner desert. Indian Army. The mounted band of the camel corps.

Crocodile in the Amazon.

Building 8,000 miles of the Trans-Amazonian Highway
through the impenetrable rainforest.

Jaguar in the Brazilian rainforest.

Prostitutes in Crepuri, attracted by the gold found in the mines of Para, Brazil.

The gold diggers are the customers of a handful of prostitutes living in wooden huts of Crepuri, Para.

Digging for gold
in the jungles
of Brazil.

Young Indian girl.
Brazil.

The "madam" of the whorehouse in Crepuri, wearing all her golden jewelry.

Chief of small group of local Indians, who rarely
have any contact with any outsiders.

North West American Indian art: totem poles in the cemetery of Alert Bay,
on Cormorant Island, B.C.

Image of the Thunderbird, Kwunkwanekulegyi, omnipotent ruler of the
skies and protector of the Kwakiutl Indians.

Grass whiskers sprout from fallen totem pole on Guilford Island, B.C.

Himalaya, India: Buddhist monk with trumpet used in temple ceremonies.

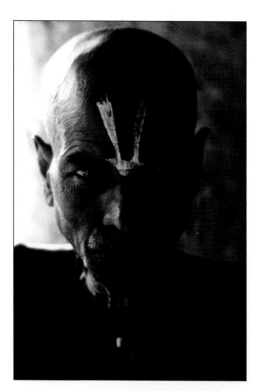

Bihar, India: Village priest of Vishnu Shiva with religious markings.

Rainy season on the market of Shillong, Assam.

Buddhist monks at the ocean near Kanchipuram, Chennai, India.

Hill tribe woman sitting on her roof in the Himalayan foothills,
Himachal Pradesh.

Boy playing a flute, Kashmir, India.

Dal Lake, near Srinagar, Kashmir, is famous for its houseboats.

Elephant in Serengeti, Tanzania.

Masai warrior in Kenya, Africa.

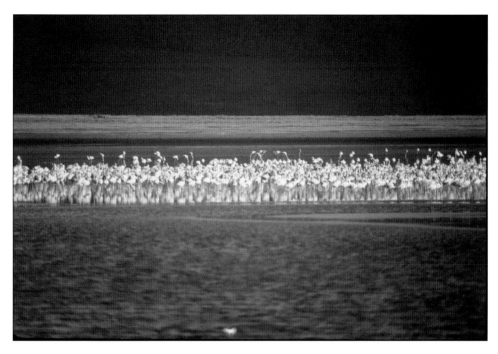

Flamingo dancing in lake, Tanzania, Africa.

Wildebeest in Serengeti, Tanzania.

A walk in the wilderness of Lapland.

Ice on a pond, Lapland.

A religious holiday at the Erdene Zuu monastery, Mongolia.

An outdoor concert in the Mongolian steppes.

Mongolian Woman in yurt.

Mongolia: here wood is worth its weight in gold and is
transported for miles by oxcarts.

The steppes of Mongolia.

Toby on UNESCO expedition in Mongolia.

The world of the Pathans.

Pathans: the women.

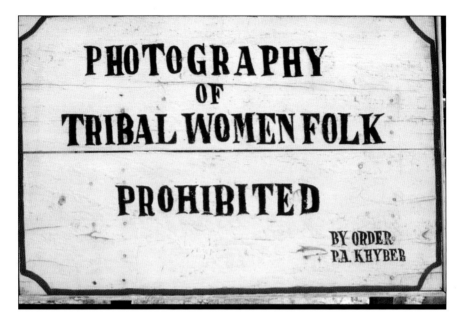

The world of the Pathans.

Three Pathan women.

Pathan children at play in the backyard.

A Kazakhstan welcome.

Kazakhstan women sitting in front of their yurt.

Where a yurt is home.

A home enterprise: the family breeds falcons, selling them
to Saudi princes for small fortunes.

La Mancha of Don Quixote's tales.

These women remain the very essence of La Mancha.

The pride of the Spanish Foreign Legion.

real name. His past is his own affair and he can disappear at any time, go downriver to another camp, and change his story. With a little luck, a man without a name or an education still has a chance to make a fortune. The gold is there for the taking, but the taking takes courage and the huts of Crepuri hide as many tragedies as the bleak ghost towns of the Klondike. For miles around, deep in the steaming jungle, the placer miners stake out their claims, clear the trees, dig through soft earth and gravel until they reach clay. Standing knee-deep in the yellow muddy water that seeps through the walls of the pit, the men wash the gravel in cylindrical pans, sloshing out mud and water until only the gold is left at the bottom of the pan. It is backbreaking work but what bothers them most is the knowledge that beneath the surface layer of gold-bearing gravel lays a second one, always too deep to reach with pick and shovel. So they move on to dig another hole, farther and farther away from the main camp, leaving the jungle scarred with empty pits and wondering all the while what riches they might have left behind.

The talk around the table centered on the hardships of *garimpo* mining camps, the high cost of living and the indebtedness to the *patrao*. "The *garimpeiro* is a slave," said Barriga, a big man with strong Indian features and a scar running down his left cheek. "You know, I am fifty-three years old, I have washed gold since I was fifteen and I have nothing. Everybody but the miner gets the dust in the end. Everybody—the *patrao*, the shopkeeper, the pilots, the women, *curaiu*, anybody but me." The low burning lamp cast a soft glow on blue-black hair and high cheekbones, the long shadows crept into the corners of the room. From outside, came the sound of quarreling voices, but no one moved to see what was happening. Kauby turned to me: "Tomorrow is Saturday and the men will come in to do their shopping. In the evening there is sure to be some trouble. Be careful where you go and with whom." The talk died down and soon we all got up to leave. The rain had stopped, a white mist floated just above the ground and the abrupt change from stifling day to chilly night suddenly reminded me of the Sahara. My shack was empty but for a hammock strung from hooks on the wall. A rusty kerosene cooker stood in a corner, there was no light and no furniture. Grateful for a borrowed blanket, dirty and full of holes, I put my cameras, my gun and flashlight within easy reach and went to sleep.

It was barely dawn, I was sitting on the doorstep sipping instant coffee from an old beer can and watching the jungle steam under the first rays of the sun, when a man came walking out of the forest. He looked about fifty, tall, gray-haired, tough, and rather drunk. His shirt was torn, his dirty toes stuck through broken rubber sandals and the holes in his socks. Standing in front of me, he held out both his hands, which were calloused and full of scars. His eyes were of a surprising blue against his dark skin. He performed a slight bow, doffed his straw hat, and said politely, "What is your Grace's name?" I told him. "They call me Pernambuco." He said, "I am a good electrician. Once, a long time ago, they sent me a radio all the way from Sao Paulo, it arrived in pieces and I put it together. I also had a wife. I left my village. It is now very far. *Meu Deus*, life is a whore. I have worked them all, iron and tin, diamonds and the dust. *Garimpeiros* are good people. You see, I do not wear a gun." I offered him some coffee, but he preferred a cigarette. "Your Grace, where are your people? What is the name of your village? Does it have a Deus? What is his name?" I spelled the word GOD for him and he asked me to write it down. Swaying slightly on his feet he carefully folded the slip of paper, put it in his pocket, and walked away. Halfway down the path he suddenly raised both arms high had above his head, shouted "G-O-D, G-O-D!" and disappeared into the forest. The whole incident seemed unreal and for a long time I sat there listening to his voice, full of a mad joy, repeating the same word, over and over, rising from the jungle up to the heavens like a desperate prayer.

Later that morning three planes arrived. Two were just here to borrow some fuel, as they had been unable to land in any of the other camps because of the rain. The third brought a police lieutenant and two troopers. A new law prohibited distilling the local brandy, *kasashi*, which was taking a death toll considered unacceptable even by Crepuri standards. The police were here to smash any bottles they could find, leaving the miners to drink beer, raw spirits, even snuffing spray deodorant, until someone could smuggle in a fresh batch. The plane with the police officers took off and all seemed quiet, but soon a rumor went around: the lieutenant had smashed a dozen bottles in one bar and accepted a bribe in the other. Everybody gathered at the bar. Neco, the owner, confirmed the story and the case of kashasi was dragged out in the open, standing rather forlorn in the middle of the circle. Obviously nobody wanted the liquor destroyed or blamed Neco, but they all resented being shaken down by a police officer and letting him get away with it. A heated discussion followed. In the end Elizeu, a short narrow-shouldered man who ran the new miners cooperative, suggested to send a report signed by all present to police headquarters in Santarem and, for good measure, a copy to the office of the miner's foundation in Brasilia. I was dumbfounded when everyone agreed. This group of lawless men, many of whom signed with an X, men who would not lose a moment's sleep over a miner killed, wrote an official letter denouncing the police! I had to photograph the scene of crime, with the men triumphantly holding up the bottles and Neco, in a gesture of poetic justice, declared the whole lot on the house.

Elizeu invited me to see the men arrive to buy their supplies for the week: farina, rice, beans, salt, matches, coffee, tobacco, ammunition, sugar, a new pan or a shovel. Their full baskets weighed about eighty pounds and most would walk about five hours back to their pit. The gold dust was poured on the scale and carefully weighed. Prices seemed high to me, but they were nothing compared to what the private shopkeepers, the *patrao*, charged. They gave the miners credit, but bought their gold at about half the official rate while selling them food at astronomical prices. They usually owned the supply planes as well.

Every man who entered the store carried weapons: a gun—like the one dangling on my own hip—plus a rifle and a machete. They came from every corner of Brazil and from beyond the Guyana border. They looked me over, but did not talk to me. My cameras made it doubtful that I was here to join my fifteen sisters. Rene Mande, a tall black miner from Cayenne with gold front teeth, spoke English, which he decided to try out on me. For almost forty years, he had drifted from place to place, last in the Porto Velho tin mines. When they were automated, he ended up here. "I preferred to wash gold for myself. Lady, I will bring you a friend, Madame Notte, who also speaks English. We like to speak, for everybody here speaks Portuguese, so we forget." Madame Notte was from Trinidad and sold fruit. Dark-skinned, thin and wrinkled, she could be anywhere between forty and seventy, had a cigarette stuck in the corner of her mouth, wore torn galoshes too big for her feet and called me darling. "You must be careful, not talk to everybody. Why is the reason? There are many vulgar people. I will take you to Madame Simone. She will wash your clothes." Puzzled as to what earned one the distinction of being called Madame rather than simply Maria or Consuela like the other women, I was told, and "It means Mister."

The plane had brought the mail, and Kauby showed me a letter from his mother, who lived in Cuya Cuya. It was difficult to associate this cutthroat dealer wearing mirror sunglasses, a brown fedora and a big knife stuck in his belt, with the oddly moving, misspelled message from another world. "My loved son," she wrote, "prase the Lord and I glad to hear you. Are enjoing good health and trying for your bread, thank to Allmigty God, dont let nobody full you and God wil bles you all what you do. Goodnight your sincerely mother." He seemed proud.

That evening I went to the *boite*, as they called it. I walked into a big room with half a dozen tables, a rough wooden counter, and two pool tables, the men stood leaning against the wall, the women sat at the tables, buying their own drinks. It looked much like a country dance, but the drinking was heavy and there was a strong undercurrent of violence. Kauby had warned me not to take pictures. When a scratchy gramophone played a samba, couples started to dance. A young boy wearing a small round hat, a revolver on his hip, chose a fat, unattractive woman who looked about fifty. A tall miner shuffled with a tiny girl sporting a T-shirt saying "University of Chicago," a miniskirt and huge men's shoes. Had I expected the ostrich-feathered extravaganza of the Hollywood gold rush movies?

I sat down with Julia, who hired most of the girls in town. "Usually they last about three months, then all the men know them and they move on to other camps. They can make more money when they are new. I charge them for two meals a day. They could make money, but they no more hold on to it than the men do. Most of it goes on liquor." Miranda had twelve children, whom she left behind in Santarem to take care of each other. "I send money home, but I don't make all that much," she said and added, unexpectedly, "I would like to work in a pharmacy." I asked her about a young, pretty girl who seemed very drunk. Consuela, fifteen years old, and six months pregnant. Coming to our table, she asked me, "Are you going to stay here? I will give the baby away and go to Santo Domingo. It is too hot here." Completely unconcerned, she poured herself another drink and was off to dance, only to return two minutes later: "How much gold for a photograph? Will you take a small nugget?" I had this crazy vision of myself trading pictures for gold dust. The girls did not seem to worry about the brawls continually erupting in the *boite*. They just laughed it off and one showed me a razor blade hidden in her hair. "I can't shoot as well as they can but I sure know how to handle this!" Midnight passed without incident and I made my way back to my shack. About an hour later, I woke to drunken voices, shouting, laughter, and several gunshots. It turned out to be "nothing serious, just a bullet in the arm." The argument being who had the better girl.

Early next morning I set out for a jungle camp. For nearly four hours, I followed my guide as he threaded his way along a track unmarked to my inexperienced eyes. A cut in a tree trunk, an empty pit, an anthill, a stream—though he pointed them all out to me, I knew I could never find my way back. The jungle closed around me like a curtain. We came to a stream, a thin slippery log the only way to cross. The camp dog that had followed us went over first, slipped and had to swim across, which amused the guide no end. He never looked back to see how I made it, carrying my heavy camera bag. The jungle was quiet, but for some parrots suddenly screeching overhead. My guide shrugged, signaling: no danger.

Without warning, we came to the mine. Stepping into a clearing, I saw two huts, a campfire with pots and pans scattered around it, and four men in a pale yellow pit half filled with muddy water. We had bought fresh bread and canned meat, but they invited us to share their meal: black beans, rice with garlic, and the meat of some jungle bird far better than chicken and infinitely preferable to Kauby's food. They showed me the day's yield of dust, which seemed precious little for all the backbreaking work involved, but they laughed and told me stories of nuggets and riches until I almost believed them myself. The kasashi bottle went around and after a while, one of the miners insisted, first jokingly but increasingly threateningly, that I show them that I knew to handle my gun. I tried to laugh it off and change the subject, when he got up and grabbed me by the arm. The mood had suddenly changed and I now sensed real danger. He was big, drunk, with a leering grin and bloodshot eyes; he was also carrying a big machete. Feeling like an idiot, I told them to put a beer can on a tree stump. It was like a replay of my lessons. Same gun, same distance, same beer can. Feet apart, two hands on the gun, anticipating the recoil, I prayed to my mentors and could almost hear them snicker. I sent the can flying, but did not put the gun away; it was high time to leave. "It was most good you missed not," said my guide, once we were out of sight of the pit. "They respect. Much violence is most easy." I did not tell him it was much most luck and that I would feel a lot better off without that thing on my hip.

By the time we reached the main camp it was dark, there was a rumble of thunder, a glimmer of lightning in the sky. If I did not catch tomorrow's plane, I might be stuck here for far longer than I wished. The plane made it in and many came to say goodbye: Kauby, Rene, Madame Notte, Elizeu and some of the girls. They gave me letters to mail and messages to deliver. I felt uneasy knowing that some of these people would like nothing better than to take my place and leave this way of life behind. "Darling," said Madame Notte, "why is the reason you must not eat mango? Because they give malaria." And she handed me a mango.

EAR INFECTION

I was used to the occasional bit of trouble, a bite, a sting, a light fever, an upset stomach, so when I developed an earache while in one of the camps, I did not worry about it much. There was no swelling, no discharge, just a dull hammering in my head and I did become rather deaf in my right ear. Then, in spite of drops of warm oil, painkillers, and anything else anyone suggested, the pain got consistently worse. After a week, I noticed that my right eye was discharging puss and I kept wiping it, until one morning the man sitting across the breakfast table said, horrified, "JESUS! You are crying blood!" The buzzing in my head was such that I did not quite understand what he was talking about, but the others did. There was no plane available on the dirt track outside, but within minutes we were racing to the nearest dispensary, about sixty miles back along a very rudimentary Transamazonia. The teeth-rattling ride in the jeep, the red mud ruts filled with water, fallen trees half blocking the road, holding on for dear life and trying not to listen to what the men were predicting, is not something I will easily forget or want to do again.

The pharmacist cleaned my eye, gave me an injection of what I have never asked and made me swallow some pills. One of the engineers insisted on staying with me and the men improvised a sort of bed rather than the usual hammock, including a clean sheet and a small pillow, which made me think I must be in very bad shape. I slept most of the time and woke up to noisy talking and a wet rag wiping my face. My pretty white pillowcase was a gory mess, but the pressure in my ear was gone. It had broken through and the men laughed and congratulated me as if I had given birth!

We arrived back to camp. The eye stopped leaking, the hearing came back, and about a week later I was on a plane to Europe. I still suffered from lightheadedness and arriving in London, went straight to Charing Cross, the only hospital I knew, to have a checkup. I must have been a somewhat savage sight: looking yellowish, wearing a coat over tropical clothes in November, lugging my cameras as well as a bundle of spears and arrows I had bought last minute from Indians in our camp. The doctor listened to my story, looked in my ear, folded up his instrument, said, "You should be dead," and walked out of the room. He came back with a specialist on tropical diseases and the two had a very good time. "A hole like a crater, she should be dead," they kept repeating happily to each other, as if I was not there. I left with a plastic bag of multicolored pills and took the next plane home to Mallorca. I took the pills religiously, remembering John Speke—he accompanied Richard Burton on his expedition to find the sources of the Nile—who woke one dark night with a scarab digging its way to his brain via his inner ear. Burton poured in boiling oil and took other drastic measures, finally killing the bug. Speke barely survived, but whenever he sneezed, his ear would make a high whistling noise. My crater did pretty well, I hear perfectly with my right ear and it does not whistle. Actually, my left ear tends to give me vertigo.

CHICO

One follow-up on my Amazonian journeys I was to regret deeply. While hunting in Maici camp the men had brought down a woolly monkey. It turned out to be a female with a tiny baby clinging to her back. I felt terrible, but I also knew the men never killed indiscriminately and had not seen the small animal in the dark. They gave it to me to care for and Chico spent the next few weeks hanging around my neck or riding on my shoulder. On the day I boarded the plane to leave, the engineers presented me with a small basket, neatly sewn in cloth. They also handed me a sheaf of papers, saying, "It is all here. Emilio went to Manaus for the vaccination papers, the export permit, everything!" I did not want to believe what I heard. They had wrapped up Chico in the basket and fully expected me to take a baby monkey home with me to Europe! I looked at them, my friends, my guides and protectors, a small group of tough men standing there proud and happily convinced that I loved and wanted the little thing! There was simply no way I could refuse their gift.

I flew to Rio and spent the night with friends in their fancy apartment. Chico was a sensation and everybody fed him sweets.

When we wanted to go out for dinner, we did not know what to do with him and ended up locking him in a bathroom. Coming home, we found he had emptied the medicine cabinet, shredded the toilet paper, and eaten the children's toothpaste, which was pink. It gave him diarrhea and he had pooped and vomited all over the floor, the sink and the bathtub.

I gave my friends my rare Indian chief's feather headdress and took the Pan Am flight to Madrid, where I had to change for Palma de Mallorca. The plane was half-empty and I had three seats. It was going to be a long flight, so I loosened the cloth just a little to make sure Chico could breath, and went to sleep. When I woke up, he was snuggled down in his usual place on my shoulder. His little fingers had managed to widen the small gap enough to wriggle his way out of the basket. Toward morning, a big-bellied man walked past my seat, looked down at us, and shouted, "Holy Moses, it's a monkey! My wife will never believe me!" He ran to his seat and came back with a camera; the flash blinded both the monkey and me, Chico panicked, shrieked, and took off, after which all hell broke loose. He jumped over seats, using the heads of sleeping passengers as landing pads, and was way down the isle before I could even get out of my seat. People were screaming, flight attendants came running, while I was trying to coach the frightened animal back to my seat. When at last he recognized me, he jumped on my head and would not let go of my hair. I walked to the toilet with a shrieking monkey sitting on my head and peeing all over my face. One of the Brazilian flight attendants thought the whole scene was very funny and explained to the passengers that it was just a baby monkey. She also hinted that the man should not have used a flashlight or his camera without asking me. After that, people came to look at us and wanted to hear our story. I put Chico back in the basket and closed the cover with borrowed safety pins.

Next was the customs officer at Madrid airport, who took my package wrapped in white linen and shook it. It cackled like a frustrated hen. "What's in there?" he asked. "A monkey," I said, "and please don't open it!" He called his colleagues, they poked the thing and talked to it, but in the end, the documents and my threats of what would happen if Chico got out convinced them. I arrived home in Deia after roughly forty hours of traveling, dirty, tired and smelling very bad indeed.

Chico stayed with us for several years, running free in the daytime, sleeping in a large wooden cage, complete with a blanket and a hot water bottle in winter. As playmates, he had my children and their other pets. Early morning we would walk down the terraced gardens picking fresh fruit for breakfast, Moochen or I in the lead with our basket, followed by our red tomcat, a small black goat, and at the end of the line came Chico, walking on his hind legs, his arms in the air like a prizefighter. He also rode on my shoulder in our low convertible MG, which prompted the remark of an old neighbor woman: "There goes the witch lady." There were odd incidents, such as a tourist telling a story in the local bar about a nun chasing a monkey down the street with her cane. (Chico tended to raid the convent kitchen for sweet buns.) The time I took him along to a reading by Robert Graves that took place in an olive grove. He was peacefully sitting on a branch above Graves' head, when the need took him and a stream of urine splattered on my famous friend below. (Toby, take your infernal beast away!) Once he became a young adult and needed a female companion, it became more difficult. He chattered his teeth, which frightened people, and masturbated anywhere and anytime, which was not always easy to explain to children. I had always known that this monkey, which we all loved, was not meant to be a pet and should never have left his rain forest. I was often working, my children were away at school, the cat had died of cancer, and the goat broke its neck jumping down a high terrace. Feeling guilty, I kept and cared for him as long as I could, accepting fifty-dollar bills pried from my wallet and chewed to wet wads, bags of flour strewn all over the kitchen floor or angry neighbor's complaints that he once again had stripped their precious banana tree. When we heard the Barcelona zoo was planning a monkey island and was looking for a young adult woolly monkey, we took him there. Cathy went to visit him later on, but he did not seem to recognize her. The island was still in the planning stages and Chico, living among the other animals, was simply a monkey in a zoo.

WORKING ALONE

I returned to Deia on regular visits, but things were changing. Foster continued college in Indiana, Cathy now studied in Barcelona. I stayed in close touch with them and believed they would find their place. Marc was resisting school and when he returned from a summer job carrying a certification as a qualified seaman, I could not convince him to continue his studies. Moochen and I realized that Deia was no longer the right place for him. He had been too young to remember the breakup of my first marriage, but he lived through the second alongside me. His siblings had left, I was working alone, and his father lived in the village with someone else. He had also seen me turn to a lover, something I would regret forever because I did not realize how much it would hurt him. He felt—and today I think rightly so—that for my part I betrayed him by putting my own grown-up wretchedness ahead of his needs as my child. A photographer friend leaving to do a series of articles in Germany offered him a job as an assistant. It was right for him to leave the island, but I also knew he was too young to fly on his own. Uprooted and struggling with work, I was in no position to hold him back; letting him go was one of the hardest decisions I ever made. We always kept in touch, but he would lead his own life from there on and we would not grow close again until years later.

Working alone was not easy, but I was doing well. I was building a career and a reputation. My editors soon accepted that I was willing to handle unusual situations, that I could both shoot as well as write my stories. As for me, I had learned that alone I might be more vulnerable, but also was more approachable. People talked to me, on the bus, in a restaurant or on the beach. They asked questions and answered them; they took me home and introduced me to friends and family. It made a difference to my understanding and to my stories. The Amazon articles were the first both written and photographed on my own. It was a different game; I had been used to starting out with the early morning light, knowing that Fred would be getting his story. Now I still had to get up, but made sure to be back in time for some interview, and then crosscheck the information, because everyone is biased. Tired, I spent the evening hours socializing, whether it was in a gold miner's bar or in a fancy restaurant in Rio with some Brazilian official, who was far more interested to get me into bed than to discuss the environmental problems. (This particular one had never been anywhere near the Amazon and I might as well have asked him about glaciers in the Antarctic.)

I had sometimes gone ahead and spent some time working alone before Fred joined me, but I had never been solely responsible for the story. Moreover, the Amazon had not even been an assignment, but my own mad idea. I was so scared I asked Robert Graves to read the articles before I sent them in. When he actually said, "Jolly well done, darling," I walked on air for the rest of the day. Once the articles were published, it should therefore have been plain sailing. It was not quite as simple as that. Fred had always dealt with the magazine editors and never thought twice about pushing an article. As for me, alone now, there were times I lacked the confidence to approach the right people. Friends have asked me if it was more difficult because I was a woman. I do not believe so. It had never occurred to me that my work might be judged by anything but its quality. Magazines did not pay me less or treated me differently from my male colleagues. I did not meet my employers on a daily basis; I got the assignment, and the story landed on their desk to be published or rejected. I have won awards, had one-woman shows and am not shy when I do my work. I simply have never been good at selling it.

The feminist movement burst into world consciousness. I was aware of it and had met some of the main players in New York, like Betty Friedan and Gloria Steinem. I got along very well with Betty, but was not terribly attracted to the movement as such. I knew better than to believe that bra-burning or lesbian slogans on purple balloons stood for the movement, but I disliked the close-up view of backbiting, the in-house politics and manipulations. I had no need or desire to side with Abzug and Steinem against Friedan and Holtzman, or vice versa. If I recognized its importance to all women, I also thought of it as mainly happening in American society. New to the New York scene, I lived there only part of the time and did not really feel directly involved. In Europe, few of my women friends were concerned with the movement. Many of them were professionals who liked their work, but I had rarely heard them talk about glass ceilings or obvious discrimination. Of course, all that would soon change; it was just a matter of time.

I have sometimes regretted my attitude to the movement, given the tremendous changes it did bring about. Years later, Betty said, "You were not part of it. You already had the freedom. In a way, you were an example. The question that should bother you and me is, now that we have given our daughters the power, how are they going to use it?" She knew well what power had been released. I recently read that Friedan's husband, Carl, told a reporter, "She hates men. Let's face it, they all do—all those activists in the movement." I know that is not true. Betty liked men and I think she often preferred male company to that of her women friends.

Mine was, admittedly, a rather unconventional world. I had always worked with men, facing the same exposure to success or

failure and earning the same fees. I liked men and was comfortable
with them. I was one of the Image Bank's founding photographers
and at that time the only woman. Working with journalists, I did
not find it more pleasant to share with women than with men, some
people were just easier to work with or the chemistry was better.
Women usually asked the more intimate questions. I never felt that
I had to prove to my male colleagues that I was better because I
was a woman, but only that I was as good as they were. I was also
fortunate to have worked with my husband; our children saw us work
together at home and away from it. Leaving them behind had always
been a shared decision and I learned to deal with marriage in a way
usually reserved for men. When the responsibility for my children
once again became mine alone, they were a little older and no longer
living with me full time, which made it easier to work and travel.

Through the years, I had felt the occasional sting of
discrimination. John Anstey, editor of the *Daily Telegraph Magazine*,
did not often meet his reporters personally; instead, he wrote notes
and invited them once a year to the magazine's Christmas party. One
year I happened to be in London, so I went. He looked at me and
said, "Toby Molenaar? You are a woman?" Well, yes. "You did the
Amazon stories, you were hanging from a helicopter in BC?" Well,
yes, I did. In England, I gathered, Toby was mostly a boy's name, but
after our long relationship, I wondered how he could not know that
Fred and I were married. My articles also made it quite clear
that I was a woman, I thought. At the time I met Anstey, I was under
assignment to photograph the Kurds. The story was postponed and
finally cancelled. Reason given, trouble on the borders. Maybe?

Another time, in Canada, Fred and I were covering the big
rodeo in Calgary. All went well until some dignitaries arrived as the
guests of honor. I had been shooting with other photographers from
the sidelines or from the pit in the middle of the field. I was at the
point of climbing down when the sheriff marched up to me and said,
"Sorry Madam, you can't go down there." He had seen me working

everywhere for days, so why all at once? "Well, there are important, international people watching here today. We can have a dead cowboy, we can have a dead horse, but we can't have a dead woman." And that was that. Fred took a camera down in the pit and I shot from the sideline. The discrimination, in both cases, being mostly an insurance against collateral damage: "Journalist fatally hurt in accident," against "WOMAN PHOTOGRAPHER TRAMPLED TO DEATH BY MAD STEER!" As the man said, we cannot have a dead woman. I thought that in both cases the men were idiots, but did not take it too personally: on many occasions, men had gone out of their way to help me because I was a woman. Which, of course, proved a point. Or did it?

A BUS RIDE TO A SERBIAN MONASTERY

During the summer of my discontent, restless and wanting to escape Deia for a while, I joined Robert and Beryl Graves to attend a seminar on humanism in Belgrade, a city still separated from the West by the Iron Curtain. Robert began to show slight signs of a failing memory and tended to wander, so Beryl and I were to take turns staying close to him. On my day off, I joined an organized tour with other people attending the conference, most of them from Eastern Europe. The bus was waiting; air-conditioned, with the radio going full blast, and supposed to leave at seven o'clock in the morning, which it did not. I really don't know why leaving late struck me as a very Western thing to do; nobody had promised me that Yugoslavian buses would run on time.

Belgrade was still dark, rain danced on the glistening sidewalks, but shops were lit up and I saw people buying. Beyond the suburbs, the countryside was veiled in a pale misty light. Straight furrows in freshly ploughed fields, cornstalks left standing where the rain must have interrupted the harvest, their color like old gold against the black earth. We were driving fast, never a chance to point a camera through those steamed-up windows, drops sliding down ever following, ever faster. Candies were passed around, the smiling girl guise calling me Brunhilde for some mysterious reason. The bus was quite full. After three days of humanism, I knew most people by sight and some by name, and conversation flowed over heads and seats.

"Did you hear how Robert Graves said the Oxford dictionary lists human and humane, but the Russian explained that in his language there are three different words for the same meaning?"

"I do not believe in this agony of humanism. I think there is a definite upward and promising trend among the younger generation."

Somewhere soon we stopped for coffee, slivovitz and buns filled with soft spicy cheese. Bathrooms, smiles and copper coins. Back in the bus, the first bottles of wine appeared. It was roughly two hundred kilometers to the first monastery of Sopocani, another fifty out of the way to the second one, Studenica. At noon we were nowhere near, it had stopped raining and the ploughed fields had given way to green hills dotted with farmhouses. There were some cows, a couple of sheep, but never a human soul. In a whitewashed village, the unexpected elegance of a minaret gave me a quick stab of recognition and delight: I had forgotten people were Muslims in this region. Now children came running through the mud-paved streets to stare at us, but were too shy to wave back.

"We have passed the Studenica monastery and will visit on the way back."

"It will be very late by the time we get home."

First, we arrived. Sopocani: I saw a small church on a hilltop, mist trailing through arches left standing from a ruined wall. The entrance to the church was so dark we all paused in the doorway, bumping into each other. "Excuse me, *aber bitte!*" Inside, we stared at walls covered with some of the most radiant images of the

Byzantine and Serbian art of the thirteenth century. The frescos, red ochre next to faded blue, showed scenes of adoration and damnation, of archangels and saints beside portraits of King Uros and his queen Helène d'Anjou, her young woman's face a timeless stare with unseeing eyes. The most valued fresco shows the Ascension of the Mother of God, which resounds in a symphony of yellows, blue green and violet. It seemed incredible that after its history of wars, after having been abandoned for more than two centuries following its partial destruction by Turkish troops in 1689, this church and this art was still here for us to see.

With all that beauty, however, came only the little light our rainy day provided through the narrow windows, so I took pictures to please myself rather than trying to make this a story. A cross-eyed nun wearing a flowered headscarf walked across the courtyard. Dare I ask her? She refused and told me to go and buy postcards of the monastery instead. Which I did.

"All aboard!" In English this time. An extra yell for Brunhilde with the cameras, a headcount and we were off. The atmosphere was relaxed now, as if we had accomplished a mission. "Which postcards did you buy?" "Did you notice the face behind the altar?" "We are going for lunch now and won't reach Studenica until much later in the afternoon."

By now it was nearly four o'clock and time for lunch indeed. It started to rain again. I looked back at the small monastery in the mist. Sopocani was beautiful, the walls a silvery gray against the autumn yellows of the trees.

At the foot of the hill waited the Dom turistici, the rest house. Enormous amounts of food: sour soups, dried beef, cheeses and corn-bread, more roast with potatoes, then cake, and sticky Turkish delight with the strongest blackest coffee. With the mixture of languages and the translations around the table, my own questions came back to me after making the full round, because nobody remembered where they had started. Bottles of wine and slivovitz were passed around.

"We shall now drink to humanism and brotherhood. I will be quite drunk when we get home, but I am your guide and I love you all."

"It seems we are not visiting Studenica. It does not have electricity and the driver decided it getting too late."

Some young Serbian poet read their poems. One of them could have been Chopin's younger brother and acted just as spoiled as I have always imagined Frédéric to have been. The day before, during a serious conference on humanism, he had walked across the room to present me with a red carnation, taken from a vase. "Parce que vous est belle." Now, true to type, he did not read like the others, but sang a Serbian partisan song, with a surprisingly bellowing voice for such a pale nineteenth-century face. And sat next to me, when we were at last on our way again. "Je vous aime, je vous aime." In the beginning, it always makes some sense.

Hours went by, headlights of cars, mixed with rain and brotherhood. Somewhere, a small village, shining on a hillside like a wet star. A café and an outdoor toilet, where my companions would not let me enter because "is not a supportable smell!" I slumped in my seat and wondered how much longer? To my disappointment my newly met Turkish friends, Yashar Kemal and his wife, Thilda, were not on the bus. Graves and Kemal had been curious about each other and we all had dinner together. As tall, but stout and thick-necked against Robert's long-limbed elegance, Yashar wore tinted glasses that did not quite hide his blind eye. I had become friendly with Thilda, who was a fascinating person in her own right. Of a Sephardic family—her grandfather was personal physician to the last Sultan Abdulhamit—she married Kemal, a Muslim Marxist of Kurdish origin.

Kemal's books were widely read but not popular with the current Turkish government. He spent several terms in prison and Thilda served an even longer sentence for reasons that sounded muddled and complex. She translated her husband's books into English; in everyday life she was his interpreter to the outside world. I watched her steer the big awkward man through the multilingual crowd or away from insisting journalists and overenthusiastic female fans. We had both looked forward to spending the day together. She told me later that Yashar had not been well. (After we left the conference, we kept in touch by corresponding.)

Meanwhile, in our bus, we sang, or rather, the Serbs did. Partisan songs again, with their defiant, Slavic sadness. Someone started a Russian song, but was immediately shouted down with "ruski njet!" In the front of the bus sat five Russians, guests to the government as we were all, and I wondered why this reaction? "They are not the poets we invited, they are spies, policemen! We will stop the bus and thrown them out! They shall walk!" Big uproar: the moderate (or less drunk) fraction trying to hold back the radicals. The Russians never reacted, never spoke, never stirred. "This is outrageous! These are honorable men, officers! The Yugoslav partisans could not have lasted a month without the Russian soldiers! Why do these people behave so badly? They would do better to clean up their villages!" An angry East-German writer pouring oil on the fire.

Another stop. The rain-streaked café window framed a Cartier-Bresson: meat broiling on a charcoal fires, bare wooden tables, strong faces lit by a naked bulb. This time the coffee and the fresh air were a godsend. The Serbian enfant terrible got up and translated a poem of a French poet, but the older man, sitting at another table did not notice it. "Monsieur Frenaux est un grand poète, mais il est la *meurte, la meurte!* I have translated his poem for the first time *dans la vie*, I have sung it to my Serbian brothers and he does not listen! Il est la *meurte!* Il est un mot insupportable!" Nobody seemed to know what he meant. Even the German, who acted as a go-between dictionary, shrugged his shoulder. By chance, a little later, an Austrian woman said, "Someone sent me a magazine called *Exkrement!* I find that very sad. It was a student magazine, but how are we to subsist if that is the standard we live by? Humanism is very topical." When this was translated, the Serbian Chopin saw the light: *Exkrement! La merde, la meurte!* And it dawned on us all that the French poet had been called a word "insupportable" indeed. When Frenaux finally realized what was happening, he just looked at the young man, shook his head and smiled.

We were all rather reluctant to get back in the bus and face several more hours of driving. The road were narrow and wet, darkness had set in, leaving the familiar plink-plink of the rain. Drowsing, not really listening, I was simply unhappy, hugged my private misery and had little patience for this entire disjointed venture. I dozed in my seat, isolated words and voices floating in a lazily sloshing sea of Serbian sounds, here and there pierced by more familiar words.

"Germany is the only place to celebrate Christmas."

"I was ashamed to hear what hear what the Gestapo has done in these countries."

"Yes, they were Germans, but the people back home did not know anything about all this and we have now raised a generation of good people!"

Shame, embarrassment? Then, "Some of my best friends are Americans; there are good people everywhere!"

Which jolted me awake at last.

We wrote postcard, everybody signed. Will you write, will you come again next year? And finally, the lights of Belgrade. It was still raining. The hotel was bright, comfortable and impersonal. As I crossed the hall, I met my tired face in the mirrors; the young poet touched my shoulder and said: "Madame, vous avez des cheveux qui pleurent."

KENYA AND TANZANIA

Among my favorite assignments was shooting brochures for the safari companies in Kenya and Tanzania, where the park authorities allowed us to camp in the very heart of the reserve, turning work into pure pleasure. Our small plane approached from the southeast, on the right were the ridges of the Gol mountains, behind us stood the Ngorongoro highlands and over it all the wide African skies. Below us, Serengeti. It is a Masai word meaning "the endless plains" and to many travelers it is the quintessence of Africa. Today it is Tanzania's largest national park, and within its nearly six-thousand-square mile sanctuary, it still offers one of the greatest wildlife spectacles in the world. I worked there several times and even if the routine was mostly the same, every day brought something new and different.

The guides were waiting with the jeeps and drove us to our camp. The tents were waiting and the fire made. There were drinks before dinner, served in a separate tent, complete with silver, porcelain and candles.

It was like a tuned-down version of Hemingway and *Out of Africa*, which, of course, was the whole idea. At dawn, a few yards away from where I was brushing my teeth, lions passed without as much as a glance, although smelly shoes left outside the tent overnight were your risk and a hyena's delight. Once, woken up by the drum of a sudden downpour on the roof of my tent, I found a huge male baboon urinating from a tree directly above. When I laughed at him, he bared his teeth and barked at me in fear and fury.

Lying between clean sheets, the tent smelling of grass mats, flaps open all around over screens and moonlight brushing the trees with silver, I listened to the sounds. The soft scuffle of a passing animal, a lion's throaty roar, the call of an unknown night bird, and always the hyenas (two low barks and a nasty whooping chuckle), followed by a spell of silence so deep I could hear my own pulse beating. And then, it did not feel like a tuned-down version of anything.

Cameras have long replaced guns and the animals are less shy, but one does not just leave the car and wander off, old white hunter style. Whenever I did, I have felt very vulnerable indeed. Silence can be as threatening as the soft rustle, the cough or unidentified sound that remind you with a sudden stab of fear that you don't really belong here at all. Once, on safari with Farley Granger and Bob Calhoun—my close friends and travel companions of many a year—we picnicked on top of a small hillock, tablecloth spread, feeling good and quite safe. The view from the smooth granite boulders showed the grassland below, animals quietly grazing, all was well. Farley was holding forth with a piece of chicken in his hand when, suddenly, he was rolling over backwards in the grass, long legs in the air. A large kite had swooped down at tremendous speed and grabbed the drumstick with such precision that, besides pushing him over, it left not the smallest graze or hurt. It made for a laugh, but we all realized the implication: none of us, not even Adam, our local guide, had seen it coming. As for me, I remembered the lioness rising without a sound out of the low yellow grass right next to the car that morning, at the very spot I had been staring at for several minutes without seeing anything special at all.

"No eggies, Madam, no cornbreadie before you go wildebeestie?" asked the boy, when I chose some of the tiny lemon-scented bananas with my morning coffee. "All people have much breakfast." It was barely dawn. The breeze, passing softly through the whistling thorn, still smelled of the night and the scattered bleached bones caught the first light like pale gems. Some round-rumped zebras grazed quietly, a jackal, looking over his shoulder, headed for home and two speckled guinea fowl scratched for insects in the dust. Through this silent world, our jeep moved slowly, almost ominously, lenses and binoculars scanning the horizon. I spent my days watching. There were the classic kills of the lionesses, or the swift pale-spotted cheetah running down its prey, but the days were full of smaller wonders. A newborn baby zebra getting up on four wooden legs like a rocking horse. The streak of golden dust when a serval cat ran so fast for its life, it thudded into the hole of a furiously protesting mongoose. Giraffes drifting across the plain in their inimitable silent gracefulness. A bearded, grumpy old wildebeest suddenly spooking at its own shadow, bucking in the most ridiculous way. The laughing call of the *come-away* bird or the gentle tug of the *wait-a-bit* thorn-bush at my sleeve. The tuft of a leopard's tail moving like a small white candle through the rustling, stirring grass. At times, in the lavender light of morning, it seemed a paradise untouched and I had to remind myself that most animals here drink and sleep at their peril, the flash of blinding terror and sudden death as much part of their daily cycle as the beauty and the sense of utter peace.

One of my more personal experiences was following a pack of wild dogs on the hunt. Our guide had a specific interest in them, as their numbers were diminishing. Wild dogs are merciless hunters. A full pack will make even lions turn aside and most other animals bolt at their sight. In the unhurried gait that can carry them as far as fifty miles a day, the dogs track a herd of wildebeests across the plain. Singling out a vulnerable animal from a herd, they chase it tirelessly until the bitter end. Now, on the open plain, they broke into a sudden run, surrounded a trailing calf and literally backed it against our car. Its head was right below our window, so close I could have touched it, which by some odd logic seemed to make me responsible. Minutes ago, I had rooted for those dogs to succeed in their long hunt for food, now I wanted to beat them over the head with my tripod. I shouted at them but the guide pulled me back. "Stay inside the window, or they'll tear your arm off." I could hardly bear to watch while the lead dog fastened upon the wildebeest's muzzle, tugging hard to keep its head low, while the rest tore into its belly and hindquarters, the entrails glistening. The calf kept making soft moaning sounds, but it was being eaten alive. When they had finished gulping and swallowing the dogs romped for a few minutes, batears twitching and white-tipped tails swaying, looking deceptively playful and innocent. Then the pack set out again, streaming back to their lair to regurgitate lumps of undigested meat for the waiting, hungry pups. As for what was left of the calf, hyenas and vultures moved in even while we were leaving.

The Ngorongoro crater is a legendary and mysterious place. Stamped like a hoof print deep into the green hills, the hundred-square mile volcanic caldera floor encloses a self-contained ecosystem with the greatest concentration of animal life on earth. Standing on the rim at dawn, the sun rising one side, a full moon still visible on the other, not a sound floated up to me from the crowded stage two thousand feet below. The amphitheater represented an ancient, silent and forbidding world, making it easy for me to believe with the Leakys that in this timeless region was found the origin of man. Among the staggering variety of animals, birds of all sizes and color swirled in constant motion, chatter, and song. Storks clapped their beaks with the sound of rattling bones and in the shallow soda lake, its dried crusts glittering like snow, thousands of red-legged flamingos practiced their eerie dance. It is an odd thing about birds. Once, sharing a jeep with a group of people closely connected with zoos and natural history museums, I learned that their strict dividing line was not elephants versus cats or monkeys versus reptiles, but simply *birds*. The ornithologists thought the flash of a tiny, jeweled sunbird was as good a reason to stop the car for half an hour as a great tooth-and-claw something lurking in the grass.

Just beyond the lake stood a growth of yellow-barked fever trees, where elephants liked to browse. Passing it one afternoon, the driver cut the engine and we sat contentedly, watching the dappled light turn the golden trees into an enchanted forest. Then we saw him: the biggest, blackest bull ever. Without a sound he appeared, not from the shadows of the pretty forest, but straight down the road he came, alone, the setting sun behind him like a halo. A huge male in full musth, urine dribbling down his legs, tusks curved and ears fanning out wide. Within seconds, he reached the car, hesitated and stood still, leaning on the hood. His trunk slipped through the open roof and paused in the air, inches from my face, his warm breath filling the car. No one moved. I saw the secretion run from the glands on the side of his head and the smell was so strong it caught in my throat. Patrick, a zoologist friend sitting next to the driver, had worked with elephants all his life, but he was staring up in total awe at ten thousand pounds of wild African bull towering over us. I heard him swallow, and, as if against his will, he whispered, "Good boy, good boy." Instantly the orange eye shifted, fixed and measured him: for an interminable moment, everything hung in balance. The bull could have lifted and thrown him or thrashed the entire car in seconds. There was no sound but the deep rumbling of the elephant's guts. Then, slowly, the giant turned and strode along the path toward the crater rim to find the female herd.

Every park has a different feeling. In Manyara, the golden fleck of a tree-climbing lion sprawling on a branch, looking down like an irritated old dowager on chattering clowning monkeys. Tsavo East deals with the herds of elephants leaving swaths of destroyed flattop acacia woods in their track. Amboseli herders and wildlife share a habitat slowly turning to dust. My favorite park was Tarangire, the grassy savannah beyond the slopes of the Kilimanjaro. It is a vast and secret land, crossed by the river Tarangire, the only source of water during the dry season, when the ghost-like, bare-branched baobabs stand in withered grass as brittle as straw. Red-cloaked Masai walk here, stork-legged, beaded, braided and beautiful, casually carrying the seven-foot iron spear with which their people have always faced the lion or leopard that dared to stalk their cattle. The Masai are nomads; cattle have always been their wealth, their food and, excepting war and hunting, their only concern. After milking the cows, they puncture a vein in the animal's neck and draw off some blood to mix with the curdled milk. This, together with local maize, is their staple diet. In recent years, the great herds they drive across the plains have increased beyond all calculation, which has led to serious conflicts between the tribes and those who want to preserve what is left of the endangered wild game. The Masai are spread over a large area of East Africa, but where the national parks are concerned there is simply not enough grazing land and water for both the cattle and the wild animals.

Meeting Masai for the first time is a memorable experience. We saw them dance, and had the rare experience seeing them crossing the yellow plain, single file, spears uplifted, dark robes flowing. They saw us long before we ever caught sight of them, but they passed close by without taking any notice at all.

One evening, camped not far from a small group of their round hatched huts, we heard them chant. A single voice offering a melody was acknowledged by a unanimous shout, followed by deep, throbbing, repetitive bursts of sound alternating with high-pitched plaintive calls, the first voice still leading and all blending into a seemingly endless paean. Time stood still, we might have been sitting around our fire a hundred years ago, nothing having changed. It is of course not so. The Masai no longer move around freely with their cattle or live inside the parks, since the government relegated the herders to areas outside the park boundaries. The rules are that all visitors must leave before sunset. And visitors are what these warriors have become.

LAPLAND, THE NORTHERN WILDERNESS

Joined by a guide and a botanist, I was to photograph a "nature walk" in Sarek National Park. The plan was that a helicopter would drop us off and pick us up a few days later. It sounded rather nice. I met Tore, the guide, in Gallivare, a small lumber town in Swedish Lapland, about a hundred miles south of the park. When the botanist failed to show up, we waited another day and then decided to set out without him. It was only October, early autumn, the sun was shining and we were going to a national park. What could go wrong? There would be reindeer, elk and all kinds of small animals, green valleys with lots of flowers, streams and waterfalls and I would simply photograph them all.

Our helicopter broke through the cloud ceiling without warning: "SAREK," shouted the pilot with a wave of his arm that embraced the whole horizon. I stared: below us lay a primeval black and white landscape of crags and peaks towering menacingly above snowfields and hanging glaciers and I suddenly recalled the blunt warning in a Swedish Tourist Guide: "People who have no experience in the

Scandinavian mountain wilderness should *stay away* from Sarek National Park. *It is no place for tourists.*"

The pilot touched down at the far northern tip of Lake Sitojaura, helped unload our rucksacks, said he would be back here at the same point in four days time and took off. The helicopter climbed slowly, hovering for a moment as if reluctant to abandon us to the mountains. Then it banked, the pilot waved farewell, and we watched the aircraft's winking red taillight vanish in the distance. For a moment, Tore and I gazed at our alien setting. It was a magnificent world of snowcapped peaks and glaciated valleys, of streams and waterfalls that rushed to meet the rivers and lakes below. It was also known as the most inaccessible wilderness in Western Europe. Here, a mere hundred miles from the sunlit town we had just left, swirls of snow drifted over rocks with a thin rustling sound. Behind us, the half-frozen lake surface reflected a leaden sky. On our left, the snow-streaked flanks of Takartjakka rose almost sheer, its five-thousand-foot summit hidden in clouds.

Tore broke the silence by taking out the map and showing me our route. It followed the stream until it forked west into the Pastavagge valley, which funnels deep into the mountains. For us it meant climbing the six-thousand-foot Appartjakke, descending to another lake and making a wide circle round the ice-capped massif before returning to our starting point. Most of our route lay between the tree line and the permanent snow line, a world almost devoid of vegetation, stripped naked to reveal the bare bones of the earth. Few people lived here; only the Mountain Lapps have come to terms with the park's rugged terrain, the cold that grips it for all but a few summer months and the melancholy darkness that veils it during the long winter. Now the two of us were about to invade this inhospitable world.

We set out, our boots slipping on boulders hidden under clumps of heather and dwarf willow and reached the mouth of Pastavagge in the late afternoon, with darkness sifting into the valley. We pitched camp and I stood looking into the jaws of the gulley we would climb the next day. A strong wind played among rock buttresses, an organ-like booming, carrying the distant clatter of falling scree. I shivered. Tore looked up and said, "Pastevagge is the loneliest place in Sarek. Even the Lapps avoid it. They say it is an unhappy place." I wondered what it would look like in the depth of winter, if even now it gave me this sense of foreboding. I also felt like saying, "Hey, if you knew it would be like this, why didn't you say something?" But then, this was his country, he did not seem worried, and it was hardly his fault that I had not done my homework.

We fetched water and as there was not a stick of wood around, we heated up sweet fruit soup on our kerosene cooker and sampled the food that would sustain us for the next few days: dried reindeer meat washed down with hot chocolate milk. We watched the night blot out the bulk of the mountain to the west, until the cold drove us into our tents. I had trouble wrapping myself in the quilted blanket that was to serve as a sleeping bag. The chill crept in and I lay listening to the changing voice of the wind. It seemed to keep circling around my tent, rising to a high-pitched shriek and falling to a low wail that had a despairing human quality. Later I would learn that the Lapps call Appartjakke the "Mountain of the Ghost of a Murdered Child."

We woke to find a valley bathed in sunshine. Wispy clouds whirled among rock spires and pinnacles like steam from a witches' cauldron. The wintry rays lent color to a scape that until now had possessed the stark quality of a photo negative. The dull brown heaths took on sable and purple tints, and the leaves of a dwarf willow I had barely noticed before made red and russet splashes against the snow. Where sunlight touched the frond-like growth of lichen, a green light seemed to glow within the plant and each stem of cotton grass decked with drops of melted snow was transformed into a string of liquid light. The gentler face of this wilderness showed itself only fleetingly, for as soon as the sun vanished behind the clouds, the plants seemed to withdraw into the background and the colors drained out of the valley. I had seen enough to realize that I would have to adjust my perspective, forget the profuse colors and tall trees of the lowlands. I would have to search a streambed to find a tiny mushroom, go down on my knees to explore the small scattered flowers that survive where larger blooms would be ripped to shreds by the wind. I began to wonder how I had ever thought I could manage without the botanist. There were supposed to be four hundred species of vascular plants, and I had a rather limited knowledge of arctic vegetation. Not only did I not know what I was looking for, I might not know what I was looking *at,* once I found it. I would just have to photograph whatever grew here and hoped that *Time/Life*—by whom this venture was arranged—would have a spare botanist to sort it all out! (I did not realize until after the trip that the botanist was not only supposed to point out the appropriate flowers, he was also to write the text. As he never showed up, it fell to me, and it took me forever to identify the plants in my pictures.)

We began our climb, Tore leading. Under our feet, the dwarf willow reached the limit of endurance barely above ankle height, their place soon taken by glossy cowberries. A stunted fruiting juniper defied gravity, its tortuous roots struggling across the steep bare rock face to find support. In a cranny sheltered from the wind Tore showed me tiny pink flowers of a creeping azalea framed by the bright yellow leaves of dwarf willow. This was a zone of such extremes and paradoxes that plants had to content with winter's cold, snow and darkness, survive the summer glare of ultraviolet radiation as well as rapid fluctuations between day and night temperatures.

Our first encounter with Sarek's wildlife was unexpected. We rounded a bend and found a lone bull reindeer standing directly in our path, his glossy autumn coat blending with the patchwork landscape. The wind blew directly our way and at first he did not see us. He stood still, threw back his magnificently antlered head and roared a throaty mating call across the valley. When the click of my camera shutter betrayed us, he turned smoothly, the wind ruffling his pale mane, and bounded effortlessly up the slope. Closer to the lake, two other reindeer, a young bull in hot pursuit of a cow, came running toward us. The cow saw us and swinging aside with hardly a pause, plunged into the icy lake, her would-be mate at her heels. Together they swam powerfully through the choppy water, almost a mile to the other shore. They were beautiful, but it was a reflection on the harshness of the environment that I registered these scant proofs of wildlife as highpoints in several days trekking.

We crossed the watershed that divided the valley and we began our descent around the Appar massif. To our left a debris-strewn glacier—one of ninety-six that lick down into Sarek's valleys—discharged streams of melted water. I was surprised when the air grew colder the lower we descended, but Tore said, "Mountains make their own climate." The map showed us at nearly 3,500 feet, juniper and creeping arctic were succeeded by woolly hair-moss and greenish-gray lichen with a tenuous hold among the rocks; in places even the moss and lichen carpet was ripped up by the wind. That night fresh snow fell and in the morning a dense mist descended. We slogged blindly over the broken terrain and Tore's compass did not prevent us from blundering into snowdrifts, sinking in to our hips and struggling to find solid footing. Slopes were frozen solid, and balancing my cameras I slipped and fell several times. Hard, and spraining my wrist. Where were the flowers, streams and green valleys of my imagination? From time to time we heard an eerie muffled croaking somewhere in the mist and we looked at each other, not knowing what to expect (my imagination going rather wild) and it was not until a covey of ptarmigan burst up from our path that Tore recognized the sound. A little further we came across the clean-picked carcass of one of these mountain grouse, showing wedge-shaped bites in the breastbone. "Gyrfalcon," was all Tore said.

Our last night was even colder and the wind grew stronger; toward morning a sudden gust swept the mountainside and I woke up buried under the tent. The worrying wind had slackened one of the ropes, loosened a peg, and one side had collapsed. I tried to undo the mess but could not get up from the narrow strip of foam rubber we used as a ground protection. I always had trouble staying on the thing, but this time I was frozen to the ground. I yelled, "Tore! Help!" He took one look at me and said: "You MOVED!" "Well, what do I do now?" I had visions of being thawed with a pail of hot water. He laughed and said: "I take the tent down, I pull you up, you take down your pants and we'll rub your behind with snow until it is red!" "I think not!" I said indignantly, but that is what happened. It was the only way to prevent a nasty frostbite. As it was, the skin did turn brown and came off in long thin strips, like sunburn. I felt pretty stupid standing there half-naked in the freezing air, my butt being rubbed down by a ranger, but later I regretted not having taken our picture; it was too good to miss. Tore was very matter of fact about the rubbing, but he chuckled to himself for the rest of the day. When we reached our starting point, the helicopter was waiting. The pilot said we looked like survivors of a shipwreck, limping, my arm in a bandage, our faces burned and eyes reddened from exposure. Tore of course told him my buttock story. My Swedish was not good enough to follow all the embellishments, but their snorts and hiccups did not need translation.

I was now free to go home. The thought of a return to civilization was tempting, but our experience had left me somehow unsatisfied. I was not expected home for another few days and I felt there was more to Sarek than the cold, the sparse animal life and the miniature vegetation, however fascinating. Tore had told me of an elderly Lapp couple who ran a weather station at the border of the park. He said they spoke some English because of their radio traffic and would be glad to take me in. He also explained to me that the widely used name Lapp, or Laplander, was regarded derogatory by the Sami, who are among the largest indigenous groups in Europe, which I had not known. An hour later the helicopter set me down by the lakeshore, and Tore introduced me to my hosts.

Sigurd and his wife, Sitje, were in their sixties, gray-haired, rather short, with the slightly Asian features often found among their people. They welcomed me to a roomy hand-hewn log house made comfortable with homespun wool, linen and reindeer hides. The helicopter took off and Sitje showed me the guest cabin, a smaller edition of their home. I was told to rest for a while and had not realized how tired I had been until I woke up to the noise of snowmobiles. It was dark and guests had arrived for supper. Sigurd knocked at my door and we crossed to the main house. A group of people were sitting on wooden benches covered with colorful cushions. I had been told the Lapp costume was becoming less common, but three of the men were dressed in the blue tunic decorated with red and yellow strips of felt, reaching below the knees over narrow trousers. The women wore embroidered vests and skirts of homespun linen. On a coat rack hung modern anoraks and several cushion-like caps of dark felt with four stuffed, protruding corners, resembling a medieval ladies headdress. Below them stood a row of heel-less boots, turned up at the toe. Sitje handed me a pair of felt moccasins and I saw that all the guests were wearing similar slippers, obviously provided by our host. My boots and socks were put to dry before the kitchen fire.

We sat down to fish soup and home-baked bread, followed by reindeer stew and a pudding made of hair-moss and milk. In the days that followed I ate fish balls, fish loaf, fish cakes, raw fish, grilled fish and fish boiled with small birds in a broth. As wild reindeer became less plentiful and hunting more restricted, most local Sami had turned to fishing, while meat was usually dried or smoked and kept for winter when the lakes were frozen. The stew served that evening was a special treat. The moss pudding was a standard for breakfast and desert and I quite came to like it. (I long believed I had been among the happy few to have tasted that traditional local treat, but in 2010 the fashionable restaurant Noma in Copenhagen was voted "best restaurant in the world" by some serious foodies on strength of its "moss pudding with mushrooms and a reindeer tongue slow-cooked for twenty-four hours.")

After dinner we sat and talked. One couple had a small farm; their son studied in Stockholm and spoke good English. We were chatting away when I suddenly noticed that Sigurd was telling a story that held all the attention: people were roaring with laughter and looking at me! Tore and the pilot had not spent much time with my hosts, but it had obviously been long enough to pass on my "rubbing the bottom until it is red" tale. Sitje came and sat next to me, putting her arm around my shoulder, but Sigurd's smile was so open and the laughter so good-natured that I could only join in. It was, after all, a pretty ridiculous image. I was asked about frostbite on my toes. Sami rarely wore socks, they said. I had noticed the bare feet in the moccasins, but thought they had taken off their socks with the boots. No, they had another way of keeping their feet happy. Even in summer it was almost impossible to keep dry among the bogs and brooks of the delta. Socks became wet, cold and uncomfortable. The secret was to pack your boots with fine sedge, picked from the marshes. Beaten and dried, it remained warm and comfortable in the wettest conditions. The next day Sigurd showed me how it worked. The sedge must be rubbed and teased out, folded around the fist, shoved into the boot and arranged to the correct and even thickness. It had sounded easy, but I should have known better. I tried it, ended up with a lumpy mess and blisters, and went back to wearing wet socks.

When the guests had left, Sigurd walked me back to my cabin. It stood no more than a few hundred feet from the main house, but he showed me a large brass bell hanging next to the door. "Never cross over from the cabin without ringing it," he said. It was the time of year when bears were foraging for food, greedily devouring anything from slugs to carrion to build up the layer of fat that sustains them through their winter hibernation. They often roamed near the house, attracted by the smell of fish or cooking. "Bears are dangerous; they move very fast and attack without a sound. Do not underestimate them. Last winter they broke down the kitchen door and we now keep even the dog inside at night." He laughed. "The Sami call the bear the dog of God, because it has the strength of ten men and the wit of twelve." So every time before I crossed the short distance in the dark to join them for dinner, I clanged the bell, Sigurd opened his door and met me halfway with his lantern.

Winter had come to the mountains and on the lakeshore some fresh snow had fallen, but the sun was shining and late autumn colors still glowed like embers. Pines grew thick at the water's edge and from them came the exited chatter of small birds. Crested tits flickered through the leaf canopy and a pine grosbeak was busily extracting seeds from clusters of rowan berries. Sigurd offered to guide me through the forest and for several days we explored the surroundings. He had a fierce, proprietary love of his wilderness home. After explaining that the black lichens that festooned the pine trees were the food of reindeer during severe winters, he would point to a nest about fifty feet up where three goshawks had been raised that year and showed me the compact pellets of feathers and bones at the foot of the tree. I saw the marks on bark where a bear had sharpened his claws. In a grassy glade nearby stood the tall stems of angelica's multi-branched heads, a delicacy not only favored by bears: a local specialty was reindeer stomach stuffed with angelica greens.

We emerged from the shade of the forest to see the convoluted form of the delta spread out against a black and white backdrop of snow-streaked mountains. The labyrinthine maze of the delta is a paradise for waders and waterfowl. Most species had already migrated south, but scanning the sky I saw a fast-moving white speck flying arrow-straight down the middle of the lake. As it passed us I caught the sonorous bugle note, the call of a whooper swan. We climbed till the pines petered out and gaps in the conifers were filled by silver birches or the blood-red leaves of rowans. Sun slanted through the trees fragmenting in dapples against their silver bark. I sat at the foot of a tree and looked at the mountains reflected in the lake below. It was peaceful, a hidden something scrabbled among the rocks, somewhere a hooded crow called raucously, answered by the scolding chatter of a red squirrel. A vole bustled about, driven by the imminent approach of winter to swell its larder of nuts.

On the three peaks that guarded the head of the lake, Sigurd showed me the tracks of hare, of vole and wolverine. Once he grabbed my arm and whispered, "Lie down, look!" Below us, two elks blundered through the snowdrifts, snorting and puffing like heffalumps. At the summit we looked back. From this height the delta's network of channels and lagoons looked as if it had been created by a child drawing its fingers across a paint palette, mixing soft colors in an abstract pattern of sinuous lines. Behind the delta reared the bulk of Mount Nammatja, isolated from its neighbors by two glacial valleys. Pink clouds floated motionless in the sky. Two rough-legged buzzards sailed past on splay-tipped wings, mewing plaintively to each other. They found thermal rising off the shady forest and we watched them soar effortlessly up into the darkening sky. This, too, was Sarek.

SIMPLY BIRDS

Often, in the first groping moments of waking, the bird sounds tell me where I am.

As a child in my grandparent's house in Holland, I heard the jackdaws quarrel *chyak, chyak,* in the chimney. In Saché, the wild ducks squabble on the river and the plucky black crows make rude noises in the old oak tree. In our Paris garden the brown owl hoots at my insomnia from his hideout in the crumbling garden wall and the small tits nestling in the ivy just below my window start their shrilly *peep-peep-chirp* at the very crack of dawn. In the Hamptons, the mourning dove cries its plaintive *oowooo-woo-oohoo*; in Mallorca, it asks for *justiiciia.*

While working in the Amazon, a small brown, unprepossessing bird got me out of my hammock many a morning with the loudest, wickedest wolf whistle I ever heard. It was so raucous it made me laugh out loud. The little thing would watch me sideways and fly away as soon as my boots touched the ground. I never knew its name.

The full moon floods the valley of Deia with liquid silver so bright that the olive trees show their color. The summer of my discontent, lying sleepless through the fragrant nights, I listened to the glorious song of the nightingales, wondering how, aching with unhappiness, anger and despair, one continues to breath.

On the steep village path to the sea, a young nightingale had landed, half-frozen and exhausted. It shared my featherbed that night, sleeping in the hollow of my shoulder. A small bird, a small, frightened heart beating fast. Came morning it hopped around and soon took flight. It did not come back to serenade me.

Above the darkening ocean wild geese honk in passing. Lower, closer to the frost-white fields, a skein of ducks, necks stretching, trace their own V-shaped pattern across the lilac sky.

The most desolate sound to touch the heart: the wailing call of a black loon over a moon-brushed snowscape in Alaska.

A BEND IN THE ROAD

I continued to return to Deia, but my contacts were more and more in New York and I was seriously thinking of moving there. It would mean another culture shock, from village to skyscrapers, from Europeans to New Yorkers, but this time I would be following my own career. The children agreed that Deia was no longer the family home it used to be. Fred was living in the big house we had built together, with another woman. Foster was in the United States Cathy studied in Barcelona, Marc was living his own life. We decided we would not sell the house right away, but personally, I no longer could think of Deia as my real home. We began to think in terms of a second family base across the ocean.

It was the early 1970s, and New York was a special experience. It had passed through some truly scary times, tattering at the edge of bankruptcy. President Ford vetoed its bailout by the government, spawning the famous headline in the *New York Daily News*, "Ford to City: Drop Dead." Security was low, the subway cars were dirty, and the only thing weirder than the graffiti that covered them were the passengers themselves. The public services were in shambles, and friends warned that the streets were dangerous after dark. I realized it was different from the way I remembered it, but to us, it was New York, and I was ready to embrace it all, fully and gladly. When once again, a chance encounter changed everything.

Fred and I had known Sandy Lieberson and his wife, Marit Allen, for years. Sandy was vice-president of 20th Century Fox, while Marit worked for *Vogue* and would become a well-known costume designer, dressing the films of Ang Lee, among many others. They lived in London, and spending a weekend on my way from New York to Mallorca I found they had another guest, an American lawyer friend, Stanley Cohen, who lived in Paris. They had recently been sailing together in Greece, and Stanley brought pictures and films to show. We were both old friends of the Liebersons, but we had not met before. He was interesting and good-looking and we all went for dinner that evening, ending up in Annabelle's, then the *in* club. The next day, a family crisis sent our hosts off to Manchester or some such place, leaving the two of us to entertain each other. I thought at that point that it was exactly what I wanted, a weekend affair without any strings attached, ever. I was building a new life and had no desire either to find a partner or commit myself to a relationship, and most definitely not to get married again.

I went home on Monday and later that week left to do a story for the *London Observer* in Mondragon, a remote mountainous area in the Basque region of northern Spain, where a young Catholic priest headed an important social movement. Coming back to my small inn in the village after a day of shooting, the proprietress said: "Senora, *ha llegado su esposo.*" *My husband had arrived?* I stared at her, having no idea what she was talking about. Until I remembered that, not only my estranged husband had asked me where I could be reached, but so had my partner of the London weekend. My husband? Walking up the stairs, cameras clanking, I was not at all sure what or whom I would, or even wanted to find. "You look very Spanish," my new lover said, and the affair turned out to have long and very solid strings after all.

THE PARIS YEARS

Stanley Cohen and myself

I do not think I would have chosen to live in France had it not been for my new Francophile husband. However glorious the city, the museums, the food and the countryside, the French had never made me feel that I wanted to live among them or with them. When they talked about their everyday life it always sounded like such an uphill struggle, *complots* lurking everywhere, good things being done for bad reasons, bad things a par for the course. (They were always asking why the Americans did impeach Nixon. "He used the police to stay in power. Everybody does those things! But he did not do anything wrong!") When I moved here in the beginning of the 1970s. I vaguely hoped it might just be the French way of making things sound more interesting, but in the end, it actually made very little difference, there were so many things to learn and enjoy. I soon realized that the impression of unfriendliness and intolerance that foreigners often take away was not necessarily aimed at them. It sufficed to ride the bus and the metro to discover that Parisians have little patience with each other, to say nothing of the world in general. A foreign face or tongue simply aggravates any ordinary problem. What is more, when

I began to understand the nuances of their complaints and arguments, they could be very funny. The French attitude toward tourists has of course markedly changed since my apprenticeship years. The younger generation travels the world and is far more sympathetic to foreign visitors in the city of light.

Paris itself hardly needs my eulogy. It simply became ever more beautiful; domes and statues were regilded, buildings cleaned and the Eiffel Tower relit to resemble a golden filigree. It would be my home for more than twenty privileged years that could fill a book by themselves. I lived with its beauty, but never took it for granted. Every day the light was different, the shops displayed their fruit and vegetables like jewels, small water channels gurgled along the sidewalks, their soft music muffled by bundles of old rags. Like New York, it was a city for walking and I discovered something new every day: a button shop, a small museum or a puppet theater, a young woman restoring paintings in a shop window or a kosher delicatessen that sold bread-and-butter pickles from brimming vats. When I moved on, I missed them all: friends, museums and great restaurants, the Jardin de Luxembourg and the glorious views crossing the bridges at night, the Grand Boulevards, the busy neighborhood markets and elegant shops in narrow rues.

Stanley, a brilliant, cosmopolitan lawyer, and, unbeknownst to me, one of the more eligible American bachelors in Paris, had come to France in the 1960s. Working for a law firm in New York, he convinced the two senior partners that they needed a French office. If I understood it right, it was a case of one the oldest children's bluffs in the world: "Mom, Dad says I can go to the party if it's all right with you." And vice versa. Arrived in Paris, he set up a small office. His French still far from fluent, as showed one of his first cases: a Chicago businessman wanted to sell some property he owned in Paris. They worked their way through all the stages of negotiation and closed the deal. Walking home together, the older man turned to Stanley and said, "Well son, you did just fine. But tell me, did we sell the property or did I just buy another one?"

By the time I met him in 1971, Stanley's *cabinet d'avocats* was one of the most respected international law firms in Paris. If I had thought law was writing contracts and going to court, I soon realized that every case represented real and very different people. Besides "normal" people, Stanley worked with government agencies, international companies and film studios, embassies and well-known artists. It was all very impressive, but the successful lawyer I would marry in the Mairie of the 14th Arrondissement in Paris was not that far removed from the young man who worked summer jobs on a Brazilian tanker and interrupted his law studies at Harvard for a year to run a Seaman's Club in Yokohama. He had a wicked sense of the different and the ridiculous. At the point of signing a huge contract on international pipelines, he was quite capable of looking at the dozen executives sitting around the table and asking, with a serious face: "What makes this day different from all other days?"

I felt strongly attracted to this man, who constantly surprised me, and the attraction turned to love. Living together, we slowly learned who we were. We were different. I had been married twice, had adolescent children and a career I was not ready to give up. He in turn might have chosen a younger partner for a first marriage. I hug my children, my friends and my lovers. It took me a little while to understand that Stanley's kooky way of saying "What are you all dressed up for?" really meant, "You look great." I loved Asian and primitive art, Stanley collected contemporary artists. We did agree on pre-Columbian, German existentialists and art deco. He liked to sleep in a dark room; I preferred to know when morning came. I was on time; he was late. I was used to sharing work, which is different from telling a partner about it after it is done. I did not know anything about international law or the stock market and when Stanley complained about falling numbers I actually once said, "Oh, stop moaning. I'm sure they will go up again." Soon none of it really mattered and we simply shared. Still, thrice-warned child, I look back today and wonder whether I unconsciously held back part of me. Sharing what I could, but never again the total surrender, just in case?

My rather unconventional lifestyle had not prepared me to deal with the rules of Parisian society. I remember not having the right clothes to act the part, nor was I ready to live up to a standard *plus royal que le roi,* a faint echo of my Swiss "that is not done." I certainly did not have the connections and had never heard of the *petit carnet,* the elegant little notebook that is a *must* if one wants to finds one's way through this particular kind of jungle. Most of my women friends were professionals, busy with some project or other. In Paris, when I innocently asked new acquaintances, "What do you do?" I was liable to get a blank stare *(Do?)* from wives or mistresses who not in their worst dreams could imagine that they might have to work for a living. It was a little like exchanging a free-roaming existence for a settled urban life and reminded me of the Mongolian nomads who, when the government forced them to move into apartment buildings, built their *yurts* in the courtyard and continued living in them.

The French do not easily invite people to their homes, and social life mostly takes place in restaurants. Our friends were of mixed backgrounds and interests. Some, like the Malkins and my Brazilian friend Sergio Correa da Costa—now retired in Paris—came from my earlier life. Barbara Chase Riboud, Joe Barry, or Joseph Heller were Stanley's friends, but soon we shared them gladly. We found an apartment in Montparnasse that was probably among the nicest in Paris and perfect for entertaining at home. Pure art deco, the duplex had a curved silver-banister stairway leading down to a living room as large as a nightclub and painted the dark purple of ripe eggplant. The glass doors opened on a garden surrounded by ivy-covered walls, the dining room had mirrored sliding doors that might reflect the table set for a dozen, or the red rhododendrons blooming in the garden below. Ideal for entertaining, we gave dinner parties, book parties, costume parties or just plain parties, the guests a mélange of writers, artists and ambassadors, fashion designers and old friends.

Dorothy Bis, who was certainly used to mixed crowds, once wrote me a note saying she had rarely seen so many people who had nothing in common having such a good time together. Stanley had his poker evenings and at Thanksgiving unsuspecting French friends sat down to "turkey à la Franklin." We were involved with Democrats Abroad, and the apartment became a favorite for meetings and fundraising dinners. I recently came across a letter from Betty Friedan: "I truly had a wonderful time. You all organize book parties in three days, find Armani jackets at bargain prices and generally made me feel at home in Paris as I've never felt before." It reminded me that I too had wonderful times in Paris.

Our daughter Laura was born, our much-wanted child, making Stanley a proud and happy father. He carried her around, pushed the stroller, and before we knew it, she was a toddler holding his hand, and the right age for bedtime stories. She decided early on that Stanley's American accent did not qualify him to read her the French stories, which were reserved for me. Truth is, his vocabulary was far larger than mine, but I probably sounded more European. A cheerful, happy child, she traveled with us from a very young age, conveniently falling asleep in cars, trains and planes as soon as they started moving.

I had expected our home routine to change, but it hardly did. Gerard had started to work for Stanley when the household was that of a bachelor. A cook by profession, he had last worked for Edmond de Rothschild, but left there because he did not get along with the chef's wife. Flying solo, he cooked for Stanley, drove him to the office, shopped and cleaned. Then I moved in, Laura was born and soon Vicky arrived as her nanny. She lived in and Gerard came for the day, bringing his small dog, which Stanley called our rent-a-dog because it made our household complete, but we did not have to worry about it on weekends. The domestic scene had changed, but Gerard stayed on, and now cooked for all of us. He adored Laura from the moment we arrived from the hospital and let him carry the baby into the house. He would spoil her through years to come and staged memorable birthday parties. When she was small, he arranged a merry-go-round or a popcorn-ice cream cart in the garden; later, he turned the downstairs living room into a disco with revolving lights and prepared teenager's dream buffets.

Vicky was a special case. Daughter of Russian aristocrats stranded in London in 1917, she grew up in France. She answered our ad, her voice on the telephone very British, the accent genteel, but when she arrived for the interview, it was not what I expected. Her English was still beautiful and her French perfect, but she did not quite look the part. My friend Mati Klarwein said she "spoke like an English duchess and looked like a Polish maid." I objected to the callous remark at the time, but he was not far wrong. Her only reference was a letter from a cousin in England saying that she had taken care of their children and horses. Still, she intrigued me. The cousin—who was head of Christie's in London—told me, yes, she had been satisfied with Victoria, who was of course "a little different." I could see that. Stanley took one look at the new candidate and said, "You must realize what you are doing. Either you send her back today or she'll be here forever." Vicky lived with us until Laura went to college and we have kept in close touch. Gerard is still with me forty years later. They became part of the family and added a note of constancy to our movable feast.

Our calendar now adapted to work and school vacations and my life was somewhat more predictable than it had been for years. We still traveled more than most of our friends, but I also discovered and enjoyed a new kind of family life. If our evenings were for socializing, the days took on a more domestic tinge. Laura had the usual after-school activities, and I watched her perform in school plays, arranged ballet classes and sleepovers. On weekends, the three of us went to the circus, rode ponies in the park or might go to Versailles, bicycling around the grounds. We also became more available to our families, which was rather new to both of us. Now and then, Dutch relatives dropped in for short visits; Stanley's mother, Essie, came to stay, as did his brother Howard with his wife, Shirley. It seemed only fitting in my variable life that our Moochen, Fred's mother, also came to see us when she passed through Paris. She loved Laura and got along very well with Stanley. We kept close contact with my older children. Foster worked for *Connoisseur Magazine* in New York, taking every opportunity to do research in France. Cathy now studied in Paris, lived in a studio nearby and we saw each other almost daily. Marc reemerged, and we were both grateful to find a way back to each other. He stayed with us for a few months, bringing a nice English girlfriend, but they were at an age where everything was possible and Stanley arranged for them to settle in New York. From there Marc moved to Mexico, opening an office of the Image Bank, and then on to California before returning to the East Coast, settling on Long Island, where we would later share another stage of our lives.

Stanley ran his offices and I worked on my own projects. It had not always been easy to switch from a purely professional life to being a wife and mother again, while having a social life that dominated our everyday. I had always worked freelance, not bound to an office, a magazine or the same colleagues, I had been instantly available and my main interest had been my work. Now it was rumored that I had "copped out" even the Image Bank people in Paris raised an eyebrow ("Slumming, are you?") when I came to a meeting. I admit that there were moments I regretted my former freedom, but never for very long. I had sent for my archives from Deia, thousands of slides still in their boxes. Turning a maid's room into a studio, I built a light table and started to make some semblance of order in my transparencies. It was the first time in years that I found the time to do so. My old enlarger also arrived. Once again installed in a sort of glorified closet behind the kitchen—and sending a small blessing to Dad—I spent long hours printing. Soon the Image Bank was preparing my one-woman show and I was in contact with magazine editors, who did not care where or with whom I lived, as long as we could communicate. In the end, it was really a matter of making room for assignments that were important to me.

If his work had little in common with mine, Stanley always backed me, whether I fussed around in my studio, made documentary films or went on assignments. He understood what my work involved and cheerfully joined me on a venture in the Amazon, sharing such delights as living on a tiny houseboat with the captain's pet—a big fat boa constrictor—or swimming among fish that as far as he knew, might be piranhas. (They were.) Once, stung by a spider—or maybe we sat in some sort of poison ivy on the island of Marajo— the medication proved a powerful diuretic, which made a special experience out of flying over the rain forest with no place to land for several hours. When we did, on patch of dirt, he ran straight into the jungle, to the alarm of the engineers, and stayed away so long that one of them went to see what had happened to him. He reappeared with a beatific smile on his face and ants crawling all over his legs.

Stanley's clients also drew us on trips and I went along to the Cannes Film Festival in May or Acapulco in December. It was fun, but we were not interested in sharing the celebrity life too long and wandered off by ourselves when business was completed. In Tokyo, we took time to visit Yokohama, where the young lawyer Stanley from Harvard once spent a year running the Seaman's Club. The city had changed and it took us a while to find the street and the club, where a blond Danish bouncer guarded the door. "You have your card? Are you a member? What do you mean, after twenty-five years, you come back to see this place?" Inside, an older waiter looked at my husband, looked again, and said, "Staniliiisan?!" When Stanley laughed and nodded, the man ran off shouting to the kitchen or wherever and came back with people who were still working here after all these years. They had not forgotten the young American and it was moving to see the real affection on the welcoming faces.

I was comfortable with our busy social life, although at times it could also present a challenge. My genes may make me wander, but they have denied me a peculiar social grace: I have almost no memory for faces. I muddle introductions, for I often do not recognize people who had dinner at my home two weeks ago. After Stanley asked me twice why I had been so distant to some people at a party, I went around with a dumb grin on my face in case I was supposed to know the next couple. It is a horrible handicap and it always seemed very odd to me that a photographer should suffer from such a defect, until William Klein confessed to me that he had the same problem. We recognize every picture we took, even thirty years later, time, place and exposure if need be. Real, living people are a different story altogether, especially when we meet them out of context. I have only recently learned that I am "face-blind," i.e., I suffer from a form of *prosopagnosia* and that there are many others like us, among them the neurologist and author Oliver Sacks, who wrote extensively about it. I still don't always recognize my guests, but after reading Sack's account of his own troubles (not recognizing his own front door) I feel slightly more legitimate.

Stanley and Laura on the Rakkassa

A longtime dream came true for us when we bought a boat. Searching small shipyards in Scotland, Holland and Mallorca, we found a solid ketch, built back in the 1930s. Several times a year we set out, our children and friends sailing with us. Mat and Ellen Mallow joining us in Greece, Joe and Vera Lafollette fishing with Marc in the Caribbean, Cathy wandering around with me in Ephesus, her little sister Laura in tow, and later Cathy and her husband Toni crewing for a season. Laura was not yet a year old when she came on board and I can see her sleeping on her father's shoulder or sitting on his lap while he was at the helm. One of the first things she learned to say was "up the saiws." The times Stanley and I spent together on the Rakkassa remain among the happiest memories of my life. Slipping into Bequia at dusk, a forest of masts against the red sky, the jaunty notes of a steel band skipping like pebbles across the water. The smell of frying fish as the boats lit their barbecues, small stars at the bow. The coast of Maine, with unseen birds calling in the morning mist. Anchoring below Delos, thyme growing between the rocks, the smell of warm figs, wild mint and rosemary, or climbing the hill before dawn, bare feet brushing Hellenic pottery shards. Arrived, we watched the sunrise wake the famous lions. Waxing poetic? I never had a better excuse. No two loves are the same, no more than two people and I fully embraced the new happiness it gave me.

Stanley was associated with a branch of the Rothschild family in France. We were friendly with Nathaniel, then head of the bank in Paris, and his wife, Nilli, the daughter of the Israeli ambassador to France. When Mitterrand nationalized the Rothschild Bank in September 1981, Stanley helped Nathaniel to move to New York, where they started a new company together. At the time, Baron Guy–patriarch of the French dynasty, who in 1940 had joined General de Gaulle's Free French forces in London—wrote the famous front-page article in *Le Monde* accusing the Socialists of pandering to French anti-Semitism. It concluded "A Jew under Petain, a Pariah under Mitterrand—for me that is enough." Before the small group left, there was a strategy session at Chateau Lafitte and we were all invited down for the weekend. It was memorable, for at one dinner Nathaniel served every great year of Chateau Lafitte since 1790, among them 1898, 1934 and 1945.

FRANKLIN AND MONET

Meredith and me in Southampton

Among our Mallorca connections, Olivier and Meredith Frapier lived in Paris. Friends ever since we first met in Deia, where they had a house, we now saw each other regularly. Meredith and I worked together on an article about Benjamin Franklin for *Antique Magazine*. We both loved Franklin, the man, and we had done our research: during the eight years as special ambassador in Paris, Franklin lived a fascinating story of political intrigues and romance. It became clear that we could do something far more exciting than an article on his residence. Just about that time Stanley, having lunch with the Maisly brothers and Sandy Lieberson, mentioned that the film camera manufacturers Eclair owed him money in a settlement. Harry Maisly suggested that he accept a camera instead and Stanley brought home a professional 16mm Eclair. I had never held a movie camera before, but the timing was perfect: Meredith and I decided to make a documentary movie on our favorite American. One morning soon after, we had our first appointment in the Louvre to film some drawings of Franklin and his entourage. I loaded the film in the camera, silently praying I was doing it right. I did not. The film slipped through the sprockets and our first proud day of shooting what would become the award-winning documentary *Benjamin Franklin, Citizen of Two Worlds* resulted in an empty clip and a rather humiliating request for permission to return to the exclusive *cabinet de dessin*s another day.

Contacts and friends introduced us to galleries and private collectors who might not have so readily admitted a larger film crew. Elegant *hotels particuliers* in Paris, apartments on the Upper East Side in New York and rundown castles in Normandy yielded unexpected treasures. Sometimes it meant standing on a ladder in a gloomy hall full of poorly lit ancestral portraits, filming by hand with my camera wobbly as badly as the ladder. I would despair of how to show a detail of a miniature or, having dragged all the equipment up several flights of stairs, find out that the painting had been removed to another wing of the house. Meredith traced a rare portrait of Franklin's beloved Mme. Brillon, as well as some sketches held in private collections never shown to the public before. We filmed in Versailles on their closed-to-the-public Tuesdays, and I remember walking in one morning on a most amazing sight. The magnificent Hall of Mirrors was empty but for half a dozen women wearing gray aprons, gray headscarves and large felt slippers, all pulling a heavy wooden square fastened with long ropes around their shoulders. The platforms, cushioned with woolen rags, were hauled back and forth the length of the enormous room to buff the newly waxed parquet floor. The straining, bent-over women, incongruously reflected in the glorious mirrors, reminded me of *burlaks*, the barge haulers on the Volga River.

Meredith and I enjoyed working together; there was no real division of responsibilities, we both looked through the camera and edited the final text. David Schoenbrun of CBS agreed to do the narration and for the soundtrack we chose the music Franklin heard in the salons of his friends, some of it actually composed by Mme. Brillon to celebrate the victory of Saratoga. The film showed on European and American television and was nominated for a Blue Ribbon award at the New York Film Festival. Later we remastered it for the Franklin Anniversary and the DVDs accompanied the BF300 exhibition throughout the United States and France. Large posters announced the exhibition in the Musee Carnavalet. It was rewarding to see the film in the museum stores.

A year after we finished Franklin, we were working on Claude Monet in Giverny. We based our film on an article by Lilla Cabot Perry, an American painter who for many years was both Monet's friend and his next-door neighbor. Another French-American subject, it allowed us to use all our earlier contacts and resources. We had learned something while working on Franklin, knew a little more about editing and no longer blindly followed anyone's lead or criticism. Still, we kept more or less to the same routine of finding material through private collectors and galleries, besides approaching the Louvre, the Metropolitan or the Tate Gallery. Some museums would let us take our own pictures or film directly, others, such as Sidney or Tokyo would sell us the right to use their photographs. In the end, we showed over a hundred paintings in our half hour film.

In the Louvre, the guards soon recognized us with a smile. "Ah, les deux petites dames." They were more used to arrogant crews of twenty-five, huge rolls of cable and heated arguments over floodlights than to two middle-aged women pulling a luggage trolley holding a camera and two lamps on spindly legs. We looked so harmless that sometimes they let us work alone while they went for lunch, a trust that was not quite deserved. We, the "two little ladies" actually once took down a cathedral painting hanging on those sacred walls and put it on an easel to get a better angle for my camera.

Giverny took longest because of the seasons in the garden. Monday was *their* closed-to-the-public day, and we would set out from Paris at dawn, buying hot apple turnovers at a bakery just opening in a village along the way. It rained so often on those Mondays that the gardeners said, "We knew you were coming, just looking at the sky." It was fun, but for the morning when we brought my seven-year-old Laura, little blond girl in a white floppy hat, along to spend a day in Monet's garden: scared out of her wits by a gardener stomping around in an astronaut suit and a goggled helmet, spraying plants with nasty chemicals, she tumbled into the pond.

To recreate the play of light in Monet's paintings was a challenge. The row of poplars against a sky powdered with wispy clouds, the morning sun gently touching the flowering wisteria on the small bridge, or the reflections in the pond, "forever changing" as Proust said. To film the haystacks we drove for miles, trying to find a field where they still piled them up the old way instead of sending in machines, leaving square cubes. Having dragged camera and tripod through fields and ditches to get the sunset on the elusive stacks, I know I never did get it right and still cringe when I see them on the screen.

Through Meredith's long-standing friendship with Princess Grace of Monaco, the latter had agreed to do the narration for the film. Then in September 1984, the fatal car accident occurred. Meredith lost a friend and, on a much less tragic level, our film lost its narrator. We approached several actors, among them Olivia de Havilland, who agreed on the odd—and to us unacceptable— condition that we took out the Ravel sonata, which she disliked. Claire Bloom took over and did a wonderful Perry with a perfect Boston accent. *Memories of Monet* received five international awards and became a favorite on PBS and A&E. The Metropolitan Museum shows it in their film courses, and DVDs are still sold in the shop of the Marmottan Museum in Paris. We played with the idea of making other documentaries, but our private lives became complicated and professionally the trend had turned to digital cameras, for which we were not ready.

Paris Continued

Stanley and Laura

At the age of six or seven, we discovered that Laura suffered from a mild form of dyslexia, and my priorities started to shift. There would be no long absences for a while. I had seen this before. Marc was left-handed and wrote his capital letters C, P, and R backwards, making it look like Cyrillic script, which was not acceptable to Mallorcan village schoolteachers. I also had a young Dutch nephew, tall, strong, and good in sports but never a bully, who kept getting into trouble for fighting in school. Finally, his parents realized that he was ridiculed as a slow reader. Laura had trouble telling the difference between *p* and *q*, or *d* and *b*, which turned a pig into big, a bear into a dear, and a dump into just about anything. French schools made no concessions, no individual tutoring or extra times for written exams were granted. Even Laura's Montessori school, with its very small classes, wrote her problems off as "being on cloud nine, everything goes in one ear and out of the other." The teachers blamed bilingual education, which did not get much sympathy from me, with my five-language family. I have since learned how difficult it is for dyslectic children to deal with something that they themselves do not understand and many parents do not recognize. In fact, Laura was very bright, her French was fluent, and she had an exceptional memory. She knew all the other parts in the school play by heart as well as her own and was furious when children did not act out their roles. When very young she showed a gift for editing and later, as an actor, a remarkable talent for directing.

When we discovered that the American Marymount School was the only school in Paris offering specialized tutors, Laura changed schools and they worked wonders. At home, we rearranged our own schedule. When she came home, there was a snack, a little time off and then our daily reading exercises together. I spent more time with Laura growing up than I had with my older children. Fred and I had not always been home for things that counted, but at least they had formed their own close little clan. Now I traveled less, Laura was an only child and, in a way, we grew up together because this sharing was also new to me. We took piano and riding lessons with the same teachers. I applauded her theater performances. I cried on her graduation ceremony when she walked down the aisle and handed me the rose the school board had just given her. On weekends that Stanley was away, we cooked pasta or went to a favorite neighborhood restaurant; we walked two blocks to our favorite Jardin de Luxembourg and spent rainy Sundays with outsized jigsaw puzzles.

The reading at home routine worked. It also left me with free mornings, and a growing restlessness. Pulling out drawers I had not opened for years, I found notebooks, pictures, used envelopes with scribbled notes, music tapes wrapped in plastic bags. There, emptied out on the floor was the untidy heap of my life in Mallorca. On the very bottom sat something fluffy, which I first took to be a dead mouse; they did tend to wander in from the garden and one might have scuttled into the drawer never to find its way out again. It turned out to be a small bird, badly stuffed with dried herbs. It had lost a leg and the little head with its sightless eyes hung sideways, barely connected. I held it for a moment without any recollection of how it might have gotten there, and then, suddenly, I was walking through the jungle. Not in gentle Mallorca but deep in the Amazon forest, near the gold mining camps of Crepuri. My guide, a native hunter, walked ahead, carrying his rifle and scanning the dense canopy of trees, where monkeys chattered, birds fluted and laughed. We were not hunting for food, just hoping to make it home to our own camp before nightfall. When he suddenly swung around and fired, I froze, thinking of snakes or the jaguar the jungle people call *onca*. He made a gesture for me to stay still and disappeared among the trees. When he returned he put something feathery in my hands: "*Uirapuru*," he said proudly, repeating, "*Uirapuru!*" Uirapuru, the mythical bird of the Amazonian Indians. A small brownish bird, it sings only during the mating season, but legend has it that when its magical call trills through the jungle all other animals fall silent. Its feathers and tiny bones sell on the witch markets for their weight in gold dust; women believe it will bring them fertility and men will gamble a fortune on a drop of its blood. The little man pranced around me, laughing, clapping me on the shoulder and repeating, "Sí, sí," while I just stood there looking back at him, feeling numb. All I could think was, "How could you do this? How did you dare to kill this?" We set out again and I walked on, tired, hot, and deeply disturbed, but following carefully in his footsteps, the way I was taught. Past the spiders, the hornet's nest, the snake or whatever else might be dangling from a branch. I walked, and cried without a sound, carrying the little warm body seeping blood through my fingers, the eyes already without light and the small feet curled. Walked and cried, asking forgiveness from a small dead wondrous bird and the living jungle around me.

Now, standing in my home in Paris, I looked at the dry, dusty little body bringing me its memories. I had never been sure it was really was a uirapuru or just my guide's wishful thinking. He had stuffed it but never asked for a single feather. I in turn kept it, but never tried to find out more. All I knew about the bird was its

legend and that Villa Lobos wrote his symphonic poem Uirapuru
after hearing its fabled song in the rain forests of his native Brazil. It
made little difference. I had long realized that my tears had not been
for the bird alone, that by crying as if my heart would break I had
at last admitted that I would no longer "search incessantly without
ever finding," that childhoods leave scars and love does break hearts
on the way. Finishing the drawer, I found the tiny dried leg stuck
like a small twig between some papers. I wrapped everything in my
prettiest handkerchief, took it down to the garden and buried it.
Watched with total indifference by my Siamese cat.

There were other loose ends in that pile on the floor. During the
years in Mallorca, Fred and I had collected art and music, stories,
proverbs, facts and legends. We produced a documentary on Chopin
and George Sand in Valldemossa, recorded radio programs on local
work songs, wrote articles and guidebooks. When things were finally
sorted out, I saw the material for a book on the culinary history
of Mallorca. The island's food reflects its way of life. The recipes,
the work songs and lullabies with their Moorish intonations, the
children's games, and local proverbs, all dealt in their own way with
food. Together they provided a faithful record of a colorful history
that began with Punic porridge and Roman stew, added Catalan pies
to Arabian spices, finally to arrive at the hamburgers and fast food
now offered at Palma's Plaza Mayor. The book was first published in
English in 1988, then translated into Spanish and Catalan and won
an international award. Recently, almost twenty years later, I wrote
an updated version in German.

Based on my few pages of culinary fame, the French chef Alain
Ducasse asked me to contribute a chapter to his new *Grand Livre
de la Cuisine Méditerranée*. I was assigned to write the recipes for
the Balearic chapter, including notes and anecdotes on the origin
of the dishes. All my adult life I have had a cook and if I learned to
eat well, I am still not a good cook. I know something of the food of
many places, but have for instance—and for good reasons—no fond

memory of dishes we ate as children at home. Writing my Mallorca book, I had dealt with an island's food as part of its history. Still, I found it impossible to resist the temptation and—with a nod of apology to M.F.K.Fisher—I joined Gerard, our French cook, and labored on twenty authentic dishes, allowing nothing to be added or left out, however hard he grumbled. Fifteen recipes appeared as part of a most beautiful volume, over a thousand pages thick and as heavy as a family Bible. The Ducasse cooks *did* add and leave out, turning the humble Mallorcan soups and stews into the most exquisite compositions, every dish allotted its full-page color photograph. I figured in the list of "sources," which at first made me feel slightly insulted and then actually much better, for they had turned the modest originals into celebrity copies.

My home was now definitely in France, but moving there had never really meant a clean break with Mallorca. The Deia foreign community consisted of one large gossipy family, living and working in New York, London, Bali, Paris or Madrid; anything that happened to any one of them was immediately known and passed on to the others, with comment. Fred had also kept in touch with me, usually about the children, our properties, or photographs for articles and books. We sometimes crossed paths at mutual friends, which could make for curious situations. I also vividly remember going to Mallorca with Stanley to attend Cathy and Toni's wedding and finding myself seated between my two latest husbands. It thoroughly confused all the elderly aunts on Toni's side of the isle. The years had eased hurt and remembrance and for my part, there was no more "searching in vain." Now, when Fred came to Paris we would sometimes have lunch or spend an hour at the flea market. Still, we both knew very well what had been lost. At one point, he conceded that having left me had been a "suicidal act." Adding, rather accusingly, "But I always thought you would wait!" Was that supposed to make me feel better? At ease with each other, we continued old quarrels, agreed on good times and actually talked about doing a story together in Burkina

Faso. Then, in December 1987, the phone rang and I had lost him again, this time for good.

It was a great waste, his death at the age of fifty-eight, with so much still to create and share. His books dealt with subjects as diverse as *Prophets without Honor* (Freud, Kafka, Einstein, etc.) and *The Hitler File* (a history of Nazi Germany), to *The Art and Times of the Guitar*, *Games of the World* or *The French Kings* and *Wild Spain*. His biography of Rodin was published to excellent reviews—including on the front page of the *New York Times Book Review*—just a month before his death. Besides his two older children, he left a new young wife and two small boys to mourn him. Cathy had been very close to him and hers was a bitter loss. As for Moochen, she never mentioned her son's name again for the rest of her long life.

SACHÉ

Long before we met, Stanley bought a country house, an old mill, near the city of Tours. The village of Saché on the river Indre counts fewer than a thousand people, its church and inn date back to the twelfth century. The valleys of the Indre and Loire were birthplace and home to kings who left castles, palaces and hunting lodges along the sandy shores. Lush and lazy, they have been called and are renowned for their soft light and gentle climate. It is the land of Rabelais, Ronsard and Alfred de Vigny, while Saché claims its own hero. For many years, Honoré Balzac made extended visits to the manor house owned by his mother's lover. In his little room on the second floor, he sought refuge from his tumultuous Paris life and financial difficulties. (Known today as the "Chateau de Balzac," it has become a local tourist attraction. It stands a mere few minutes from our mill.) Roaming our riverbanks, Balzac wrote *Lily of the Valley*, describing neighborhood farms and families whose names remain the same today.

Most recently, the mill property had belonged to Alexander Calder's daughter Sandra and her journalist husband, Jean Davidson, who lived there before moving to a nearby farm. Calder himself lived across the road and there was a small studio, known as the "gouacherie" on the mill grounds, he still used most mornings. Stanley had met the Calders in 1964 when Louisa Calder and Gloria Jones arranged the first demonstration in Paris against the Vietnam War. They asked Stanley to present a petition, signed by many well-known writers and artists, to the American embassy. There, instead of being handed to the ambassador, as he demanded, it was intercepted by a CIA representative, who in turn sent a report to the Saigon embassy. Neglecting to mention all the famous names, it read, "Stanley Cohen, a lawyer in Paris, led a demonstration . . ." Both Calder and Jean thought it was very funny that Stanley was now on a CIA list and offered to rent him the Moulin at $100 per month as a "hideout."

The two buildings of the Moulin Vert de la Chevrière—its full name—straddle the river. The main house and the mill stand on their own islets, linked by bridges to each other and the riverbanks. My first impression was of something truly beautiful. Two old stone houses—one dating back at least to the fifteen century—rising from a river that looked transparent in the slanting morning light. A weeping willow bent to see its trailing branches mirrored in the water, silvery cascades tumbled over stone walls, and birds chattered in the trees. We spent quiet weekends; we puttered in the garden, painted shutters and rode our bikes, Laura in her small seat behind Stanley. Growing up, she would bring her friends, to fish off the bridge and row on the summer river. They were good years. I loved gardening and for me spring in Saché was pure joy, with the snowdrops followed by crocuses and daffodils "that came before the swallows dare" swooping down with their shrill, happy cries. Summer sent out its sweet scents and autumn dressed the old stone walls with trailing vines of scarlet and gold.

Truly exceptional and truly beautiful, but also badly maintained. The main house was built long after the mill, sometime in the nineteenth century, and nothing much seemed to have been added since then. The electrical wiring was rudimentary and the toilets (one stashed away on an outdoor balcony) had cracked cement pipes flushing straight down into the river. Stanley had made improvements. The small attic alcoves used for storing grain and keeping pigeons had been turned into large rooms with skylights. He repaired gates and built a greenhouse. The house was large, there were a few handsome pieces of furniture and every room had its fireplace, but overall the place was rather bare and the comfort left a lot to be desired.

The mill itself had not been in use for many years, the waterwheel was missing, and the sluice gates needed repair. Inside, an American pool table—imported by Stanley and much in favor with Sandy Calder—was the star on the ground floor, which also featured bicycles, wheelbarrows, crates and buckets. A long wooden table with benches stood before a raised fireplace and, in a show of bravura, a small hexagonal window displayed the rushing river below the burning logs. The floor above was virtually empty. The top floor, however, accessible by the sort of narrow ladder used in chicken coops, housed a fascinating collection by the American sculptor Jo Davidson, Jean's father. They were mostly busts of celebrities, ranging from Roosevelt to Gertrude Stein, Gandhi, Russian writers, an American general and other known political figures. On their rickety wooden shelves under a leaking roof, I often imagined them coming to life when no one was looking and complaining to each other. I was tempted to do a short film based on their conversations, but one day they were removed to Davidson's gallery and I was left with one of those small regrets.

As much as we loved Saché, we used it mainly as a weekend house. We had little time to spare for improvements, while the caretaker was more interested in his self-bestowed fishing monopoly than in the damage the flooding river did to house and grounds. Stanley ran his Paris office and was often away, we were coping with a new marriage, our small daughter and a hectic social life. Besides, I did not really think of it then as my house or my responsibility.

It was only later, when Paris, too, would come to an end, that I looked at Saché and made it mine. And a home.

Teddy Kollek, the popular mayor of Jerusalem, had contacted Calder about donating a sculpture to the Jerusalem Museum. As Calder's friend and lawyer, Stanley acted as mediator and in the spring of 1975, we accompanied Sandy and Louisa to Israel, where they were to choose the location for the stabile. They stayed overnight with us in Paris and all went well until we landed and passed immigration, where men and women were separated to be checked. Three of us went through without a hitch, and we were waiting for Sandy when we heard a commotion, a familiar voice raised in loud protest. Louisa was summoned and found her husband standing in a cubicle, dressed down to his underwear and furious. For no particular reason security had picked him out of the line and treated him to a thorough search. It was not a typical beginning of a VIP visit.

Martin Weil, the young director of the museum, was waiting nearby; things were smoothed over and we were whisked off to the Mishkenot Sha'avanim. The historic building had recently been dedicated as a government guesthouse for visiting artists and academics. Built in honey-colored Jerusalem stone, it was simple and beautiful, and all the rooms opened on a covered porch with a breathtaking view of the Old City. Settled in, Sandy and Louisa discovered that an old friend, the violinist Alexander Schneider, was staying in the room next to theirs. The following day the sound of Chopin's Piano Concerto No. 2 spilled out of an open window: Arthur Rubinstein was rehearsing his concert for that evening. Things were looking up.

Then it was meetings, visits to the museum and dinner with Teddy Kollek. Everybody was enthusiastic about the red stabile that would become a symbol of modern Jerusalem. *Homage to Jerusalem* was the last major sculpture Calder would plan before his death only a year later. It now stands in Holland Park, on the site he chose.

The golden city, with its sites, museums and markets embracing five thousand years of history, deserved more than our few days visit, but we made use of every minute. I remember we ate very well, whether taken to small local restaurants or buying fresh sesame bagels from street vendors. Sandy had also come around and enjoyed the company of new friends. On the last day, we all went shopping together in the crowded streets of the old city. And there, as a mischievous fate would have it, a wretched pickpocket *stole Calder's wallet.* Stanley chased the thief but finally lost him in the maze of alleys of the souk.

LAWRENCE DURRELL

"*On vient,*" called a muffled voice somewhere behind the closed door.
I stood in silence and looked around: a large, completely neglected
garden with scrawny bushes, some palm trees and groping vines, all
conspiring to swallow up the tall, somber Charles Addams house with
the closed shutters and the rusty iron banister leading up the few
steps to the front door. Where I was waiting for Lawrence Durrell. It
was ten o'clock in the morning and I had taken the early flight from
Paris to Nimes, driving the few remaining miles to Sommières, where
he had been living these last six years or so.

Shuffling steps of slippered feet, a face peering through the
narrow crack: "Oh, it's you!" We had never seen each other before in
our lives. "Come in, I had a burglary last night, you see. My paintings,
my papers, my typewriters, my Encyclopedia Britannica, and all my
wine as well. Puts me back on gin, just as I was cutting down."
The door left open, I trailed behind him as he walked back into the
corridor, talking all the while. "The police are here, come this way."

Inside a room with the walls painted dark red, a single bulb hanging
from the ceiling, I watched him explain the loss of irreplaceable records

and tapes, memories of Alexandria and Bitter Lemons, to a young French police officer. Durrell was leaning against the wall, hands in his pockets. A short man in his late fifties, corduroy jacket and sport shirt, mouse-colored hair, a fleshy nose in a rather attractive and oddly familiar face. He once described himself to Henry Miller as a "short, fat obelisk of a man, with the features of a good-natured cattle-driver." He was stocky rather than fat, his hair thick and graying, his eyes a quick flash of blue when he turned to smile at me: "They lifted the door right off the hinges. Imagine the nerve, helping themselves to everything, my best wine, the caviar, everything! Ate it right here, too, leaving pieces of corned beef all over the furniture. One of them actually wrapped up the leftover ham and put it back in the refrigerator!" And, as an afterthought, "It *was* a very good ham."

The police officer had his own problems. "I have not read your books, Monsieur Durrell," he said apologetically, "but I have seen you on television. I will buy a book today, for my wife will want to read it now that I have been here with you." He flattened out his notes, looking self-confident. "Please do not worry about the burglars; we are sure to find them. There are gypsies in the neighborhood. Would you please sign here?

Durrell saw him to the door and came back looking amused and somewhat bewildered: "How convenient for the police, *n'est pas*, to have the gypsies. . . . All at once, I am famous. The phone has not stopped ringing since seven in the morning. Nobody has ever made such a fuss about me in all the years I have lived here. Even the woman who owns the bar where I behaved like as absolute pig last night called me to tell me she loves me! I thought she'd never let me back into the place, but I guess all you need is a good scandal or a burglary to be popular. Now she will tell everybody what a good time I was having while it all happened. You know they took my own mini-bus? Loaded the stuff inside and just drove off, *voila!*" Chuckling, he poured himself another drink. "My God, I actually made you breakfast hours ago, you must be starved! They never serve any food on that flight!" He handed me a large gin. I looked at the glass and he eyed my cameras.

"Mr. Durrell," I tried, "you think we could go outside for a while? It is rather dark in here." "Of course, the pictures. I quite agree, but why hurry? We have lots of time and I suspect your magazine wants those awful close-ups, spreading them over two pages, showing every pore and blackhead in my face. It needs a little courage to be sacrificed like that. And you a woman, too." We walked through the house, opening shutters here and there. In the big living room he sat down at the piano and played old tunes, "My Foolish Heart," "Ménilmontant," "Tea for Two," singing along effortlessly, like he must have done while playing in the nightclubs of his Bloomsbury days. Sunlight slipped through the panes of colored glass, streaking his face with green, red and purple bars. "*Fleurs d'autrefois*," he said. "Do you like curry? I made some for lunch, having gotten up so early. Have you ever been to India? I was born there, you know, my father was an engineer, he built the little railway going up the mountains to Darjeeling. I remember living in a construction tent right underneath the Tibetan monastery." When I answered yes to both questions, he touched my shoulder and said, "Yes, I thought so. You must of course stay."

We climbed the stairs and he continued to show me rest of the house. Carrying his glass in one hand, pointing to empty spaces where the paintings had been removed, he said: "What really insults me is that they only took one of the pictures I painted myself. You think there was actually someone here who knows what is good and does not like mine?" Durrell had been painting for years, albeit not signing his pictures by that name and few art lovers knew the work of Oscar Epfs. "We all painted in the thirties," Durrell/Epfs said. "Miller, Nin and all the rest, even though we did not really know what we were doing. I think I'm absolutely bloody marvelous." (About a year later, I saw a nice review of his watercolors at a show in the rue de Seine Gallery and was sorry not to be in Europe. I would have loved to see the show, and him, again.)

Glasses were refilled. Breakfast—if it had ever been made—never appeared. Through lunch, the two of us sitting at the kitchen table, eating the bright red curried peppers with a bowl of his own olives, fresh bread, cheese, and local wine hurried in from the village store, he touched on a thousand subjects. "My younger brother Gerald writes about animals and has a habit of putting me in his books, choosing the most horrid personifications. As boys, we argued all the time. I remember he once hurled the worst insult at me he could possibly think of: 'You . . . you AUTHOR!' I am very fond of him. Tell me about yourself. Have some more wine. My wife bought this oven; she loved all these buttons and technical gimmicks. I find that most women do, oddly enough. You must take a picture with my secretary; there are never any women in the pictures with me and I would much rather be called a dirty old man than an old fag, which the British are quite capable of doing. Do you realize I am sixty now? I think love is fantastic; sex is fantastic. The older I get the more I think so."

His face reflected all his moods, his hands underlined the sentences with impatient little movements, as if he was pushing the words ahead to keep pace with his thoughts. He has always loved beautiful, or what he calls "smashing," women and, so far, has married three of them. His first marriage broke up during the war, but soon after he wrote to Henri Miller about a "strange smashing woman, who sits for hours on the bed and tells me all about the sex life of the Arabs, perversions, sweetmeats, removal of clitoris, cruelty and murder." He married her and they called their daughter Sappho. He said once that what he liked about the sexual scene in Alexandria was that the "women were madly violent, but not weak or romantic or obscure like Anglo-Saxon women, who are always searching for a tintype of their daddies." Watching and listening, I could see why Durrell has always been attractive to women. One feels he likes them, understands them. He also makes them laugh, which is a big step in the right direction.

His third wife, Claude, died of cancer five years ago and he started to drink "rather a lot, about a bottle of gin a day. I gave it up and now have no more than three glasses of wine a day." By then we were on our third bottle of cold Vouvray. "It has cured my fear of flying; it's cured my fear of loneliness." Claude did not only love stoves, she gave him the beautiful Pleyel piano he plays so well and when at last we walked outside, he pulled on a short blue sheepskin jacket, saying, "It is the lining of Claude's raincoat." Sitting down on the top rung of the empty swimming pool, still holding his glass, he mused, "You know, writing used to come to me as natural as breathing, so easily, I never stopped to think. Maybe I have lost that innocence. I think about it now. And so many people would just love to see one fail. Especially in England."

I remembered that not all his twenty-odd books had the same impact as the famous Quartet that tipped him for the Nobel Prize. Anthony Burgess wrote about *Tunc* and *Nunquam*: "The prose is languorous, a dope-soaked failed sixth-form master discoursing in a greasy mandarin dressing gown, - - - tawdry verbiage." How does one take such criticism? "Of course, I am self-indulgent," he admitted. "Overwriting has been the mark of all great writers. We do have a marvelous language and one tends to be a bit voluptuous with it. I like lucidity, but temperamentally I can't do it." He nurses a deep hatred of what he calls "the English way of death," and complained to Miller that the "mean shabby island up there wrung the guts out of me." I asked him if he goes back to visit and he said of course, but admitted with a grin that he is capable even today of writing a postcard from a London sparkling with sunlight: "Here I am, back in the fog and the snow . . ."

We talked about Deia and Robert Graves, who loves to tell a story about Arnold Bennett carrying a five-pound note in his pocket to give to the first person he saw reading one of his books; on his death the note was found, still folded, in his wallet. Durrell said: "I have always had a high opinion of myself, but I too have been surprised to find other people sharing it. I remember exactly how it felt when I went to a beach in Cyprus and saw a whole row of people lying in the sand, reading *Bitter Lemons*. I kept telling myself the book probably came as a free guide book with the package tour!" He laughed when I told him that he actually had been my tour guide to Alexandria, as Mahfouz was to Cairo and Graves to Rome.

We sat on the garden wall and watched the light grow golden over the vineyards. "I don't think one should live anywhere else but near the Mediterranean. One needs the tolerance. Why are so many people afraid of the gross and grotesque things in life? They are very necessary. Last night I went out with a woman who was really wonderful. On the way home she kept dancing off the road, she kept losing her shoes, I had to pee, and I had to dig her and the champagne glass out of the mud all the time. It was wonderful."

He turned and stroking my head rather absentmindedly, kissed me on the cheek as if I were his pet. I pulled back and he looked at me in surprise: "You are not afraid of me, are you?" "No, of course not, but I am wearing a wig, you see, and..." I never got any further. For a moment, he stared at me incredulously and then exploded, in sheer delight. "How fantastic! How absolutely fantastic! Are you bald? Completely bald?? All my life I have wanted to sleep with a woman who was bald!" It was no use explaining that I was not bald at all, but had been working and traveling nonstop and had grabbed the wig that god-awful-middle-of-the-night-early-morning purely for convenience. He simply loved the idea too much. "We must go to bed!" Sitting there on the wall, looking at each other, laughing through our images, temptations, Justine, absurdity, the why-not and the oh-well, when the hired car drove up to the house and sounded its horn: my clue to leave the set. Still laughing, we gathered up the cameras and he helped me carry them to the car, holding my hand. "Come back soon." Kissing me goodbye, he walked back to the house, but turning around midway, he pointed his finger at me and shouted: "It would have been beautiful!! Imagine, bald!"

JOSEPH HELLER

I first met Joe in Paris at a party for Stanley, who had received the Légion d'Honneur for services to France. They were old friends and Joe was in Paris for the publication of the French edition of "God Knows." The next day he introduced us to his editor, François Bourin, and his wife, Shoba, who were to be our friends for years to come. I did not know then how much time we would spend as Joe's neighbors on Long Island. Our friendship developed over the years and he was dear to me.

At one point, he was diagnosed with Guillain-Barré syndrome and spent a long time in the hospital. Stanley was the first friend to visit him and realized how very close he had been to death. They talked about it and Stanley asked Joe what he had promised God to let him live a little longer. "I asked him whether I should go back to my wife," Joe answered. He did not.

Returned home, our pool had the easier access for his exercises, so we saw each other regularly. When Joe later married Valerie, who had nursed him back to health, the marriage took place in our house in New York. They stayed with us when they came to Paris and we would visit them in Oxford, with Laura, when Joe was a fellow at St. Catherine's College. We also traveled to Italy together. Joe, having been stationed in Florence during World War II, was erudite about its art and the museums, as well as the restaurants. He loved to eat and after a lunch where he ordered just about everything on the menu, he would give a great sigh and say, "So, where shall we go for dinner?" (In Easthampton, within a week of being neighbors, there had been an ice-cooled martini glass in our freezer, just in case, and the big smile was worth it every time.)

He was a complex man. He readily came to Laura's birthday parties; he liked my grown-up children and my grandchildren and at our Seder, he would answer the questions, white-haired elder to curious child. But I also used to watch dumbfounded how rudely he could treat people and how they would allow him. When our neighbor and good friend, an impressive dowager in her own right, approached him at one of our parties, she was told, "Why don't you go and talk to someone else?" She never forgave him and I am not sure she forgave me. One day Joe was rather rude to his wife, but later, when I said something to him, he looked surprised. "What do you mean? I am never rude to Valerie. I wake up in the morning, see her head on the pillow and I am happy."

I watched an interviewer tell him that he had never written anything as good as *Catch 22* again, Joe looked straight into the camera and said, "Who has?"

THE PATHANS: THE WORLD OF PURDAH

I said goodbye to Stanley, who had accompanied me as far as London, and flew to Peshawar to meet André Singer of the BBC. We were to work together on a *Time/Life* volume called *The Pathans: Guardians of the North-West Frontier*. André, who had just published his book *The Khyber Pass*, was writing the text and I would do the pictures. The stretch of Afghan/Pakistan border called the North-West Frontier is a chaos of mountains, an area of twenty-five thousand square miles inhabited by ethnic Pathans, one of the most warlike and fiercely independent peoples on earth. Most Pathan tribes live in both Afghanistan and Pakistan and do not recognize official borders. They never have. They never will. If they evoked the romantic world of Kipling and the Great Games, they also belonged to the very tribes that left sixteen thousand English dead, strewn along the mountain paths on their flight through the Khyber Pass, in the first British-Afghan war. Winston Churchill, who served on the Frontier in 1897, wrote, "Every man is a soldier. Tribe wars with tribe. Every man's hand is against the other and all are against the stranger."

In our twenty-first century the NW Frontier is known as AFPAK, a place where young soldiers from different nations die in the effort to dislodge Al Queda and the Taliban. The Mohmand Tribe, with whom André and I lived for about six weeks, has been at the very center of the struggle. The population suffers greatly, their villages the target of terrorists and Allied troops alike and I have good reasons to assume that many of the people we photographed and befriended have died, and others taken side with the Taliban. A hundred years ago, Churchill also added, "I wish I could come to the conclusion that all this barbarity—all these losses, all this expenditure—had resulted in a permanent settlement being obtained. I do not think, however, that anything has been done that will not have to be done again."

KADO

At the time André and I arrived in Peshawar in 1982, neighboring Afghanistan was involved in a civil war. The insurgent Mujahideen tried to overthrow a Marxist government that fought back with the help of the Soviet Union, and hundreds of thousands of refugees crossed the border into friendly Pakistan. Peshawar was a hub of ISI-trained Mujahideen, moderates, liberals, extremist Taliban, and Pashtun nationalists. André and I had always known that we could not enter the Tribal Territories without a special permission and the tense atmosphere in the city did not make the authorities very lenient toward foreign journalists wanting special favors. Luckily, Dr. Akbar Ahmed, the Pakistan government political agent for the territories, was also an anthropologist, who had spent time in the Mohmand Pathan village of Kado. He understood our situation and was willing to help.

"The journey you will be taking is not a long one in terms of miles," he said, "but it will take you beyond the reach of my government. No one really rules the Pathans. The government influences by negotiation, not by force. Our laws are not enforced in the Tribal Areas, and anyone who leaves the official government road does so at his own risk. It has always been this way but right now, it is even more sensitive than usual. I can arrange a permit to get you through the police checkpoint into the area, but you will need more than that once you cross over. If you want to visit the Mohmand tribe, you need someone who will accept responsibility for you. I have spoken to a friend who lives in Kado and he has agreed at least to meet you.

"Will they accept me too, allow me to live with the women and actually photograph them?" I asked. Akbar shrugged. "I cannot guarantee anything. They observe a very strict rule of *purdah.* Women live for the most part in seclusion. They will treat you with respect, but will probably also treat you as an honorary man." I readily nodded agreement, but had no idea what he meant. We knew that if we achieved our goal, I would be the first Westerner to penetrate the high walls that, literally as well as figuratively, surround the lives of Pathan women. I would experience at first hand not just the everyday life of Muslim women living in seclusion, but women living under an uncompromising tribal code that insists on revenge for injury or insult and death for slight of honor.

This was not just a matter of *Time/Life* contacting the Pakistan Government Tourist Office and asking for their assistance in doing a story in a certain area. To be able to live in a Pathan community, it was of paramount importance that one of the senior families took us in and we waited anxiously for the meeting with Dr. Ahmed's friend. Our introduction to Shams-ud-Din took place in Peshawar; we saw a distinguished gray-bearded man, dressed in the white baggy trousers and long cotton shirt traditionally worn by tribesmen. A Mohmand Pathan, he was also the headman of the village of Kado. He and his son Ihsanullah were in Peshawar on some business matter and had come to look us over before he staked his name and reputation by inviting and taking responsibility for two unbelieving foreigners. They greeted me, as they did André and Akbar, with a simple handshake. Did that mean I had a chance of becoming an honorary man? Shams-ud-Din spoke at length with Akbar and then conversed with his son. Turning to us, he said that they were returning to Kado next day and we were to leave with them. We had passed the test. The most respected and most senior member of the Mohmand tribe had accepted to be our host and protector during our stay in the territories. Ihsanullah, a handsome man in his twenties, had learned English at a Pakistani government school and was willing to be our interpreter. It would make things a lot easier. André spoke some Pashto and I carried a thin, used dictionary bought years ago in a secondhand bookshop in Madras out of pure curiosity, never dreaming that I would actually need it, but here things were sensitive enough without having to rely on gestures and basic phrases.

The next morning we left Peshawar in a battered hired car driven by a grizzled, silent Pathan. The road stretched flat and straight across the plain. The fields were remarkably lush, wheat was turning from green to gold, and tall sugar cane gave the region a near tropical look. After about twelve miles we turned into a narrow dirt track that led northwest to where the hills rose on the hazy horizon. "Slow down," said Shams-ud-Din: a chain was strung across the road from two posts. I saw two dusty tents in the bushes beside the road, and beyond stood the squat towers of Michni fort, remnant of the British Empire. There was no sign of life. "It is the police checkpoint," Ihsanullah explained. "They are supposed to prevent any smuggling between the settled area and the tribal lands." We sat in the hot silence. Whereas André or I would probably have honked our horn, the Pathans waited stoically in the car. Eventually, a pair of sandals swung out of the nearby tent, followed by a yawning police officer in a wrinkled uniform. "Will he want to see our papers?" André asked. "I doubt it. It is too hot. Around noontime, we can smuggle in anything and anybody. Even you," said Ihsanullah. He was right. A cursory glance inside the car and we were waved through. A foreign woman with cameras, riding into forbidden territory in the back of an old rattling car with three armed Pathans did not wake that young soldier enough to ask a simple question? Ihsanullah looked at my face and grinned. "No, don't worry. They know my father as a respected elder and are not at all interested in making trouble." Looking back, I saw the road empty, the chain fastened. We were now inside tribal territory. From this point on, our safety rested on the goodwill of the tribesmen alone. A few miles beyond the fort, we came to the Kado River, running high with melting snow from the mountains. We said goodbye to our car and its driver. Crossing the fifty-foot-wide river meant wading through thigh-deep water, carrying our belongings. I kept my camera bag safe and managed the slippery stones, but Ihsanullah, worried about guiding us across, slipped and got hopelessly soaked, much to his father's amusement. A hundred yards further down, I saw a man struggling to float across on an inflated goatskin.

I had understood that the village of Kado was just across the river, but we continued to walk along a narrow track and all I could see were a few mud walls, about ten feet high, and more paths disappearing in various directions. I had expected a traditional village, some thatched huts, a square or some other sort of center. Echoing my thoughts, I heard André ask, "Where is the village?" "Why, here," was the answer. "It is all around you." The walls were built around compounds and each compound was a dwelling. "Are the walls for defense?" "Partly," answered Ihsanullah. "But also for *purdah*." Here was that word again. It seemed impolite, even dangerous, as strangers and guests, to inquire too deeply into a subject that involved the honor of the Pathan women and André did not pursue the question. Continuing along a twisting, dusty path, the only people we saw were children—boys and girls— most of them extraordinarily handsome. The majority had brown eyes and dark hair, but among them ran fair ones with eyes of blue or green. Pathans in general do look very different from the people of the plains. Tall and thin, lighter-skinned and with more aquiline features, to say nothing of the ubiquitous rifle on their shoulders, the tribesmen tend to stand out even in a crowded bazaar.

As we continued, I straggled behind the men through sugar cane so tall I lost any sense of direction. At last, Shams-ud Din called a halt. We stood in the middle of a clearing and all I could see was another mud wall. Suddenly, from a scattering of trees, a group of men appeared, dressed in loose shirts, baggy trousers and sandals, the limp ends of their untidy turbans hanging in loops around their neck. Each man carried a rifle and a fearsome-looking bandolier of cartridges across his shoulder or strapped around the waist. Most had an additional knife. "My relatives," explained Shams-ud-Din. First came his brother, behind him were various sons, cousins and uncles. For all their warlike appearance, the men seemed friendly. They greeted us with a nod of the head, a clasp of the hand and an exchange of the traditional welcome "May you never tire" and the reply "May you never see poverty." When I say *us*, I mean some of us. I had been advised to buy local dress, the *salwaar kameez*, and was wearing the baggy trousers and long loose shirt, my veil draped like a scarf over my head and shoulders. I thought I would fit in better that way, but I might as well not have been there, for they simply ignored me. Later, I came to understand that it would have been impossible for any of these men to address me directly. I was a foreign woman, unveiled and unrelated to them. In this society, there simply was no code for someone like me: not until Shams-ud-Din established one. This was indeed a first.

In the clearing, under a shelter built of carved poles holding a thatched roof, stood a dozen charpoys—the wooden bed frames crisscrossed with rope webbing—covered with a thin mattress and a cushion or two. What was this place? "This is our *hujra*," Shams-ud-Din explained. "Every large household has a gathering place like this. Men get together to talk and unmarried men and guests spend the night." I nodded and wondered what the rules might be for a foreign-married-honorary-man-female-guest. Ihsanullah directed André to one of the charpoys and me to another, both facing in the same direction. It was now after one o'clock in the afternoon and very hot and I wondered what was next. Just when I reached the assumption that the men lying on the charpoys were here to take their siesta, they all got up and removed their sandals with that peculiar single-handed movement of Muslim men in a mosque: it was time for prayers. Each man prayed individually, with his own gestures. While one knelt with his hands raised to his chest, another was pressing his forehead against the ground and a third stood reciting a prayer. To get a better view of all this André turned around on his charpoy, but Ihsanullah immediately came over and asked him to change back to his original position, as his feet were now pointing to Mecca. It could be interpreted as a deadly insult, shaming Islam, and foreigners had been killed for that very offense. André apologized. I did not even dare to turn my head.

After prayers, André asked if we might go and explore the village, to which the men agreed at once. Joined by a few armed tribesmen and followed by an entourage of giggling children, we set out, cutting through wheat fields and leaping across irrigation ditches. One of the boys always walked ahead to warn any women who might be out in the open, that unrelated males were approaching. The women could then retreat inside their house or veil their faces. We began to realize that life among the Pathans was likely to be full of social pitfalls. We climbed a hill, visited another armed cousin who offered us more tea, descended to the river to see men fish and it was late afternoon on our first day in Kado when we finally arrived back in the hujra. We had not seen a village, just more mud walls, wooden doors, children, and armed men. The elders were still lazing on their charpoys, idly gossiping, but now food was brought from the adjoining compound— chicken and eggs, flat leavened bread and a plate with boiled spinach, tomatoes, onions, and potatoes. We did not realize it then, but by Pathan standards this was a feast—bread, vegetables and curds formed a standard meal—and it had been prepared especially for our benefit. It was dusk when we finished eating and, so far, no one had referred to my status within this male company. I had still not seen a single woman and the men still politely ignored me. Then, suddenly, Ihsanullah turned to me: I should come with him and join his wife, his mother, and other women in the adjacent courtyard. I had been waiting for this, but it happened so quickly that I did not even have the chance to speak to André or make any plans for the next day. Ihsanullah simply got up and expected me to follow him. I picked up my cameras and travel bag, smiled a rather wan farewell, and walked through the heavy wooden doors that sheltered the hidden part of Pathan society.

Not without some trepidation. From what I had seen that day, I realized I would have to tread very carefully. I could so easily cause offense. I had just heard that taking too little food at a meal would be insulting, whereas eating too much was seen as greedy. There would be the veil, the language, the respect I owed to Bebeha, Shams-ud-Din's wife, who ruled the inner courtyard. She had been asked to accept me, but would she? What if she simply did not like me? As a woman, I knew only too well how we could make life difficult for each other without seeming to do so. This was not a polite teatime visit: I was to move into her household and live within the compound for weeks. We knew from Ihsanullah that some of the women, as well as their husbands, resented my intrusion into the most private area of their lives. After all, whenever it suited me I could dispense with purdah and mix with their men at work and at play. Who could tell—so the talk went in the hujra—what alien and contaminating ideas I might bring into the quiet routine of the women's world of the compound?

That first evening, I walked into the compound, the heavy doors closed behind me, and I faced a straight line of women of all ages, staring at me. Neighbors and friends who had come to have a first look at the infidel stranger. Ihsanullah sat me down on a charpoy, again, said something to his mother, shrugged his shoulders and left. Bebeha came and sat close to me and smiled. I smiled back, then simply sat still and waited, having wrapped my veil tightly around my face, just in case. The younger women followed Bebeha.

Coming closer they first looked at me, then touched me shyly, but within minutes, they had undone the veil so they could see my face, feel my hair, and examine my skin. I was prodded and inspected to the accompaniment of babble in Pashto. The women were bursting with questions, but that first night it was almost impossible to understand each other. Finally, I simply lay back and Bebeha shooed the women who did not live in the compound away. I just began to relax a little when much to my alarm I felt strong fingers digging into my thigh. It was Ihsanullah's wife. Despite my protests, she smilingly pushed me back down and proceeded to knead my legs from the hips to the feet and back again in quite a painful manner. I would learn later that this pummeling is regarded as highly refreshing, and a sign of affectionate esteem. At the time, all I could do was wonder when she would stop and how long the bruises would last. In the weeks that followed, one of the young women would administer the massage whenever I came home from a long day of dragging my heavy bag around and I actually came to look forward to it.

Meanwhile, I had been wondering what Pathan women used for a toilet, but was not quite ready to use sign language to indicate what I needed. Nowhere in the courtyard did I see a place that might serve. Just then, Ihsanullah walked in and I plucked up my courage to ask him in English. He turned me over to Bebeha, who took me to a room off the courtyard, inside which was a small stone platform. Several jars and some folded clothes waited nearby: it was their washroom and instead of being able to go the toilet, she insisted I have a bath! Something had been lost in translation. It had been a long, hot day and a wash would not hurt either, so I showed her my pajamas and toilet kit, but she instructed me to undress and handed me a set of clean clothes. The shower consisted of a bucket of lukewarm water thrown over me by one of the daughters-in-law, followed by a rough dryoff. There was no privacy and my Western underwear brought oohs and aahs from the young women: they did not wear any, and especially wanted a closer look at my bra. I handed it over and it did the job: within an hour of having arrived here among total strangers, I stood naked among a group of girls trying on lacy underwear from Paris. The contamination had indeed begun.

In the courtyard, charpoys had been arranged in a rough square, cotton quilts were handed out, and everybody was clearly getting ready for bed. The children were tucked in. I was getting desperate about going to the bathroom, when a buffalo helped me out by peeing loud and long. I was just happily pointing to the stream, when Ihsanullah walked in on my pantomime, stared and said, "Oh, the *laatriiins!*" He took me to a brick enclosure in a corner of the courtyard, while Bebeha ran after us with a handful of kapok that looked as if she had just pulled out of a quilt. When I showed her my roll of toilet paper, she stroked with one finger and shook her head in disbelief. The enclosure had a dirt floor and a large shovel leant against the wall. Everybody obviously buried the waste immediately and there was no smell. The men and boys did not make use of this toilet.

Ihsanullah had left again and there were no men in sight. The women lay down in the same clothes they wore when I arrived. Dressed in Bebeha's clean trousers and tunic I curled up under my flowered quilt and looked up at the stars. Somewhere in the shrouded village a dog barked and another answered it. I eventually fell asleep. It was all of nine o'clock.

When I woke up, it was not quite light. Bebeha had obviously been up for some time; a small fire glowed and she was brewing tea. I joined her and asked if I could help. Breakfast was leftover *naan* from the night before, warmed over the fire and softened with *ghi*, the clarified butter. She was actually boiling the tea with pungent buffalo milk and lumps of brown sticky cane sugar. I watched with mixed feelings: I liked strong coffee in the morning, no sugar no milk, and maybe a slice of toast with bitter orange marmalade. There was of course no question of hesitating. I was the guest of honor, served before anyone else and watched by one and all. I ate, drank, and smiled my thanks. For several days, my first thought at awakening was 'Oh, Lord, the breakfast,' but I soon became used to pungent buffalo milk and sticky brown sugar boiled in black tea. I have always liked the flat naan bread, so that was fine. I was also very much aware that every day these people generously shared with me whatever little they had. As an after dinner treat, Bebeha sometimes brewed green tea and spiced it with cardamom seeds, a great luxury. Many years later, I still add them to my green tea or my coffee, and think of her.

The courtyard itself had a kind of biblical feeling. Mud-walled and dirt-floored, it was kept immaculately clean, despite being used by three men, three women, six children, two buffaloes, a dog, and a collection of chickens. A mulberry tree stood in the center, there were some rosebushes, and a thatched porch running along one side provided shade. Doorways led to the private quarters of the three married couples and by Western standards no one seemed to have very much private space, but I never noticed any wrangling or irritation on that point. The courtyard was where everyday life was lived. The weather was warm, we all slept outside, and the men spent the night in the hujra or inside their room.

Bebeha, by virtue of her age, character and high status as the wife of an important elder, exercised a kind of matriarchal authority over the other women in Kado. With her husband, she had decided to extend to me the rights of a guest and even those women who were clearly antagonistic to my presence kept a grudging silence. Bebeha guided and protected me; she became a close ally and a good friend without whom my work would have been virtually impossible. When I strayed too far from the protected area I would sometimes face gestures like the veil pulled across the face as a sign of rejection, some fist shaking, some shouting, or even a stone held ready in case I came within throwing distance. As time passed, I was slowly included into some of the daily rituals. I have always lived with fireplaces and had no trouble starting the small early-morning fire of twigs and cow-dung patties. Helping Bebeha to fetch water from the river, we passed the *hujra* where André watched without a word as I juggled veil, camera, and water jar. I tried to milk a buffalo once, it looked so easy, but the hairy brute totally rejected me. It made for a good giggle among the girls. Bebeha baked fresh bread every day. She put the dough to rise early morning and shaped the loaves just before lunchtime. The *naan* was baked in a clay oven shaped like a huge jar, sunk neck-deep in the ground. The charcoal fire on the flat bottom of the jar heated the sides of the oven to scorching point about half way up. I watched Bebeha slapping the dough from hand to hand with the deftness of a lifetime's experience, making that look easy too. "Try," she laughed, "a whole loaf for an adult, a half for each child." One end of the dough was pasted on the hot wall of the clay oven, its weight pulled the loaf, hanging free above the hot charcoal, into the required teardrop shape, and the naan came off clean when baked. Or so I thought. I slapped, shaped and pasted. My loaf either fell half-raw into the cinders or refused to come off at all. Once again, the young women looked on, amazed and amused at how inept I was. Still, all those small gestures brought us closer.

Life is hard for anyone in the tribal territories and poverty is a fact. Men have the satisfaction of playing a full part in the masculine society of *pukhtunwali, tor* and *hujra*. The women have no such compensation. "For a woman, either the house or the grave," runs one Pathan proverb and it aptly summarizes *purdah*. From birth to death, a Pathan woman's existence is one of submission and servitude, enforced as much by a sense of unquestioning inferiority instilled by her upbringing, as it is by the threat of angry men intent on revenging any slight on their honor. After a few weeks of reaching out to each other, Bebeha and I had formed a real friendship. She supported me, told her daughters and in-laws to let me photograph them, which in turn persuaded some other women to confront my camera. One day I decided to ask her what it all meant to her as a woman: the seclusion, the strict rules, and certain punishment if disregarded. It was a sensitive subject and I was not at all sure that

I would get more than an evasive answer. But Bebeha looked at me and then made it very clear to a rather reluctant Ihsanullah that she wanted him to translate. I listened carefully.

When a girl is born, Bebeha began, her birth goes at best unmarked, and if she is the second or third girl born in succession, her arrival is actually the occasion for general mourning. It is hardly an auspicious beginning. In her few years of childhood, she'll know the only freedom in her life: she can run freely around the village and may even accompany her father on a trip to markets or fairs in the outside world. Still, her brothers receive the lion's share of such entertainments—just as they receive more food, more education and yes, when they are sick, more medicine.

A girl is rarely referred to by her name, at least by the menfolk. "Daughter" or "sister" it is, and even after marriage her husband will call her "wife," or "mother of my eldest son." Approaching puberty begins with the veil. As a child, Bebeha saw her mother wearing veil and *burqa* and, copying her in play, always knew that the game would one day be reality. The transition is therefore gradual, but, she said, the arrival in the state of purdah meant more to her than a restriction, it also meant respect and security. The adults of her own family may love a young girl, but will always see her as a temporary visitor to the compound, for marriage—usually at fourteen or fifteen—means moving to her husband's house. In her new family, she has to learn to adapt herself to new rules, as well as accommodate her mother-in-law, who dominates the compound. Most important of all, she must produce children—male children. If she does not give birth to a boy, her husband may well consider taking a second wife. There is no divorce, for although Islam law allows it, Pathan honor does not.

The question of *purdah*. The word means curtain in Persian and originally gave privacy to the women's quarters. It has come to mean the whole system of restraint under which many Muslim women must live and few people adopt a more rigid observance than the Pathans. The women spend most of their lives behind the high mud walls, out of sight of strangers. Still, in tribal villages the restrictions of purdah are often easier to endure than they would be in a large town. A woman must conceal herself from strangers, but may walk freely—though always discreetly—in the presence of her male relatives. Among the Mohmand in Kado most marriages are contracted between relatives and here the kinship of blood and marriage extend the circle of the women's freedom from a single compound to most of the village.

Bebeha never went to market, not even in the nearby town of Shabkadar. The men did all her shopping, from her clothes to items of food not supplied by the family fields. She and the other women did heavy work around house and field. Although young men do field work, they are not expected to lend a hand to the women. When I went out alone with Shams-ud-Din, he would always insist on carrying my camera bag—because I was a guest, not because I was a woman. The few times Bebeha was with us, she was supposed to take it: Shams-ud-Din could not be seen carrying something for his wife. When Bebeha and I then carried the bag together, he smiled and looked away. Despite all the things in her daily life that I would have felt as unacceptable in mine, Bebeha seemed a contented woman. Pathans are hardly given to public endearment between men and women, but there was a strong feeling of mutual affection and respect between her and her husband. In the evening, I watched the two of them settling down together by the small courtyard fire to have tea and discuss the day's events: it seemed a comfortable conversation between equals. One day I heard Shams-ud-Din repeating the words of a song a neighbor woman was singing. It was a sentimental song, every verse ended with the refrain "My beloved." Smiling at me, the dignified, gray-bearded Shams-ud Din sang the last line, "My beloved" and put his arm around his Bebeha.

Bebeha had done well: she bore four sons and three daughters. The two older daughters married in the same village, staying in close contact with her. Her two elder sons, Ihsanullah and Farman, brought their wives into the family and three little grandchildren now played in the compound or slept in their cradle. Much to the family's anxiety, Ihsanullah's marriage had been childless for four years, but Bebeha formed a close relationship with her daughter-in-law and the two women had helped each other through the years of waiting for the first baby, luckily a boy.

The two younger sons went to school and helped the men in the field. Polio left fourteen-year-old Ghani with a limp that put him at a disadvantage in the hard physical world of a Pathan village. He was betrothed to a cousin of his own age, who was deaf and spoke with difficulty. A girl of considerable intelligence and beauty, both partners seemed content with the match. In about three years, there would be a double marriage, for Roquia, the youngest daughter, was to marry the brother of the deaf girl. Until they reached puberty the children's—both boys and girls—day-to-day existence was remarkably carefree, while parents and grandparents alike indulged the youngsters. The lanes and compounds of the village echoed with their noisy enthusiasm as they roamed unhindered, with high, swooping voices and the patter of sandaled feet, playing the games that the world's children have invented since time began. I watched pretty Roquia, eleven years old, at play with other girls, outlining a rectangle on the ground with loose stones to make a play compound and peopling it with little twig dolls dressed with strips of cloth . She seemed so young; it was hard to imagine that she would enter this particularly hard form of adult womanhood in a scant three years. I thought how I would feel if I had to ready my young daughters for a lifetime of such a constricted marriage, instead of watching them grow through adolescence, receive a solid education, and finally, choose their own partners.

The compound was a women's world, but the men of the family entered and left without formalities. One morning Shams-ud-Din and Ihsanullah, planning a visit to Peshawar, came to consult the women about what to buy in the bazaar. I was to go with them. Putting on my jeans and long-sleeved shirt made it brutally clear that I was different, a visitor, and I felt guilty somehow, leaving these young women who had but few memories of having visited the city. Outside the gate, André was waiting with some neighbors. I had to look twice to make sure he was there. The tall, thin Englishman with a suntan, dark hair and light eyes, dressed in tribal dress complete with soft rolled hat and sandals, looked just like another Pathan. All that was missing was a rifle. There was nothing about him of the "faint note of foolishness which clings to the European in the East," as Jung saw it.

In the bazaar, the men went on their shopping tour. Some tools, some rope, a length of cloth. Shams-ud-Din chose a pair of leather sandals for his wife, producing a piece of string cut to the length of her foot. I bought a bag of cardamom seeds, plenty of sweets, the usual notebooks and pencils for the children, a little blanket for Ihsanullah's new baby and a necklace of colored beads for Roquia. I had been tempted to find a doll for her and asked Ihsanullah, who vetoed my suggestion; it could be interpreted as introducing anti-Islamic values. Wandering off on my own, I spotted a stall with Western clothing and managed to buy several plain cotton bras of various sizes before the men caught up with me.

Back at the river, the water had risen and Ihsanullah simply put me, with my cameras and two large baskets full of their purchases, on an upturned table and floated it across. The village owned a small wooden boat that leaked very badly and was waiting to be repaired. Until then people waded or floated across, sometimes on an inflated goatskin bag. The bag would retain the air just about long enough for a strong man to kick his way across the fast-flowing waters of the snow-fed seasonal river.

It was about six o'clock when we returned to the compound. Tonight charpoys had been arranged to provide seats for everyone, the table was spread with dishes: bread, curds, vegetables, potatoes in curry sauce, and green tea. Bebeha and I joined the men, while the younger women and the children stayed in the background until we had eaten. When they in turn had finished their meal, Ihsanullah fetched the baskets. He showed his wife the cloth she had ordered and explained why he had bought a different pattern. Shams-ud-Din sat on a porch step with his arm affectionately around Roquia, watching Bebeha critically trying on her new sandals. The children received their presents. Several relatives had slipped in to join the party, filling the darkening courtyard with jokes and laughter.

One by one, the men and the visitors left, and the women cleared the table. The children had already pulled the quilts over their heads and were sleeping quietly. A little cry came from Ihsanullah's baby in his hanging cradle under the porch. Last of all, Bebeha moved around the courtyard, her kerosene lantern making a point of light in the soft darkness. She checked that the animals were comfortable and bolted the double doors. She touched me gently on the shoulder, and then she too lay down and slept.

The bras, brought out next morning once the men had gone, were a great success, judged by the giggling while exchanging sizes in the bathhouse. The two young women did not really need to wear any but they loved the idea; I never knew whether their husbands were impressed, but did not think it wise to ask Ihsanullah.

As befitted her status, Bebeha received visits from female friends and relatives who were seeking her advice or simply came to spend some time. I sometimes saw her climb the ladder that was leaning against the outer wall of the compound. From the roof of her room, she could look straight down in to the compound of her neighbor, a close relative and friend. The two women would exchange news and discuss local gossip. Once she allowed me to follow her up the ladder, but asked me not to take pictures. During the months I was there, she left the village only on two occasions, once to go to a wedding— to which I was not invited—the other time to visit the tomb of a holy man to pray for her grandson's health, to which I was. It was interesting to me that the tomb was well-kept and decorated, a far cry from the usual Moslem graveyards that, in seeming indifference to the dead, offer small stone stumps scattered in fields of unkempt grass and weeds. Ishanullah explained that holy men or great heroes are revered for having imparted to us a lasting value by which others can measure their lives. What is left of the rest of us is turned back to the earth and we are remembered in private ways for private reasons. It was not a sign of disrespect to the dead, he said, simply a different attitude toward death.

On this outing, Ishanulla rowed us across the river in a borrowed boat. When Bebeha left our courtyard to visit the other compounds she wore her light veil, but that day she and the neighbor who accompanied her wore the burqa. I had been asked to wear my Western clothes, with a scarf covering my hair. I had of course tried the burqa; a heavy, closed garment, it was like wearing a tent and my view of the world through the rectangular screen was rather limited, to say the least. I had trouble breathing, did not know what to do with my arms, and kept turning my head to check on noises. Which helped not at all. I lost track of the narrow screened opening, tripped over the hem and stumbled about blindly, with Ihsanullah, Bebeha, the girls and all the children enjoying the show.

I discussed with André how simple, everyday tasks became complicated for women like Bebeha. He in turn had listened to the men's stories in the *hujra* and begun to understand why no one took any risks. The code of *pukhtunwali* rules almost every aspect of Pathan life. Broadly speaking it decrees what is honorable for a man and what is not. It requires that hospitality be extended to all strangers and refugees; it demands that the chastity of women be protected, but above all, it insists on revenge for injury or insult. The enmity between the tribes themselves caused endless feuds and bloodshed. The seventeenth-century Pathan warrior poet Khushal Khan beseeched his people, "If the different tribes would but support each other, kings would have to bow before us." An old Mohmand headman told André that the fights with his fellow Pathans such as the Afridi tribe had been as bitter and bloody as anything his father had experienced against the British. This was saying a lot when Churchill wrote, "All who resist will be killed without quarter. The Mohmands need a lesson, and there is no doubt that we are a very cruel people—with fire and sword—in vengeance. No quarter is ever asked or given. The tribesmen torture the wounded and mutilate the dead. The troops never spare a man who falls into their hands, whether he be wounded or not. The picture is a terrible one."

André told me that one long, grievous feud had involved members of Shams-ud-Din's family. It began when a cousin, in a dispute over a marriageable widow, killed his uncle. Once the first blood had been shed, the quarrel acquired a momentum of its own. The feud lasted for more than twenty years, and by the time passions were exhausted eight men had died. Shams-ud-Din had lost several uncles, the widening ripples of the quarrel had drawn in his wife's family, too, and Bebeha's father and brother were among the dead. That was *pukhtunwali*. Then, there was the matter of *tor*, literally *black*. "Suppose," André had asked, "that a man was thought to be guilty of dishonoring his neighbor by making approaches to his wife. Would the neighbor be justified in killing the man?" Half a dozen men sitting around in the *hujra*, nodded gravely. "But then, would it not be the duty of the dead man's family to take revenge?" One of the Mohmands shook his head: "Not in a *tor* matter. If the dead man's father believed the accusation, the killing would be justified. If he did not, he would certainly take revenge, but no one would make such a charge without proof and in any case, the truth is seldom hard to find. Usually we encourage the father of the guilty man to kill his son. That way there is no excuse for more killing later." He hesitated. "I will tell you now. I lost my brother, peace be upon him. My father was an important elder in a nearby tribal village. A couple, driven from their home district because of a dispute over landownership, asked him for shelter, which was granted. Living in the household of strangers, the wife could not observe strict *purdah*. My brother saw a good deal more of her than he should have and the inevitable happened. Soon others, including the husband, discovered what was going on and he took his suspicions to my father, who realized that his guest was telling the truth. Head of his household, he took the matter in hand. A few days later, he organized a small feast for his family and his closest friends. At the end of the feast, he asked everyone to pray. After the prayer, he drew his pistol and shot my brother dead in front of all the guests. He had no alternative; it was a matter of honor. Once my brother was buried, my father called the betrayed husband and handed him the pistol. The aggrieved man knew what to do and with everyone's approval, he killed his wife. Finally, to show that *pukhtunwali* had been observed and that there was no need for revenge, my father gave his dead son's wife to the widowed husband. The families became linked." He looked around the circle of men. "It was my father's duty to kill my brother. But if he had not, I would have done it myself." We discussed it later with Ihsanullah, who remarked that the man was right, adding that there is not always need for evidence of illicit sex or even flirtation. Husbands have killed their wives for the mere sin of having spoken, unveiled, to a stranger.

The treatment that André and I were receiving was determined by *pukhtunwali*. When Shams-ud-Din first took the decision to invite us to his village, he had become responsible for us. His fellow tribesmen would take note that any interference with us would be regarded as an insult to him and would be revenged. The code was simple, said Ihsanullah, "If my father did not retaliate when insults were done to him or you, even very small matters, people would not believe he was a true Pathan." Even very small matters? I thought of my shouting, fist shaking, and ready-to-throw-stones ladies behind their high walls and was glad I had never mentioned it to anyone. It might have started a small war.

By Pathan standards, Ihsanullah was a well-educated man and although he believed strongly in perpetuating the traditions of the tribe, he decided to teach the children what he had learned in the outside world. Until Pakistan's independence, education was regarded as unmanly and Mohmands going to school in British India were taunted for their softness. Limited education for girls was grudgingly accepted, but as late as 1977 female teachers brought from Peshawar were threatened with abduction and protected by armed escorts. Ihsanullah, who taught the boys in the village, was willing to help in ways that would have shocked his ancestors. In the *hujra*, the male bastion temporarily deserted by its habitués, I found him teaching young girls to read. There were about half a dozen of them, ranging in age from five to eleven-year-old Roquia. Sitting with their back against the mud wall, the girls clutched a tattered exercise book or a small plank on which to write with a piece of charcoal. When I photographed them, they pulled at their hair or just giggled and looked down at their feet, poking out of baggy flowered trousers. I left them to it and walking away, heard: *"Alef, Jimah,"* called Ihsanullah. A girl's voice repeated timidly *"Aa- alef,"* another whispered *"Jii-mah."* And so it continued.

The day before we left Kado, we were treated to an impromptu entertainment that reminded us how deeply the Pathans cherish their traditions. A local poet, Jalal-ud-Din, arrived to recite and sing to us. Shams-ud-Din's *hujra* quickly filled up with men and children, there were no women present (I knew they were all sitting just on the other side of the wall) and I wore my "foreigner's" clothes. Three young Kado men brought local music instruments; one was somewhat akin to a zither, another a kind of guitar, the third was a small drum. These village men, tough and heavily armed, sat quietly listening to seventeenth-century ballads teaching that:

"As long as he lives, he'll never change his promise, to honor his word, the Pathan will give his life."

But actually hummed along with:

"I am deeply wounded in my heart, by the bullets of my beloved's eyes."

As the evening wore on, the younger children were sent to bed while older boys and more men replaced them. The recital continued well into the night, reminiscence and reverie punctuated with shouts of laughter. It was a fitting end to our last evening in Kado.

In the morning, when it was time for us to take leave, Shams-ud-Din did an astonishing thing. He brought André into the family courtyard where I had spent these many weeks with the women. In a touching gesture of friendship, he was quite openly breaking the rules of *purdah*! Called from their work, the unveiled women timidly crossed over to the men, shook André's hand, smiled and disappeared again. André and I looked at each other, realizing that no other action could have shown more clearly Shams-ud-Din's regard and trust. The men of the family showed no emotion, they embraced André and clasped my hands. The children danced around us and shouted: they had just been taken to see the new wooden boat André and I had offered the village (courtesy of *Time/ Life*), to replace the broken one. Personally, I had bought a shiny sewing machine in Peshawar and Ihsanullah had carried it home as a gift for Bebeha. She and I now also said our goodbyes. We had lived in close intimacy, had exchanged confidences and real friendship, and there was little chance we would ever meet again. She held me close, called me "little sister," and sobbed quietly. When the heavy gates closed behind us, André and I walked in silence; we both knew these had been privileged days in our lives.

THE SILK ROADS

It was the assignment of my dreams. In a formidable venture that was to span nearly ten years, UNESCO's Silk Roads project planned several expeditions following the ancient trails, assessing cities and sites for classification or restoration. They would not just set out to travel the distance, but explore the different routes to recreate an image of the people who lived along them. As their photographer, I would document the architectural and cultural aspects for archives, publications and exhibitions.

The Silk Road. For a thousand years, traders, pilgrims and scholars had used the local terms the Chinese gave to the routes that connected their lands to the Western regions. When in 1877 the German explorer Baron von Richthofen coined the catching name *Seidenstrasse,* or Silk Road, it suited the Western image of a great highway to Asia. One of the most evocative names of all times, conjuring up caravans laden with bales of silk and chests filled with ivory, rubies and jade, trekking through deserts and snowcapped mountains to arrive at exotic markets bustling with colorful people. It stuck like a good commercial and was equally misleading. In reality, there was never a single continuous route along which goods traveled, neatly wrapped, from Xi'an to Rome. Our UNESCO expeditions would retrace a maritime route from Venice to Osaka, a desert route from China through the Central Asian Republics, a Buddhist route through India leading to a humble grove of *sal* trees in Nepal, known as the birthplace of Buddha. And finally, a Nomad/Altai route across the mountains and steppes of Outer Mongolia. It took a close look at maps and charts, where the span of a fingertip covered a trail that might take a camel caravan a months' march, to realize what an immense distance and effort those journeys represented.

Joining such an expedition, even for part of the way, would mean leaving home for at least a month or longer. When I went with André Singer to do the book on the Pathans, Laura was still very young; between Stanley and the staff at home, she was well cared for. This time, she was thirteen when I joined the expedition, and we talked about what it would mean to her if I accepted the assignment. I like to think that she understood. I have never pretended that my children did not resent being left for such long stretches of time. Years later, I asked her about those long absences, whether she ever wondered if I cared enough. She assured me that she had always understood and accepted my idiosyncrasies. Stanley and I were drifting apart, but he knew that this assignment answered a deeper need in me than a mere wish to travel, and he made sure to spent extra time with our daughter. Vicky and Gerard had been part of our household since she was born and added constancy. A hundred years ago, the young Swiss Isabelle Eberhardt wrote about "loving a city where at last I feel at home" and in the next sentence her "deep-felt joy knowing that, nevertheless, tomorrow I will break camp at dawn and leave all the things that are so truly sweet and endearing to me tonight." I understood her only too well, both the happiness and the qualms.

I signed up and traveled the fabled roads. I had read everything I could, from the contemporary, terrifying accounts of Timur's piles of skulls and Genghis Khan's hordes to the novels and orientalized poems of Englishmen who had never set foot in Central Asia, among them Oscar Wilde:

The almond groves of Samarcand,
Bokhara, where red lilies blow,
And Oxus, by whose yellow sand,
The grave white-turbanned merchants go.

Or, probably most famous of all, James Elroy Flecker's:

We travel not for trafficking alone,
By hotter winds our fiery hearts are fanned.
For lust of knowing what should not be known,
We make the Golden Journey to Samarkand.

(Flecker, at least, had some experience in the Near East, working in the consular service in Constantinople, Smyrna and Beirut.)

How could I not have dreamed? What fascinated me most were the traveler's journals. The classics, as well as those closer to my own times, such as the missionaries Mildred Cable and Francesca French or Peter Fleming and his strong-headed Swiss friend Kini Maillart, or Owen Lattimore, born and raised in China. Although their journeys along the Silk Roads were different from mine, I could associate with their everyday troubles, with the heat or the monsoon, the food, the outlandish customs and the danger of uncertain receptions. Their description of animals, bazaars and the profusion of costumes and languages were both familiar and always new. "The Kirgiz wears a heavy fur even though the day is hot. His boots have high heels and he rides his bullock right up to the shop door. He sometimes carries a hooded falcon chained to his wrist." So noticed Cable and French, and so one day would I. For more than two thousand years, a ceaseless stream of travelers, dynamic and full of knowledge about distant places, moved along the legendary roads. I loved these men and women for knowing that whatever the end, their travel was consequential in itself, that what mattered were the lessons learned along the way. Few travelers reach such distant goals unmarked.

The maritime expedition, our first and longest, covering twenty thousand miles, was allotted a full five months. For this adventure, the rumor ran, the Sultan of Oman had offered a supply boat, a term that to me evoked a sort of container barge. Waiting for us instead was H. M. Sultan Qaboos bin Said's personal yacht, the *Fulk-al-Salamah*, a beautiful ten-thousand-ton white ship with comfortable double cabins, dining facilities, a spacious deck and a crew of forty Oman sailors. The commander was British, the engineers were German or Scottish and a jovial Dutchman ruled the Italian kitchen staff. Our own team counted about sixty people. Besides UNESCO staff there was a medley of international scientists and historians, several media people and an Omani television crew. Like the original merchants, most of us traveled only part of the way. I joined the ship in Chennai and left it six weeks later in Brunei, having passed through Thailand, Malaysia, Singapore and Indonesia.

It was the first time I traveled and worked with a group, and it was a world away from my self-contained one-woman show. Decisions were made for the greater good, involving long and sometimes petty arguments, space was comfortable but limited, and one was never alone. I shared a cabin with a young Turkish archeologist and we became good friends, but I read in bed and probably kept her awake, while she snored and talked in her sleep. The cabin next door housed an elderly Israeli linguist who argued nonstop with his American roommate. The Chinese historian invariably arrived too late for breakfast, upsetting the Dutchman. Still, after a little wriggling to find our place, we got along well enough.

Part pampered students, part pilgrims, we were bombarded with stacks of literature, and most evenings there were briefings and lectures. We discussed religion, architecture, languages and music, the origin of golden ornaments in nomad's mounds or the plain blue beads on camel's collars. On landfalls local specialists briefed us on what we were about to see. At the time of "Cleopatra's baleful beauty, white breasts revealed by fabrics closewoven on the shuttles of Seres," wealthy Roman patricians cheerfully exchanged heavy gold for a fabric light as spoondrift. For centuries, the Silk Road traffic responded to an extraordinary appetite for luxury and opulence that went far beyond the moth-spun filament. The continuing passion for silken weavings, in step with a Japanese emperor filling his treasure room with the most beautiful objects in Asia and shrewd Dutch merchants bent on profits, sent thousands of traders and sailors on their adventurous journeys. The maritime route we were following was as much a route of spices, porcelain and artifacts as of the precious fabric that gave it its name.

Learning about great upheavals and the fate of peoples, we sat cross-legged in tents, visited temples, palaces and libraries, but simple things often taught me their own, silent lessons. A shard of soft-green Persian pottery I found on an empty beach in Java, a Roman coin bearing Caesar's image bought for a few pennies at a market stall in Chennai made me wonder, how did they get here? How did a South Indian merchant know the value of a Roman denier in the days of Tiberius, a village potter in Fujian how to make a bowl that pleased a European housewife living halfway across the globe? Carrying my small treasures back to our cabin, I touched them gently, with a new understanding of the immense distances they had traveled and the human contacts they represented.

Our sheltered life at sea alternated with a marathon of visits and ceremonies that had nothing to do with our ordinary lives. In every port of call, we stepped into a new country, a different culture with its own sounds, smells and tastes. The local authorities carried us off to be wined, dined and shown the sites. Staggering back on board after a particularly grand reception, we sometimes—rather ungratefully—wondered how many more governors, speeches, flowers and folklore dances, how many more outpourings of warm hospitality we could handle. Rare were the days that saw a few of us, thankfully silent, sway on an elephant's back on our way to a picnic or climb the steep slope of Java's Mount Bromo on a wiry pony simply to enjoy the view. Personally, I was so used to arriving alone at an airport or train station that I never ceased to be delighted by crowds waving banners, rows of honor guards, caparonised elephants, musicians and dancers. (My very best surprise was to find Stanley and Laura standing on the quay in Thailand, having come to spend a few days together before he took her on a Christmas trip to Chang Mai!)

Trying to reconstruct the history of the great mercantile epic was like a treasure hunt. There were tangent clues, historical places, heroes and events, but we spent as much time with the invisible companions in whose wake we traveled. Journals and letters revealed the mortals behind the writing, from unknown Buddhist monks and Christian missionaries to Marco Polo and Xuang Zang or the extravagant Portuguese adventurer Fernao Mendes Pinto, pirate, merchant and slave, who ended up a Jesuit. My favorite was Ibn Battuta, whose story I found by far the most personal and humanly engaging. In June 1325, at the age of twenty-one, Battuta, then a law student in Tangiers and driven by what he called an "overmastering impulse from within," set out on a pilgrimage to Mecca. He returned some thirty years later, having traveled most of the known Islamic world, roughly seventy-five thousand miles through Africa, the Middle East, and Europe before crossing over to Asia and China. On the way, among countless adventures, he married and divorced several wives, bought and sold small harems of slave girls, was appointed ambassador by Sultan Tughluk in Delhi and found himself stranded on a beach, barely alive, his only possessions ten *dinars* and a prayer rug. Once he was back in his home country, Ibn Battuta settled down as a respected judge with a well-deserved reputation as a traveler and teller of tales.

These scholars, traders and adventurers left us testimony that, more lasting than the perfumes, more valuable than the gold, the musk (and, oddly enough, *rhubarb*) stowed among pearls and silk, were the ideas that traveled with the merchant's bundles. Buddhism spread through all of Southeast Asia, Zoroastrians and Nestorians left traces in China, while Arab traders sowed the seeds for Islam that took root in the subcontinent of India, in Malaysia and Indonesia. Changing the world as they knew it.

I would later realize that the maritime expedition differed from all the others in that we traveled in a sort of time capsule. Thoroughly immersed in past events, tales and chronicles, we barely wondered why heavily armed bodyguards surrounded our host at a seminar in Chennai, what was actually happening with the guerillas in Shri Lanka, or what caused the villager's revolts in Thailand. It took a few odd encounters to remind us that there was still a world outside our Noah's ark. First, we met the seventh US fleet on its way to the Saudi coast and Operation Desert Storm. It was an impressive and chilling sight, the seemingly endless parade of huge gray ships silently and ominously pursuing their set course across a shoreless ocean. Thousands of young soldiers going to war. Navy planes buzzed us and asked for identification. What indeed was a ship carrying a group of international scientists doing in the Arabian Sea, heading out into the Indian Ocean?

Later, somewhere in the South China Sea, the captain suddenly stopped the *Fulk-Al-Salamah* and turned her around: he had seen an unidentified, stationary object on the radar screen. The turbaned sailors reported to their deck stations and we were asked to follow orders. No one knew what to expect, anybody's guess was good enough, and there were plenty. The object turned out to be a junk, barely afloat, its sails in tatters, eight Malaysian fishermen hailing us, waving their arms, shouting and crying. Surprised by a storm that left them without an engine, they had been drifting for over two weeks. By now water and food had run out, they were ill and exhausted, the damaged vessel was taking water, and we saw sharks circling the wreck. After several ships passed them by without reacting to their signals for help, they had given up all hope. To be rescued at this late moment by a luxurious yacht belonging to an Arabian Sultan must have been one of the most unlikely events in their lives.

The day came that I waved goodbye and saw our beautiful white ship sail away without me. Grateful for all I had seen and learned, for new friends made, I knew that among the things I would miss most was the sea itself. The long days of empty horizons and the sunrise of a perfect dawn. The night a befriended engineer knocked at my cabin door: come and see! Up on deck the jeweled sky wheeled about its axis. Our bow set the sea hissing like silk, drawing a shower of brilliant sparks from depths of green fire and leaving a long glowing furrow of phosphorescence in our wake. A night of beauty, of infinity so vast, it hushed us into silence.

THE DESERT ROUTE

A year or so later I met the team in Samarkand to continue past Tashkent, Penjikent, and Pyshkek to Alma Ata and Panfilov on the Chinese border. The names were magical, evoking their past, their opulence and culture. For centuries mysterious and rarely heard in the West, the recent political upheavals had made them familiar reading. But what were these cities really like today? Would there be anything left of the legends and myths that had surrounded them? Not bound to the UNESCO schedule, I arrived a few days early, for there were places I preferred to see by myself, and one of them was Samarkand.

On the midnight flight from Moscow the plane was old and rickety, some of the seats literally tied together with string and rubber bands. Next to me sat a very fat, very rude, and very drunk Uzbek, who kept sliding sideways, emitting foul breath and the smell of sweaty clothes. At about three in the morning, an attendant asked, "Breakfast or lunch?" I opted for breakfast and she handed me—and everybody else—a stained paper plate with a piece of gray rubbery chicken and a greasy glass of vodka. On my way to the lavatory, I glanced into the pilot's cabin: women's underwear hung drying on pegs and two girls were sitting on the men's lap, laughing and drinking.

We landed in the early morning on a small dusty airport already bright with the promise of a hot day. My first impression of Samarkand was that of a dreary and rather modern city. High-rises towered, construction cranes loomed everywhere and over the mud walls that hid the lower houses I could see the bristly quills of television antennas. On the sidewalks bearded men in biblical robes hawked transistor radios, hairspray and pictures of Michael Jackson. Venturing into narrower streets, I glimpsed dark shops and small courtyards. I wandered around, shared ice cream with beggar children in a park, bought dried apricots, and tasted a spoonful of curds offered by a smiling peasant woman with a full set of metal teeth. Tired and jetlagged, I wondered: Was this what had become of the Afrasiab of Genghis Khan, the fabled city of Timur the Lame? The city that, more than any other, evoked the Silk Road? Was it all in a name and a few yet unrestored ruins? Did I even know what I was looking for? Trying to cross the street against a roar of trucks and buses, I felt more like Crocodile Dundee in New York than a visitor in a legendary city that was the contemporary of Babylon. Having left behind me what had become a rather shaky marriage, I was feeling wretched, depressed and full of doubt. I needed an uplifting experience, something to justify my childhood dreams, a belief in past or present beauty. Not this grotesque travesty. Jet-lagged, cranky and disappointed, resenting all and everything, I was ready to accept defeat.

Until I turned the corner of a dark alley and walked into the Registan. Bare of shrubs or trees, the vast square stood splendid and aloof in the intense sunlight. Three sides enclosed by the blue and gold *madrasahs*, the fourth side open to the wind and its corners marked by tall round minarets it was unlike anything I had imagined. I had seen lovelier buildings but rarely one with such majesty lent to it by simple lines and the richness of its colored tiles. Here it was, the center of medieval Samarkand, witness to the splendor of Tamerlane's capital. Here ambassadors were received, the spoils of victories piled up for all to see; the enormous brass trumpets announced the wrath or mercy of a ruler whose empire reached from the Volga to the Ganges, from Tien Shan to the Bosporus. What could it have been like in its days of glory, when kings, soldiers, students and pilgrims walked these grounds? In the fourteenth century, Ruy Gonzalez de Clavijo, ambassador of Henry III of Castile, reported that pavilions were covered with tasseled hangings of a "rosecolored stuff" ornamented with emeralds, pearls and other precious stones, which fluttered in the wind. At receptions the tables were of gold and tents lined with ermine, elephants painted green and red, fruit trees for shade and fountains with red apples bobbing beneath the spray. After regaling us with all these pretty details, however, he also noted that the drinking was heavy and competitive, that trespassers were killed on sight and their corpses left on the grassy borders as warnings to others who might follow them at their peril.

Nearly seven hundred years later, I sat down on a bench in this grand square, tired and grateful. I had spent hours looking at the bee-hived ceilings of luminous gold, the intricate weave of ceramic animals and flowers, my fingers trailing the sun-warmed tiled walls.

Tourists and schoolchildren filed through, craning their necks at the azure and turquoise domes, the slender minarets, the giant portal of the Shirdar madrasah decorated with a tiger and a gazelle in the rays of the rising sun. It was hard to believe that these marvels were built with bricks formed of chopped straw, camel urine, desert dust and clay from the Zehravshan River. A mere mud building, until artisans faced the ribbed domes, the arches and minarets with tiles of a lustrous radiance *sans pareil*. All around me much noisy restoration was going on: it was a living place, Samarkand rebuilding its past. And at the entrance of the square, a large red banner read, *"Welcome to the Silk Road Expedition."* Meaning *me*!

The next day I saw the world with a far more sympathetic eye. Small rosebushes bloomed against walls washed a pale blue, children sold tied bunches of rhubarb stalks and spring onions, which they wore on their heads like little caps. The bustling bazaar, right behind the shattered turquoise dome of the great mosque of Bibi Khanum, was filled with color and the sound of unfamiliar languages. People bought turmeric and crystalline sugar resembling chunks of quartz, prayer rugs from Bokhara, saddlebags, furs, and robes of shaded *ikat*-weave silk. Barbers did a brisk trade, protesting mules were shod, and the stalls served broiled mutton kebabs with carrots and rice *pilau*, with small paper screws of red pepper and coarse salt. I lunched on a slice of an omelet made in a copper pan over two feet in diameter and bought pastries of almond and pistachio nuts.

Earlier, at dawn, I had wandered into the necropolis of Shakhi Zinda, an ensemble of mausoleums and mosques built by Tamerlane, Lord of Asia. Entering a narrow passage, I stepped back in time, past monuments whose structural and cultural layers embraced almost the entire 2,500-year-old history of Samarkand. In the silent alleys between the tombs of the ruler's kin, the light glowed softly on blue-glazed tiles in shades ranging from the palest opalescent turquoise to the darkest cobalt and lapis. A triumph of fourteenth- and fifteenth-century artists from Shiraz, Isfahan and Herat, they made this city one of the most fabled places on earth. There was a dreamlike quality to these empty lanes, leading where, echoing what voices? A small vaulted arch framed a round courtyard, dominated by a twin dome with strips of Koranic writing running along the base. Rising out of a grove of acacia trees, the entrance hall was lined with precious stones, the soft light filtered on writings in gold and on the crypt below. Doves cooed and a white mulberry tree dropped its fruit on the stone steps. The gatekeeper who had so kindly let me in at that godly hour long before opening time, sat quietly smoking, his back against a carved door. He offered me tea and we sat together, peacefully. Just before the first visitors began to arrive, the turbaned old man, touching my forehead, gave me his blessing. "Look well, daughter. The day will come when you remember this sight with gladness," and watched me walking through the arched gate, back into the present. Behind me the turquoise and gold-flecked domes lit up the sky, doves cooed in the trees and I knew why I had come to Samarkand.

To describe what is was like for us to travel the storied Silk Routes I would need far more than a chapter, for the paradoxical reason that spectacular events were rare. If we spent but a month or so where others traveled for two years, their journals too dwelt on seemingly unimportant details such as the availability of food, the extremes of temperature or the lack of animal life. They simply gave us their world as they lived it. Now as then it was a day-by-day trek, time was of little consequence, and every step was part of the goal. The timeless image of the Silk Road owes as much to the unembellished accounts of men and women leading camel trains through desert wastes, mountains and wind-blown steppes as to the terrifying tales of murderous attacks or the glorious romance of its great cities.

We traveled in buses and jeeps. Normally one kept the same place, once chosen, so one could leave things like books and personal items. I shared a seat with a director of the Leningrad Museum, a specialist on nomad art, who spoke half a dozen local languages. A good-looking, big, and friendly man who liked to sing, especially after some of the local vodka. At which point I usually tried to get out of my seat because he tended to declare his everlasting love to the collective mirth of my colleagues and fall asleep on my shoulder. Actually, he had a beautiful deep basso, perfect for the Russian operas he preferred and we did become good friends. The traveling was well organized. Unlike our intrepid predecessors, we did not risk starvation or to be robbed and executed for not being circumcised. Moving from site to site, we were welcomed in hotels, tents and army camps. I liked the tents, and the clean camps always had hot showers. The Intourist hotels were usually modern buildings with uniformed attendants at the door, mirrored dining rooms and large conference halls.

They also held small surprises. The elevators rarely worked and young male employees stood watching indifferently while elderly professors lugged their bags up the seventh floor. The first night in Samarkand, wanting to use the bathroom, I suddenly felt the room swaying. Did I have one of my dizzy spells? An earthquake? No such thing: the shiny new toilet was not attached to the floor and simply keeled over when I sat on it. In the new, but already shabby hotel Uzbekistan in Tashkent the door handle came off, locking me out of my room. In Alma Ata, when I brought the floor guard an armful of laundry, she gave me a tin bucket. Insisting in my basic Russian that I would like to have my things washed by the hotel staff, I was sent back to my room, still holding my laundry, "*Da, da*, you wait." A knock at the door, a young girl handed me a piece of string and a skiver of soap: "*Da*," she told me, "you tie on balcony."

On our expeditions, I would find it increasingly difficult to accept the local security people, and even our own crowd, interfering with my work. It had already been a factor on the maritime route, for if I came to regard that expedition as a highly educational cruise, it was a cruise nevertheless. We were on board ship, spent time with other passengers in a limited space, walked down the gangplank, visited prearranged sites and got back on board. But it was our first expedition, I learned from others, saw countries new to me and the sea journey was so wondrous that it far outweighed my frustrations. The overland expeditions offered closer contact with the peoples we visited, but also meant an hour-by-hour schedule designed for specialists who in due course would draw conclusions relevant to themselves. I was used to working alone, my criteria were light and timing, the moments often irretrievable. I was willing to make concessions; I was not willing to keep taking pictures of seventy-odd people climbing up monuments offering their backsides to my camera. Our work served UNESCO'S purposes as well as our own, so, with two other journalists, we asked for a meeting. We were promised more leeway and a jeep, so we would not have to wait until everybody finished their breakfast porridge, and we would be able to stay at a site after the others left. It helped, but security personnel still often barred our way, one commander dragging me back to the car and shouting "YU, KAMMARA NOT MORE!"

All that time I was well aware that I could not have made this journey on my own. Today I could probably join a biking-tour around Outer Mongolia through my local travel agency, but until the collapse of the Soviet Union, the Central Asian Republics were a remote and closely controlled region. UNESCO was an institution associated with economic and cultural benefits for which all doors were wide open and all assistance guaranteed. Alone, I would not have been allowed to travel very far. It had happened before. Russian soldiers pursued Fred and me in the Danubian marshes of Soviet Rumania, accusing us of photographing forbidden installations and men in striped pajamas working in malarial marshes, instead of wild birds. Arrested at gunpoint, we were locked in an abandoned museum for two days—no food, just water—while the police confiscated my films and threatened us with horrors unless we signed a "confession." When we demanded to contact our consular offices instead, they backed off, but we had a very hard time convincing the authorities that our poor Rumanian ornithologist had shown us nothing but pelicans. As they could not develop Kodak color film—a monopoly at the time—they finally gave me back all but the one they had ruined by trying. Then, with some face-saving shouting, they pushed us out of the door. Remembering that, I was truly grateful for our current privileged situation and for all it offered, but I missed the excitement of an unplanned tomorrow, of making my own choices and mistakes, while exploring a new world. It had taken long and careful preparations to guide our unwieldy expedition to the many sources of knowledge, new sceneries and new people; by the same token, it left small room for surprises.

The impact of archeological sites often depended on what insight I brought to it. Certain buildings or landscapes were accessible through memory or recognition; others needed to be seen through the eyes of those who know their history. A sand hill resembling a misshapen mud pie along the dry riverbed of the Syr Daria did not volunteer the fact that it was once one in a string of heavily fortified villages. That a desolate place where we came upon a child's skull and some small bones was once full of life, of people traveling between the fortresses, the high watch towers with their signal fires reassuring beacons in the desert night. Archeologist friends assure me that their work is incredibly rewarding, but I also have watched them spend years digging, sifting, hoping, and believing. I loved to spend time on sites in the mauve or golden desert, but somehow fear that one season on a dig with some self-absorbed colleagues and a few young volunteers must be very much like another. I am grateful to enjoy what they find; to stand in awe before pieces of broken flint, polished and burnished from use, forming a sickle used ten thousand years ago to cut the spare stalks of wild grain at the brook's edge. To learn about a people through the beauty of apricot-colored pottery, Peruvian gold, a pyxis of carved ivory, or the fabulous ram of Ur, its horns of lapis caught in a flowering thicket.

The initial site of ancient Samarkand lies in a suburb still called Afrasiab, where we found a cluster of lifeless hills pockmarked by recent excavations. The day was dark and windy, a chilly rain slanting this way or that and to an unsympathetic eye, the gaping cuts on the slopes might as easily suggest an abandoned quarry as the distant glory of the citadel. The place had an eerie, menacing feeling and echoed the words of the historian Ibn Ak Asir after he witnessed the massacre by Genghis Khan on that spring day of 1221: "They pitied no one and evil covered everything, like a cloud driven by the wind." Our archeologists, of course, had no such morbid thoughts and were happily arguing the merits of a young Swiss colleague, whose team had been digging here long enough for a slender tree to grow out of a mud hole. Its feathery top fluttered in the rain like a small green flag. The famous site of Penjikent, just across the border of Tadzhikistan, was an enormous jumble of mud walls, caves, steps, and narrow paths leading to two temple ruins. Here, the rain had brought an explosion of colors, bright red poppies and golden yarrow blooming everywhere. The warm air smelled of herbs, the river gurgled just below, there were butterflies and fluffy clouds and the muddy ruins of Penjikent were every bit as lovely as Afrasiab was not. It was all in the weather. Or a matter of personal interpretation? On one timeworn stela the runic inscription read, "O Creator. Of Life, with my people and my Khan, Alas, I did not get my fill." The regret of this young warrior, dead for centuries, touched me much like "Where have all the young men gone?" Long time passing, and the flowers, too, had fallen.

Agatha Christie, working in Nimrud with her archeologist husband Max Mallowan, once found a clay tablet buried under the threshold of a house. It represented a small dog and inscribed on it were the words, *"Don't stop to think. Bite!"* Christie wrote, "You can see it being written on the clay, and someone laughing!" I could almost hear *her* laugh, ("The little dogs and all, Tracy, Blanch, and Sweetheart, see, they bark at me.") and short of finding golden sarcophagi or winged heads, I will cherish a young soldier's regret for life not lived to the full. And small dogs, too.

In these arid regions, gardens are a delight and a legend, sung by poets and recalled in the nomad's tents. The Persian word paradise means walled garden. The Koran, created among the people of the desert, describes paradise as a celestial garden and medieval texts held that if a paradise were to be found in this world, it would be in the gardens of Samarkand. Most cities in Central Asia still allow generous space for parks, wide tree-lined avenues, and small gardens are filled with flowers and homegrown vegetables. Despite seven decades of Soviet domination, they have remained an essential element of life. Moscow imposed its language and its ways, but the very colors in the market stalls and public parks, the blooming roses in small private courtyards told of the attempt to hold on to a cultural heritage. Some men wore western suits made in Russia, but most preferred the quilted coats and the embroidered square skullcaps common in Central Asia. In the teahouses serving kabobs, cheese, piles of flatbread and sticky cakes, we were received with the standard greeting among Uzbeks: *"Salaam alaikum,"* the century-old Islamic welcome, in spite of it being banned by Moscow. Uzbekistan seemed to have no shortage of food, although people told us it was getting more expensive every day. Tashkent's two-story market offered plenty of everything, butcher stands showed long strings of sausages, chopped beef sides and some sold pig's feet, a Russian delicacy that infuriated local Muslims. Women hawked pomegranates and watermelons, scallions, radishes, tomatoes and the ubiquitous potatoes. Crowds wandered among street stalls laden with fresh vegetables, fruit, herbs, bread, cheeses, nuts, and spices that were the wonder of our Russian team members used to the meager shelves of Moscow. They wanted to buy it all, but it made little sense, as our meals were varied, tasty and more than adequate.

Away from its greenery and gardens, the Republic of Uzbekistan is highly industrialized, counting uranium, oil and natural gas among its riches. The legendary Fergana Basin, once famous for its horses, vineyards, orchards and mulberry trees, is today the most densely populated area in Central Asia. The distant grape-colored mountains still trace the horizon, but ugly villages and monstrous factories with their belching smokestacks blight the countryside. The region ranks first among those with irrigated agriculture and while still part of the USSR, produced 70 percent of the total cotton output. Cotton needs heavy fertilization and the gigantic irrigation systems rely mainly on the Syr Daria and Amy Daria rivers that once fed the Aral Sea. Together, they led to a disastrous level of pollution and the slow death of the Aral Sea, a catastrophe approaching the scale of Chernobyl. Driving through these regions, I had the terrifying sense of an unstoppable devastation, a dehumanization taking place in slow motion even as I watched.

Kazakhstan is a region four times the size of Texas and could hold half a dozen European countries in its vast plains and steppes. Together with Kyrgyzstan, its population suffered most under the forcible introduction of collective farming. While untold numbers died, more were sent to labor camps or fled into exile. Of the nearly five million horses that wandered their steppes, fewer than four hundred thousand remained. We were invited to a collective farm in Osh. Embroidered cloth spread on the grass, decorated yurts and enormous bowls of noodles, mutton and freshly baked bread. Men wore the high-peaked Kirghiz hat, girls danced in flouncy skirts, dark hair covered with small caps of silver lace. The women sold their handicraft, children shrieked on painted swings: like just another summer fair. There was however more to Osh than a fairytale name and quaint costumes. A year ago that very day, the region was torn by religious and tribal unrest, Russian troops were sent in: several hundred mosques were burnt and over three thousand people died. It had not been forgotten. Our hosts could not have been kinder, but all day we were accompanied by security personal and the Russians in our groups were silent and uneasy.

The peoples of Tien Shan, Kazakhstan and Kyrgyzstan share the same language and customs. I spoke to Turkmen and Tadziks, who are Afghans and Persians; there were Uigurs, Tatars and Kazkas with their Mongolian antecedents and Turkic tongue. A nomadic people who have nothing in common with the Russians and spoke with great bitterness of the callous policies of the Soviet government. The secret nuclear tests in the Semipalansk region poisoned the air, the water, and the very earth. Decades later, women continued to die of cancer and leukemia, their children born deformed. I became friendly with some young women in Alma Ata who were putting together a documentary film on the subject, hoping to smuggle it out of the country. All I could do was to accept some pictures, promising to show the unspeakable damage inflicted on the area and its people. If Czarist Russia's conquests aimed above all to check the English in Afghanistan and India, the Russia of our days feared the force of nationalism and set out to Russianize Central Asia in one of the bloodiest chapters in its history.

On the Kyrgyz/Kazakh border, no pretty girls greeted our caravan with bread and *kumis*. Instead, I saw a group of rugged horsemen, wearing heavy fur coats and on every rider's crupper sat an enormous eagle. When one set his bird on my arm, it grabbed the protective cloth with razor-sharp talons, the curved scissored beak almost touching my cheek, and I was glad the furious eyes were covered under the soft leather hood. Not all riders were big and strong: two white-haired old men, one in a bright green velvet coat with gold buttons, the other dressed all in black but for a red fur hat, galloped by laughing like youngsters, horses shying and birds flapping. They should have looked ridiculous, but they did not. Their people have hunted with birds of prey for thousands of years and are masters at handling the raptors. Falcons and hawks are for birds and small rabbits, but the brown Aquila they call *berkut* takes on foxes, wolves and deer. Prodigious hunters, they stoop at tremendous speed, braking smoothly to grip and gouge through eye and nerve to terrify, blind and exhaust. To my surprise, when the huge bird soared up into the skies on its six-foot wingspan, it sent out no clarion-voiced call, but emitted a thin, tinny sound, much like a young crow cawing.

I had long looked forward to a hunting story and carried a letter from the Russian embassy in Paris to the local authorities asking for their cooperation. My favorite commander ("Yu! no more!") read the letter, scowled at me, crumpled it up and tossed it away. That was that. On my own, I might have cajoled or bribed one of the big Kazakhs to spend a day with me, for they rather liked being asked and only showed reluctance when the police officers moved closer. There was no way, and I still regret not having had the chance. I did find a Russian farmer living near Lake Issyk Kul who had managed to breed falcons in captivity, so rare a feat that Saudi princes pay a royal fifty thousand dollars for a fully trained adult bird. The family happily posed with their falcons, an extra one incongruously perching on the baby's carriage. Among the smooth boulders along the shore marked with ancient petroglyphs, I saw a drawing of a human stick figure holding a bird of prey on its outstretched arm.

We arrived at the Chinese border, where our expedition was coming to an end. One more time, in the desert village of Tamaly Tas, the warm welcome waited. Entering through the low yurt door, I was met by an explosion of colors. Tapestries blazed in red, orange, yellow, gold and green, the upraised wooden floor was covered with damascene pillows, and a round space in the middle held trays with the traditional deep blue or bright orange teapots and cups. Bottles of vodka and lemonade stood among plates of mutton dumplings, noodle salad with grated carrots, cucumbers, and radishes. There were fresh and dried apricots, sweets made with nuts and honey. I saw furs and hunting gear hanging from the painted poles and stacks of folded embroidered cloth against the felt walls: here were all the trappings of a rich Central Asian culture.

All along, the Kazakh and Kyrgyz women had played an important part in the reception ceremonies and seemed to be in charge of their families. Unlike the neighboring Uzbek wives, who mostly wore the sack-like chador and walked an obedient four paces behind their men, they wore spotlessly white towering headdresses and heavy silver ornaments on richly embroidered dresses. They posed for pictures and asked about my life as a woman, in the Western world, laughing readily when something struck them as funny, as when I showed them a picture of my husband and myself riding a tandem.

One more time, the head of the newly killed sheep was offered to us, the honored guests. As always, we had rolled dice to decide whose turn it was to eat the eyes. The two helpings of that delicacy were reserved for the important people of our group, but on such occasions, our leaders were uncommonly eager to pass on the honor. We had all learned to swallow quickly and think of something else.

(I tried to avoid the memory of my Swiss friend Idh, who once swallowed a live slug believing it would cure her stomach ulcer.)

Before we left, an older woman burned fragrant herbs on a round iron altar, wafting the smoke over us to clear our minds of all evil thoughts. The altar, with a small, cutout iron horse standing on its edge, looked uncannily like a round bronze lamp, dating back to the fourth century BC. I had seen in the museum of Bishkek.

I left Kazakhstan treasuring another, rather different memory. Michael was an archeologist at the University of Alma Alta and, voluntarily attached to our expedition, he joined us whenever time and interest allowed him. A Cossack, well over six feet tall, with dark hair and gray eyes, he would arrive in his own jeep or, just as often, trot in on a big gray horse. The two of us worked together for about a week, photographing odds and end. He would pick me up early mornings, sling my camera bag over his shoulder and give me a lecture on whatever he had planned for me to see. They were good days, spent away from the crowd and with someone who knew the area. He understood what I was looking for and needed pictures for this own work. We drove around, found our ruins or stones, unpacked our lunch, sat and talked.

On our last evening, he joined us for the farewell party. The expedition had reached its end and we were all going home. After dinner, walking down to the stables together, he looked at me and said, "Will you come with me?" Something in me moved and before I took time to think, I said "Yes." He lifted me up on the saddle, swung up behind me and we left the compound. As simple as that. It was a moonlit night, his arm held me close, I felt his heart beat and I did not ask where to or how long. We rode through the steppe until we came to a small wooden cabin. He held my hand, walked me inside and asked, "Madonna, will you stay?" I looked at him. "Yes, until tomorrow." There were oil lamps, a fire and soft furs on the bed. It was a night without blemish or guilt, a night that did not belong to anyone or anything but us.

When morning came, we rode back through a wakening world and into reality. Back to Alma Ata, the city that boasts four thousand acres of green space, parks and tree-lined squares, where most of us took the flight to Moscow. Our expedition had traveled far together and once we parted here, not many of us would meet again. There were last-minute exchanges of addresses, hugs and a few tears or a helpless shrug. An elderly Japanese professor held on to a flowered rug, a French colleague carried her old Kyrgyz saddle bought from a horseman in Osh. When my Russian friend—the one who sang—turned to embrace me, he carefully put down his prize possession: an enormous bag of bright red strawberries, bought that morning on the market in Alma Ata.

MONGOLIA

I knew that UNESCO was preparing the Altai/Nomad expedition through Outer Mongolia. It had been two years in the making and so often postponed that many of the team were ready to give up on it. I had spent much of this time in Saché restoring the mill and the work was just about done. It was 1998. Sag Harbor was furnished and beautiful, Laura was in college and I was alone and getting restless, again. When the call came to join the last expedition along the fabled road, I could not have been happier. It was a journey I would long remember.

Imagine a pair of cranes flying low, a wolf loping over the hill in the same direction, a line of horsemen riding flat out, like on an ancient marble frieze. The sweet absinth fragrance of artemisia, the silky-leaved herb that grows in desert and steppe alike. The great silence and the rustle of heavy-seeded grasses sighing against the ceaseless chirring of myriads of tiny jumping grasshoppers.

I am glad to have these memories, for my first impressions were very different. Coming from Xian, one of the Silk Route starting points in China, our expedition spent a few days in Oulan Bator, where a first view of Mongolia's capital offered a jarring contrast of concrete and felt. The gray city blocks and the ornate, but grim government buildings fashioned in the Soviet image belong to a different age from the low, round dwellings made of felt and lattice that dotted the outskirts. Straight roads cutting one another at right angles versus narrow mud roads winding through small gardens. The squares were impressive, ringed with party buildings and minister's offices, and there were museums—mainly showing People's Republic Party Art—an opera house, and a few monasteries that survived the communist purge. Overall, I agreed with a travel brochure that advised me, "When traveling to Mongolia, do not bother to spend much time in Oulan Bator."

My real aggravation was the rudeness among its inhabitants. We had arrived at the occasion of Naadam, the National Festival, and people were getting ready to watch the parade. To keep the crowds on the sidewalks, police officers shouted, shoved, and wielded sticks or leather whips. I tried to cross a wide avenue when a guard grabbed my shoulder and pushed me hard in the chest. I showed him my official UNESCO press badge and my cameras, pointing to the group of government officials I was to join, but he shook me, *spat* at me, and shouted "TURRIST!" I tried again, whereupon he actually poked me with an electric cattle prodder! I could not believe it: we were guests of the government and this oaf tried to stun me! It did not bode well for ordinary mortals. I gave up, stayed on my side of the street, and decided to watch the parade from there. In any case, I did not expect much more than the usual display of shopkeepers and clerks dressed up in national costumes.

I was wrong. The Mongols sat on their horses as the nomads they were, their high-boned broad faces and long black hair blending inherently with the jeweled headdresses and necklaces, the embroidered silk coats, the glossy furs covering heads and shoulders. For centuries, Mongol aristocrats set the mode in Eurasian weaponry, dress, and jewelry, and here it showed. The riders wore cuirasses of fine hide, their small horses were protected by armor, the saddles and bridles inlaid with hammered silver and colored stones. The sabers and knives, the spears with hooks and the lassos to pull enemies from their horses looked utterly natural on these men, who carried them unheedingly. As they rode past, led by a fur-hatted Genghis Khan and ignoring the crowd, these horsemen did not look like a neighborhood folklore group dressed up as warriors for the day. They looked real. Real, beautiful and terrifying.

I watched the races and wandered around the fairground. Families were buying anoraks, goldfish in a bottle, a handful of nails, half a dozen knives, a string of beads or a pair of felt boots. Young men on horseback swaggered through the crowd, who made way, and I could see why. Two of them rode straight for me: one hooked his boot under my camera bag and before I knew it, I was lying on my back in the dirt, while they galloped away, shouting with laughter. People helped me up, but my impression of the inhabitants of Oulan Bator on that first day was not exactly a great one. It never got much better. Valuable books were stolen from our bus in the hotel parking lot. Coming back to the hotel, I was met by a police officer who handed me my *light meter*: someone had lifted it from my bag. I was grateful, but it proved that our every step was watched and I did not want to think of what they did to the thief. Another time, someone tried to cut the strap of my bag while we were walking down a busy street, but our Turkish delegate—director of the Istanbul museum—jumped on the man and drove him off. Waiting in line for a telephone call at the post office, a huge Mongol standing behind me literally pushed me facedown on the counter, leaned over me, elbows on my back, and took my place. The female employee watched me being squashed and helped the bully. That was Oulan Bator and these were only my personal experiences. "It is not an auspicious beginning," as one of my Chinese colleagues assured me.

We had arrived at a time of appalling economic troubles for Mongolia. The country lacked everything from money and fuel to flour and spare parts. It was not easy to send an unwieldy convoy of several buses and a dozen cars with foreign scientists and organizers, media and technical staff on a six-week journey covering about fifteen hundred miles over untracked steppes and mountains. To have organized a complex and costly excursion such as ours was a measure of the prestige the government attached to the event. Starting from Hovd in Mongolia's westernmost tip bordering on Siberia, we would traverse the Altay and Hangayn mountain ranges, crossing the spectacular Zagastain and Solongat passes before skirting the Gobi desert and emerging on the high grassy plateau of Tsetserleg into the valley of Orhon, then on to Harhorin and finally work our way back to the capital. Travel would be slow, nomad style, and we would mostly sleep in tents and yurts, here called *gers*. We had all provided the usual certificate of good health (a reminder that one of our scientists had died onboard the Fulka), but this time we were specifically asked for "patience with taxing conditions."

Leaving Oulan Bator, we started on a journey of ordeal and enchantment. Our expedition promised to travel to areas inaccessible to foreigners and often to Mongols themselves, and it did. Staring at a map, I had been hard put to imagine the rolling, treeless steppes that stretch from the Hungarian highlands to the Great Wall of China, to picture the nomad's routes that crisscross them or the lives of those who live there. As we flew east in two small planes, several of the rickety seats were broken and I had only half a seatbelt, reminding me of some domestic Russian flights. We had left before dawn and I leaned in my window seat, peering down at the haze over endless green-brown hills and some striped fields. Wondering happily, if a little drowsily, what would be awaiting us down there this time. Hovd welcomed us enthusiastically. A small, rather Russian-looking town with whitewashed houses and brightly painted doors, it sat surrounded by mountains and rocky desert. The two hotels were bare but the people were friendly and the food was very good. Eating rice with meat and plenty of vegetables, followed by fruit and cakes, I am afraid we took it rather for granted at the time and had no real inkling of the effort it represented. The usual speeches, a theater performance, folklore dances and a black-and-white flickering film about the glory of Mongol past (including horror scenes of molten lead being poured in an enemy chieftain's eyes) followed the governor's dinner, after which we slept in the comfort of a hotel room for the last time in quite a while.

We took our seats in buses and cars: our real journey began. As soon as we left town, there were no more paved roads and no traffic. Someone in the expedition later mentioned that in the first three weeks of travel we had passed six vehicles coming in the opposite direction. Rough dirt tracks led through mountainous countryside where the wildflowers, among them vast fields of edelweiss, were breathtaking. I tried to make the driver stop, but this was the beginning of a very long journey and people were in no mood to stop every time I saw a pretty flower. My Canadian college Angèle, with whom I shared room, cabin and ger on this trip, felt the same frustration, but it took days of arguing before we were allowed to travel in one of the security jeeps. The police officers did not appreciate our sudden *"STOP, STOP!"* either, but they were a little easier to manage than a bus. On this, as on all the expeditions, I was grateful for the wonderful opportunities, but would deal with the frustration of being told where and when to go, of our own crowd getting in the way of my picture

If UNESCO chose Mongolia as the country most characteristic of the steppe, it was no coincidence. The Mongols are today perhaps the one of the last truly nomadic people in the world. We entered a world where perceptions of time were radically different from ours, where the notion of movement was built into people's very existence. When the Russian-led government forced them to live in settlements, the nomads often set up their gers in the courtyard rather than moving into the apartments allotted to them. If in most other desert lands this kind of life was rapidly fading away, here in Mongolia the trend was to return to it.

The people of the steppes do not just pack up one morning to wander off aimlessly; they live and move with their animals. Their territory is linked to seasonal pastures, and the tribes ask each other for the rite of passage through a given stretch of land at a fixed time of the year. Every spring, when flowers color the grasslands, nomad families follow a traditional pattern. The women put on new cotton dresses, the gers and their contents are loaded on camels, and everybody sets out for the summer pastures. It is a most conservative and regular routine, changing only with drought or disaster. A classic image of men on horseback leading, women and babies swaying in their saddles to the camel's rhythm, goats, yaks and cattle guarded by children and young adults, dogs barking, bells clanging to the clicking sound of hoofs.

Animals are selected to make the best use of the various feeding grounds. Children herd goats and sheep, which do not stray far from the gers. Horses and yak cannot graze where goats and sheep have cropped and are the responsibility of adults. Camels are the more ornery sort and may wander off by themselves as far as a hundred kilometers away from their owners in search of food. When autumn ends, someone sets out to look for them; it may take him as long as a month, but he finds them eventually before winter sets in. "How cold does it really get and what happens to the animals in winter?" I asked a Mongolian friend. "It gets minus 45 Celsius on an average day in January." was the answer. "It is very dry, but you try to shake hands and you are stung by an electric current. There are shelters for the little ones, but horses, yak and camels fend for themselves. They dig for grass, put their heads down, and wait for winter to pass. If the blizzards are fierce and the ground freezes too deep, they die in the thousands."

I found great beauty in the broad, golden-brown faces with their high cheekbones and almond eyes narrowed against sun and wind. I also saw the traces of those winters etched in the handsome faces of even the younger people; the skin often creased early, cheeks wind-burned with red patches. To us, all were friendly and truly hospitable. An odd mixture of being shy and fearless, women and children would watch me for a while and then suddenly ask to look through my cameras or to have their picture taken. In return, they showed me their treasures, a plastic bracelet, a grasshopper in a tiny basket or a calendar showing a palm-fringed beach with bright blue water. Wherever our expedition stopped, people brought gifts of meat and cheese, sometimes even spring onions, none of which they could afford, certainly not for so large a crowd. We made sure to return their generosity, because we knew they had little to spare, but I never had the feeling that the smiles were forced. The gestures were so natural, so genuine, we could only accept gratefully, awed by such generosity. In a ger I met a family of seven playing host to another family of five *it did not know*. "They are from town and wanted to be in the country for a few days," said the head of the household. "They came our way, so we took them in." Hospitality and sharing were a way of life, and it led me to reassess our Western values.

Our standard meal was boiled mutton, served in its broth or, a rare treat, with noodles. For a while, the joke around the camp went "Guess what's for dinner," but it wore off rather quickly. UNESCO and the government paid for our food, but nomads do not grow and harvest; these people had neither bread nor vegetables and sometimes I felt we descended on them like a swarm of locusts. We adjusted to eating mutton and dairy products three times a day. There was usually hot water to make tea, on rare occasions round flat cakes made of flour and water. To preserve the meat, it was air-dried in strips and strung outside the gers like laundry on a line. When I asked if they ever roasted or broiled, the answer was, "Roasting is for rich people." Our day started with the turbid, greasy smell of a whole sheep, innards et al., unsalted, bobbing and boiling away in a huge, uncovered copper kettle, right outside our ger. My stomach gently heaving, I waved back at the smiling women stirring that pot-au-feu with a long wooden pole. At six in the morning, on my way to the outhouse.

Most families make a variety of cheeses and distill the mare's milk into the local drink called *kumis*. The milk is beaten until it begins to bubble like new wine, turns sour, and ferments. The butter extracted, one is left with a nourishing drink. It is the nomad's staple and features in every ceremony. Winning horses are anointed with *kumis* and each time we resumed our travels, mare's milk was sprinkled in our wake to wish us a safe journey. Every guest is offered—and would never dream of refusing—a welcome cup. I like *kumis*, but one had to be careful for it could be mild and light or so strong it knocked you flat. I have seen it distilled to resemble clear vodka. "It greatly delights the inner man," reported the friar William of Rubruck in the thirteenth century to Louis IX, who had sent him on a mission through Mongolia. "It intoxicates those who have not a very good head. It also greatly provokes urine." All true. We soon learned not to drink the entire bowls proffered while we were on the road, for it made for awkward stops ("not again!?") for the entire caravan on the open steppe without a sheltering bush or tree. "Boys to the left, girls to the right, five minutes for all." Most of us also paid, at one time or another, the morning-after price for enjoying the crystal-clear version and I can attest to the fact that our inner Mongols were often delighted and could get very rowdy. It seemed to bring out their love for Kurash wrestling—practiced since the days of Tamerlane—performed in bulky underpants and accompanied by loud grunts and bellows. The winner stalked around in high-kneed steps, arms spread like wings, and crowed like a fighting cock.

Most areas we traveled were seasonal grazing grounds, routes unmarked except by bleached animal skeletons sprinkling slopes and fields. As we drove for weeks on end, each car traced its own pattern on the land. We skidded over rocks and pebbles in desert sand, bumped over shrubs and old tree stumps, slowly climbed mountain slopes, splashed through ditches, forded streams and trundled across plains. The skies were high and endless, cloud shadows drifting over pale green hills. Storms gathered, emptying out black rain clouds over the small white gers, the horses shying and children running to tie up whatever ran around loose. Camels, goats, sheep, yak and horses filled the grasslands in patches of white and brown, and teams of bullocks pulled heavy wooden-wheeled cards transporting precious tree trunks. The days passed in monotonous contentment, small events followed each other in a natural sequence like sunrise and sunset, and it was enough.

Moving at our slow pace through stunning landscapes, wrapped in the ringing silence that reigns in much of this country, I sometimes entered a tranquil, flowing state of mind that allowed me to put my current medley of self-pity and near-delight into some perspective. I wondered about this undefined need, this selfish pleasure that so readily discounted bad experiences, physical discomfort, even my children's loneliness in exchange for a new country, a new morning promising unfamiliar sounds, smells and colors. Why did I often find such peace of mind, happiness even, during my wanderings? Why, since early childhood, had I always preferred to read about people— often long dead—traveling unknown roads in remote regions, rather than enjoy a good tale about my next-door neighbors? Ruminating here on the Mongolian steppes, I accepted the fact that it is in my nature to want to climb the next hill. That I love answering the inner summons, that I love the scramble, every time, and that it was not likely to change. I am not alone in this. Almost every traveler's journal has a sentence wondering why do we go, what does it bring us, and what does it do to others? Most arrive at the same, self-centered answer: we have to set out on the journey or live with the regret.

Our passage through the Great Lake region was a rather special experience. Although the scenery was beautiful, with more edelweiss covering the slopes, it also snowed, in July. At Durgun Nuur Lake, the tent pegs had to be planted in loose gravel on the beach. It was very windy, our tents were flimsy, and so were the blankets. We were cold and no one slept much. Awakened by strange rumbling sounds right above my head, I crept out of my sleeping bag and noticed an opening between the tent and the ground: someone had dug a hole in the gravel. I lifted the cloth a little more and carefully peeped out of the slit. Leaning against the tent, standing motionless, was a horse and what I had heard was the rumbling of its guts! Its rider noticed me immediately, as he was hanging head down from his horse and we were literally staring at each other *upside down*. He broke out laughing at my stupefied face, swung back up, and galloped off. Later that night the wind blew away several of the tents, scattering people's belongings all over the beach. Within minutes, while we were still scrambling to find our possessions, riders came galloping out of nowhere. Young boys, they never got down from their horses but simply reached out, picked up what they could, and took off again. I saw some holding on to women's underwear, blankets, a camera, and a backpack. They were like the flock of crows that swooped down each spring on my cherry tree on the very moment the fruit was ripe, and stripped it clean in minutes. There was no way to follow them or even accuse anyone the next day.

Lumbering through mountains and deserts, some of our vehicles inevitably broke down. We all expected that, but the problem was that it usually happened to our food truck, an old Red Army sterilization unit, a kind of chuck wagon that dragged its own oven, stoked with wood, and cooked our mutton stew while it was barreling along. The whole thing looked like an army kitchen from the Crimean war. It also produced our hot water. Whenever it got stuck crossing a river or toiling up a mountain, we would only know about it when it did not show up with our supper. On those nights, we made a fire, boiled water, shared teabags and pre-cooked noodles, while everybody brought out their reserves of cookies and chocolate. One afternoon, the truck was two days late. We could not move on without it, as it might never catch up with us again. Stuck in the middle of nowhere, we washed our clothes in the river or caught up on our notes. Some people were sleeping, others playing chess, but we were all getting rather hungry. At last, a truck came lurching uphill but to our surprise, it was not ours: out stepped a smuggler offering Russian military rations. The dates on the cans had expired several years ago, but we bought them all. I confess I did not risk the cabbage and beans, but gobbled plums and pineapple jam with the best of us. The driver then produced some bottles of whiskey with Johnny Walker labels and although it was anyone's guess what was in it, we bought those too. The kitchen truck took another day to arrive.

We were of course not always freezing or sweating or in difficulties. We spent two luxurious nights in traditional gers at a tourist encampment pitched at a riverbank in beautiful Ih Uul Sum. Each ger contained five beds arranged along the wall, painted tables and stools, a cupboard, felt rugs, a washstand and a stove. Young women served hot meals from an adjacent trailer and actually *grilled* the muttonchops as a special treat. For breakfast, there was fresh fish from the river, and I was among the lucky few to get a hot shower.

Early morning on the grassy plateau of Tsetserleg. I sat on a rock and watched the morning sun with its soft green light and long shadows slowly enforcing the colors and shapes in the valley below. Nomad families build their gers in small groups of two or three, most are simple and unadorned, the painted doors faded and the felt gray with use. For us they had put up a good dozen, brand-new, beautiful and comfortable. Standing there grouped together, the painted wooden doors showing bright red against the pristine felt, they formed a colorful hamlet. Our hosts were busy cooking breakfast, smoke rising out of the narrow black stacks. People in long purple, red or pink robes were walking back and forth, and from where I sat, the scene looked like a miniature behind-glass painting I had bought at a market stall. I walked down the hill and, entering the picture, I drank my kumis, spooned noodles in my stew, added a sprinkle of my small private salt reserve, and was *comblée*.

Among the "people of the felt-walled tents," as Genghis Khan called them, the horse is essential to survival. The center of the nomad's household, their number and quality represent a family's wealth. In Mongolian epics, the horse, not the shaman, gives wise advice to the hero in trouble. Children ride with their parents before they walk, at the age of two or three they manage by themselves and by the time they are seven they attend to the herds. It all comes natural to them, while I learned some things the hard way. Not realizing that horses kicked *sideways*, I stood innocently next to some, when a flashing hoof struck out without warning and sent me flying. I was lucky to get away with the blue-black imprint on my thigh, rather than a fractured femur.

Adolescents, the "young riders," all own their own horses and could not imagine otherwise, but many are now also tempted by the saddles of motorcycles. Heavy silver bikes roared across the steppe or stood incongruously parked against the felt wall of a ger. Besides being a lot faster, the bikes have become a status symbol, and it looks like they are here to stay. Horse-riding championships are restricted to five- to twelve-year-olds, as no one over that age needs to prove their skills. I saw those children, sitting astride their horses without saddle or stirrup, tearing away over the steppe. When a boy was badly thrown, everybody gathered around the ger to find out how seriously he was hurt. I watched an old man massage the child's body and stroking his head with an eagle's feather. He also measured it with a ribbon he would take to the nearest shaman, about twenty miles away, so the witchdoctor would be able to treat the pain from a distance. When I left, the boy rested quietly on pillows, an elderly woman sitting next to him, humming what sounded like a lullaby and holding his hand.

The people of Undursant had organized the yearly *urga*, the roundup. Urga is both the ancient name of Mongolia and of the long pole with a noose at the end that herders use as a lasso. (They also thrust it into the ground outside their ger as a sign they want privacy.) It was a great sight. Hundreds of horses were running back and forth, the nomads on their own small animals herding them.

Like cowboys in a Western, I thought. Well, not quite. These men, dressed in brightly colored tunics with silk sashes, trousers tucked into felt boots and narrow-brimmed hats on long dark hair belonged nowhere else but here, in a faraway and magic country where this scene, on these endless steppes, under this vast arc of sky, has played out since time remembered.

Surrounded by horses, riders and steppes, people talked horses, riders and steppes. We kept picking up rumors about an exclusive wildlife reserve with some very rare inmates. Talking it over with Angèle, we decided to do an article on the side. About four thousand years ago, there was a race of wild horses running free in Mongolia: the very horse one finds painted on the cave walls of Altamira and Lascaux. In the fifteenth century, Johann Schiltberger recorded one of the first sightings on his trip in Mongolia as prisoner of the Mongol Khan. In 1881, the Russian naturalist and explorer General Nikolai Przhevalsky mounted an expedition to find them, after which the breed became known as Przewalski's horse. For decades after, Carl Hagenbeck and other dealers in animals organized raids. Killing the adults, they captured the foals, strapping them to camel's backs for further transport to European zoos. By the beginning of the twentieth century, the great nomad that had found its way from Europe to Asia was mainly found behind bars. After 1945, only two captive populations remained in the zoos of Munich and Prague. The Germans shot the most valuable group in the Ukrainian reserve during the occupation, and the ones in the United States had died out.

Most "wild" horses, such as the American Mustang and the Australian Brumby, are actually feral horses, descended from escaped domesticated animals that adapted to life in the wild. In contrast, Przewalski's horse had never been successfully domesticated and remained a truly wild animal. The *Tahki*, to use its Mongol name, is stocky in comparison to the domesticated Mongolian horse and has shorter legs, often faintly striped. The dun colored velvety coat varies from dark brown to yellowish-white on the belly. It has an intelligent head, a white Roman nose, a black tail, and an upright bristly mane. The nomads have always revered the animal, as it represents all that they hold dear: freedom, solidarity to the clan, hardiness and endurance. Since Mongolia shrugged off the Soviet occupation in 1990, the country has reinstated many old national symbols, the *Tahki* among them.

At the time of our journey, there had not been a Przewalski's horse seen in its original habitat for over twenty-five years. In 1975, a Dutch couple started a program of exchange between zoos and a breeding program of their own and the Mongolian government had recently set aside a large area as a reserve for the experiment. Sixteen released horses passed their first winter, with temperatures of minus 45C, and in spring, a young stallion was born.

Angèle and I took advantage of a day of rest and bribed our driver to take us the nearly hundred kilometers to the reserve. We had no introduction and Baldir Damdin, the guardian, had strict orders to let *no one* near the animals. Angèle stressed her long and arduous voyage from Canada to Khustain Nuruu to no avail. When I tried the Dutch angle, however, the stern face under the embroidered domed hat cracked a wide smile: Oh, you are from Holland, like Inge and Jan Bouman! The Dutch couple who had saved and brought over the very horses now grazing somewhere behind us, protected by electric wiring from wolves. And from people like us. For the horses to survive, explained Damdin, there should be as little contact as possible with humans and none with domesticated horses. Once they were self-sufficient, they would be set free on the steppes. Under repeated, *"exceptionally!"* we approached one of the three enclosures and got our story. I took some rather distant pictures, but later visited the Boumans in Holland, who were happy to have direct news from Mongolia and let me take close-ups of some protégés peacefully grazing in a very domestic Dutch meadow. A census in 2005 accounted for 1,500 *Tahki*, of which 248 roamed in the wild: a miniscule down payment on our immense debt to nature.

In the towns, our team was parceled out among local hotels. Our drivers would take us and we were not given a choice. It was not an easy thing to house us all, for now about thirty local interpreters and "technical personal," i.e., police, had joined us, which brought our group to nearly one hundred souls. The town people were polite, but remained aloof, and guards accompanied us everywhere. I was constantly aware of an undercurrent of latent violence, discussions easily turning to arguments. The overall atmosphere of control and suspicion in the cities was very different from what we encountered among the gers, where hospitality, laughter, and free questioning went hand in hand. The nomads on the steppes had a naturally free, if at times fierce appearance, whereas in the towns these same people, often dressed in ill-fitting Western clothes, tended to look like country bumpkins.

One day, our driver found our little group—the Canadian journalist Angèle Dagenais, the American photographer Nick Wheeler, the British writer John Lawton, and myself—a wonderful old hotel. We always had the same driver, who knew us well by now, the owner of the hotel was a friend, and our jeep arrived a little before the rest of the caravan. We loved the place: a large room painted red with wonderful golden dragon-and-flower motives, two enormous beds built into the wall like small rooms and covered with pillows. I gave a woman some money for firewood and soon we were happily sitting around the fireplace, congratulating ourselves on our good luck. It lasted exactly thirty-three minutes: in came some officials and turned us out. The hotel owners had no right to accept us without specific permission and we had no right at all. We ended up sleeping in a cold schoolroom on narrow cots and our driver was yelled at for taking the initiative. Our Dream Room went to the only married and rather boring couple on our team, who looked at all that golden-red glory without great enthusiasm and I was sorely tempted to ask them for the firewood money.

For several days, our expedition pitched tents near Harhorin and the ruins of Karakorum. Ancient capital of the Mongol Empire,

Karakorum was an important intersection on the Silk Roads, a lively cosmopolitan town where Muslims, Buddhists and Christians met, trading in Arabic, Chinese and various European languages. In its days of glory, the Khan's palace boasted a fountain made of silver in the shape of a tree, devised by William Buchier, a Parisian sculptor. It had "at its roots four lions of silver, all belching forth with white mare's milk." (I wondered a little about all those people drinking their kumis straight from the source and being innerly delighted.) An enormous stone turtle, weighing several tons, still sat in the prairie nearby. Erected in the thirteenth century to protect the site, it saw the city flourish, destroyed and rebuilt whenever wars passed its way. It watched when, finally, the palaces, temples and schools returned to grassland.

Buddhism arrived in the sixteenth century, and the monks built the Erdenezuu monastery from the rubble of the old capital. Today the monastery complex, surrounded by a brick wall with 102 white stupas, stretches a quarter of a mile in each direction. It was a magnificent sight. Once, three hundred gers stood inside the wall, together with sixty-two temples where a thousand monks chanted the ancient six-syllable manta "Om mani padme hum," reflecting the close links between Mongolian and Tibetan Buddhism. Both incorporate elements of Shamanism, which survived in many forms. Skilled in divination and healing, taking the white warts of the hallucinogenic Fly Agaric to fall into a trance during which "his soul flies away," the shaman has secured his superior place within the tribes. We regularly passed Shamanist shrines, usually a cairn, containing animal bones, rusting tin cans, old bottles and branches fluttering with feathers or strips of cloth. Our driver always made some of us walk three times around it and added some odd item to the pile to ensure a safe journey.

During the communist purge that tried to eradicate religion in the 1930s, hundreds of monasteries were destroyed and untold Buddhist monks brutally slaughtered. In these hills, the bleached skeletons and skulls lying about thinly veiled by grasses were not just those of cattle. Erdenezuu monastery was now again a place of worships, and we took part in a noisy celebration where crowds waved banners and monks dragged wooden wagons covered with red cloth. Lamas wearing intricate yellow headgear blew eight-foot copper trumpets that looked like Swiss alphorns and produced mournful sounds, clashing with the clanging of cymbals, ringing of bells and beating of drums. I also finally heard the rare phenomenon of overtone singing called *khoomei*, the "solo in two voices," which Mongol peoples practice. The singer simultaneously produces two sounds: a high eerie fluting and a sort of long-drawn low growl. It is as if they bring out the rainbow colors of the voice, unearthly bell-like tones floating over a deep rumble. It was an awesome sound. Priests use the chanting in meditation and as a healing tool, and I could imagine the powerful impact under such circumstances. On our day, however, the sun was shining, there was the brazen clamor of competing instruments, and colored banners were tugging and flapping in the breeze. Everybody seemed to have a wonderful time pulling the chariot around and around the white walls, singing and smiling and bowing to the Golden Stupa. I know I did.

I like Buddhist temples; the carved roofs, the red and green tiled gate guarded by stone lions, while inside wait the ancient scrolls, the colored silks, the smell of burning juniper incense, and Buddhas in all shapes and sizes. In Erdenezuu carved dragons, clambering up tall columns, watched over a golden, eight-foot tall, seated Buddha. The butter lamps smoked, blackening the frescoed walls, the chants rose to the roof and in the dim light, the figures clothed in oxblood robes created a superb image. When not praying, the monks seemed delighted to talk and answer our questions. They told me how for decades local people had buried many of the temple treasures and were now bringing them out of hiding. I spoke to monks who had survived the purges. Rather old and frail, they were nevertheless intent on reminding young acolytes of the monastery's history and their own. I was amused to see that the lama's spirituality did not preclude a little entrepreneurship: I could take all the pictures I wanted outside, but was charged five dollars a *minute* to take my camera inside the monastery. Twice the amount bought me their goodwill and a very generous measure of their time.

From Karakorum, our journey almost over, we descended to the plains. Birds and frogs sounded in the early mornings, the evening light was transparent, and the breeze bowed the willows along the marshes. The steppe wore a magnificent mantle of red and yellow flowers, or turned a soft mauve that blended into khaki toward the distant hills. It was hard to imagine that so gentle a scene would soon lie buried again under ice and snow, that people and animals would struggle to survive, waiting for another spring. In these vast expanses, I had been gripped by a sense of the primeval, of an infinite space where double rainbows described a full semicircle in the open sky and herds of wild horses ran far and free. Days, years and centuries go by and nothing changes. I had seen countries and cultures stranger to my own, but in Mongolia I sometimes felt that if I would continue to walk the endless grasslands to their distant horizon I would, one beautiful morning, simply tumble of the edge of this flat earth.

THE UNRAVELING

Our marriage was slipping through my fingers like a rope of sand. If there had been a real issue, we might have had a chance to work out something, but there was nothing tangible to fight. One cannot hold someone who does not blame you for anything, but simply does not want to be married anymore. Among the warning signs of wear: the growing absences and a lack of intimacy when we were together. We rarely quarreled and if I insisted, his attitude often was "I don't want to talk about it" or "Now is not the time." Nothing was resolved, and it only furthered the distance. While trying to hold on, I also watched it happen.

I do not think Laura realized at the time how final the separation was. Growing up she had often questioned her father's absences—legitimate enough—and may simply have thought that they were growing longer. Which they did. Moreover, was it that final? Stanley and I did not sit down to analyze things as they were or chart a new course. He had no new companion and neither did I, so we continued a relationship based on habits, on the vague idea that for now ignorance would be easier for Laura than having parents by appointment. It must have seemed the better choice, but it was an unhealthy and often wearying situation for both of us and did not shelter her from hurt then or realization later. For several years, Stanley lived the life of his choice but continued to inhabit the edge of ours, spending time in Paris and sharing vacations, going skiing in St. Moritz or sailing the Caribbean, until Laura was old enough and I no longer needed to act as chaperone. To the outside world, I remained part of a couple. In reality, I shared and enjoyed life with my daughter, I continued to see friends, gave dinners and worked at my profession, but a vital part of me was being depleted.

Then one day, Laura was ready to leave for Sarah Lawrence College. There were no more backpacks, jackets and sneakers piled up in the hall, no young voices from the kitchen over snacks after school. In the evening, there was just me. The semi-separation had lasted for so long that the real impact took time to sink in and I continued to live for a while as if nothing had changed. It is a common human reflex to look the other way, pretending it hurts less. Until the days became something to fill, the nights grew too long, and I realized it was time to close the Paris chapter. It was interesting to see how people reacted when our final separation was rumored about. Friends stayed friends; acquaintances differed. Some divorced or widowed woman I barely knew would ask me to have a drink or lunch with a group, as if I had suddenly qualified for a club. Others, when calling to invite "us" to dinner, would chat until they had found out that Stanley would not be around and then postpone the invitation, saying "I'll call you next week." Men, sometimes the husbands of these very women, made advances, sent flowers, or invited me to some social event not shared by their wives.

Around that time, the proprietress of our apartment died and it was up for sale. We had never been able to buy it before and the opportunity was tempting. A unique space where we had lived more than twenty years as a family. It was also the reason why I did not want to continue living there on my own. The Paris closure was not immediate and the mill house in Saché was there. It would give me some time to ask what had happened this time. Had I not cared enough, fought enough? Had I become a lightweight person, like a summer novel with a short shelf life? Would I now want to stay in France? I could not see myself living all year round in small, isolated Saché, no matter how beautiful. Should I leave it all behind and start again, again? Alone?

Betty Friedan once said to me that the ties of intimacy, the bonds of truly shared self were crucial to her happiness. Crucial? Truly shared self? The intimacy of bed and the companionship of marriage are wonderful, but I had learned to create and preserve a space for myself and was not sure that I would ever want anyone in my life again on such close terms. Lillian Russell said to Djuna Barnes, "I lift up a golden Buddha and hold him in my hand; it is peace to me, happiness. I could never be lonely without a husband, but without my trinkets I could find abysmal gloom." It made me laugh, because I knew exactly what she meant. Sometimes I missed the sharing of laughter and grief, but it was the intimacy born of everyday things I missed then, not the sex or the male companionship. I have had lovers all through my life. When young and pretty, lovers for the joy of it, for looking at each other in bright sunlight or on a moonlit beach. Lovers later, because of Brazil or Mongolia, or because of Mozart, or simply because it was that kind of night. There were friends who became lovers and lovers who became friends. Few to regret and not all to remember, but I am glad of them, for I would not have liked to grow into an old woman envious of young love or embittered for never having known it.

Actually, I was bemused that I had been married three times, for I tended to think of myself as a person who could easily have stayed married to one man all my life. Instead, look what happened. Thinking of the three different men who had been at the core of my life, I realized that if they helped shape my every day, they had also played a part in shaping me. My first husband introduced me to a new country, a new way of life, but living together, he constantly undermined my self-confidence. I kept holding on to a make-believe world until I woke one morning and did not recognize the person I had become. Scared, I finally took the unknown road because it could only lead to a better place than the present.

Fred did the opposite. He broke down all defenses—fake and real—I had built up through the years and left me standing naked in the market. He then taught me to recognize and use the talents I did have. Pushing my limits ("Why don't you?") he gave me wings, showed me I could fly. And I did. It was a process of love and passionate involvement and if the breakup would leave me desolate and devastated, I ultimately found an inner strength that only the extraordinary trust we had shared could have built in me.

And the third time, the one that pays for all? I knew by then that what seems so solid today might not hold up tomorrow. Stepping young and trusting into the safe Swiss mode, I had lost my way. My marriage to Fred was built to last, but it did not. This time, a simple affair had grown into a real and enduring relationship. For my part, I saw a brilliant man and an intriguing lover, a new closeness in love and genuine affinity. I think that Stanley fell in love with me as a woman, but was also attracted to the image of the working journalist. When we founded a family I continued to work, but adjusting to the role of mother and wife, I inevitably changed. So did Stanley. We shared good and intimate years. I know that over time he felt tied down—unjustly so from my view—and we grew apart. I have seen other couples arrive at such an impasse, deal with it together and come through it with the marriage still standing. We did not.

A brilliant man, a lover and husband; a caring father in his own personal way. He continues to be a most loyal friend; he is family, I turn to him for advice and know that he will always be there. All that, yes. But also, a distinct individual not necessarily at ease within a long-term, emotional relationship, sharing each day at such close quarters.

Having reached another crossroad, I had to decide where to take my life from here. Having lived for years in different countries, speaking half a dozen languages, I realized I had none I called my own. Home was where I had made one. What did I really want to do? Stanley and I had never had any disagreements on financial matters, and I was comfortably off. Alone, no longer directly responsible or accountable to children or husband, I was free to live as I chose. The question was where and with whom. First, I said goodbye to Paris. In that last year I did a thousand things I had never found the time to do before. It was not a morbid gesture of mourning; I simply wanted to touch the things I loved about this city, so I could hold them close. Friends, places, theaters, music, gardens, glorious light and shadows perdu, solid stone and illusive image. Soon they would be memories and I a visitor.

Once, in an earlier life, I nursed the idea of settling down in India, in a sort of reverse of Paul Scott's "Staying On." For years, I held on to comforting images of a big old dilapidated house standing within its gardens, the peacock's raucous cry at dawn, the rake trailing along the gravel path and the sound of high lilting voices. "Pani hai? Ayah, chota hazari." My own small corner of Rajasthan, a place where I could grow old with someone I loved and share with friends for years to come. A kind of sidewalk painting I could step into, like Mary Poppins. But time had done its work, on India and on me. Moreover, even were I to find that magical place again, I had never seen myself stepping into it alone.

Assuming that India now had become another favorite place to revisit, there was room for other possibilities, and I kept running them through my head. Live near friends? Karen Fawcett and I had been close friends for years, sharing ups and downs. She was my neighbor in Paris and we both had homes in the United States. Since her husband died, we travel together to Asia most winters and had talked about getting a place in Vietnam or Hong Kong as a part-time home. Tempting as it was, I knew it was not the answer.

Go back to Holland? My cousins Akka and Ivy were among my favorite people in the world, I also had grown closer to my brother Dick in recent years, and I liked my native country. Still, it was very small and the weather was often depressing. For many years, my Swiss friend Idh was like a sister to me and being a Swiss citizen, it would be easy for me to move there, but we had lived very different lives. Honestly? I did not want to live there again. An embarrassment of choices? The more I turned over these fantasies in my mind, the more I recognized that none was realistic, that all along I had been evading the question: *What about my close family?*

I knew how rare a gift it was that my grown children were also my friends and their spouses truly dear to me, but we all lived thousands of miles apart. If I now chose to live near some of them, it would have to be a place where I would be content even if they moved away. I could hardly expect my children not to get a new job or move to another country—I, who had never guaranteed them where I would be at any given time. I cherished them all; I did not expect them to assure continuity or hold them responsible for my well-being, now or in the future.

What is decisive to make one really feel at home? Does it have to do with a sense of recognition, of having arrived at a sanctum, with peace of mind, happiness even? Years ago, in Deia, my son Marc asked me, "Mom, are you happy?" The question was unexpected, the word hung in the air and I probed it gently. Happy. It triggered split-second images: I saw the deck of the Rakkassa and felt the pull of her sails on a starlit night. I remembered my jeep on a narrow mountain road, facing a truck full of turbaned Afghans unwilling to back up, and myself laughing aloud, thinking of the coming argument. And yes, I saw myself at home in the kitchen, peeling apples, laughing and talking with family and friends, preparing Thanksgiving dinner.

"Happy? I repeated. "Yes, yes, of course I am happy." What I really meant was "I am content." To me, real contentment is not resignation for lack of anything better. Like hope, it is an act of will. It has to do with intelligence, reason and knowing about happiness. I do. Happiness wants personal effort, contentment is its very base, and neither comes free. I have seen it take the shape of a new love, a million dollar career or an ice cream cone, but one has to want happiness to achieve it, and maintain it with contentment.

I looked down at the serious young face of the boy who was my son. "Would you like to go for a swim?" I asked. Together we walked down the steep path to the sea and on our way back Marc showed me a secret: a lone mulberry tree growing among the rocks on the terraced slopes. We filled our wet towels with fresh leaves for the pet silk worms he kept in a cardboard box in his room and arrived home tired, hot again, and, yes, happy.

I have often missed things Mediterranean. I have never quite forgotten the first train ride from Holland through Switzerland, heading south to Italy, shortly after the war. It was almost spring, but I had left my lowland country in a freezing rain, slanting horizontally at a landscape fraught with war-winter memories. Emerging from the Simplon Tunnel, we burst into a different world. The air was soft as a caress and I saw—for the very first time in my life—mimosa bloom and lemons grow on trees. Later, living in Mallorca, all that became part of what I loved. Leaving Deia, I left behind more than my marriage; I left a way of life. For years to come, regret would color the memory of the dark red earth, the silver-green of the olive trees, the first luminous leaves of the fig, and the piercing perfume of the orange groves. Waking in the morning, my eyes would search for the missing pattern of dark beams on a whitewashed ceiling.

Should I go back? My daughter Cathy and her family lived in Mallorca. Cathy and I were very close, she had become an established photographer and we had many things in common; her husband Toni, a journalist and editor who ran a public relations office, was very dear to me. High-school sweethearts, they married young and now had two growing sons, Fabian and Juan Antonio. It would be wonderful to get to know my grandsons better. It seemed possible; we talked about it and actually started to look at properties. But I am not much good at walking backwards; here ghosts haunted every valley and we soon realized that Mallorca had never been a real option. Instead, we go to Holland, photographing small fishing villages and visiting our cousins; do a story together for *The Observer* on Gabriel Garcia Marquez, who invited us to spend a weekend with the family in his house in Barcelona, or travel through China and float down the Yangtze. Building memories.

THE HAMPTONS

What was to be decisive then, in choosing the set for the next chapter in my life?

I first saw Easthampton in the early 1970s, when Stanley and I spent a weekend with our friends Irene and Bob Towbin, who had just bought a house on West End. It was November and we arrived late at night, after driving around in circles for a good hour trying to find our way. My main impression had been of endless look-alike lanes lined with beautiful trees, but never a name. The next morning, pulling up the shades of our bedroom window, I looked at a living painting. A landscape of golden dunes flecked with snowdrifts, huge waves crashing on the beach, black jetties thrusting out into the surf and white birds sailing the winds over an immense ocean. A Winslow Homer, come to life with sound and fury. It took my breath away, and everything in me said "yes." Once, in the ancient city of Samarkand, among the turquoise-tiled domes, an old man touched my forehead in blessing: "Look well," he said. "The time will come when it gladdens your heart to remember this sight." Looking at this wild and untamed wintry beach, his blessing springs to mind.

The ocean of the Hamptons is not turquoise blue, nor is it very warm. There are no palm trees rustling in the breeze, nor coral sheltering fish of many colors, but its beaches are magnificent, wide and empty. Here the summer mist drifts, a silvery veil that covers the lone, distant figure walking a small dog. The surf lisps and whispers, sandpipers sprint like Looney Tunes in some mad race along the water's edge, and small transparent crabs flit in and out of bubbling holes on errands best known to themselves. I sit and watch the red disk rise triumphantly out of the ocean, revealing a dawn, pale-rose as the inside of a shell. In winter, snow flecks the dunes with white and storms scatter offerings of shells and frozen sea horses on the sand. I look for the migrating birds, the wild geese honking over the darkening ocean while lower, closer to the frost-white fields, skeins of ducks, necks stretching, trace their own pattern on the lilac sky.

We rented a big old house on Drew Lane, just off the beach. They were wonderful years, moving between Paris, New York and those glorious beaches. We already had an apartment in New York and since Stanley's association with Rothschild, we spent more time there. For a while, Laura attended the Montessori school in Paris and Fleming in New York. She learned to be comfortable in both worlds, building friendships that would still be strong when she in turn took her own children to those very same places. Our Paris household moved there for the summer months: the family, Vicky and Gerard, his dog and the family cat. Essie, my mother-in-law, usually spent the summer with us, enjoying herself and teaching Gerard the secrets of her matzo *brei* and special brisket. Cathy and Marc came with their families, Howard and Shirley often came on weekends, and the guest rooms were rarely empty. It was a large and lively crowd that spilled out on the beach every day.

SAG HARBOR

Toni and Cathy

Fabian

Juan Antonio

Sag Harbor was the least developed, least fashionable among the Hampton villages and had kept much of its old whaling town charm. It did not offer the ocean beaches or the great mansions with their magnificent trees, but had graceful captain's houses, mom-and-pop stores, a large library and a whaling museum housed in a Masonic temple. Moreover, oh glory, it had a harbor full of boats, a long wharf from where whalers once set out to the ocean beyond. I liked the Dutchness of the place, the low wooden or brick houses, the high blue skies with rounded masses of cumulus clouds drifting over flat land and mirrored in water nearby, every way you turned.

My affinity here was for the ocean, the old houses, the mourning doves and the clamoring, complaining gulls. They were all there, as well as family and friends. I had spent long stretches of time on Long Island and it was familiar territory. I felt good about the country and the people, about walking out of the door and spending the new day. Marc and his family lived in nearby Bridgehampton. My daughter-in-law Amelia, Peruvian and beautiful, had long become another daughter to me and I knew I was welcome, but I needed a place I could make my own.

Stanley owned a house in Water Mill, which we did not share. We continued to be on good terms and it seemed natural that he and Laura found the house for me in Sag Harbor, in the very location I had hoped. When it turned out to be somewhat ramshackle and subject to flooding, Marc—now a successful builder in his own right—simply tore it down and built me a new one as spacious and beautiful as my dream house in Rajasthan could ever have been. Only minutes' walk from Main Street, my garden sloped down to the water of the Cove. The newly planted trees soon screened off the neighbor's houses. The renovated cottage in the garden became Laura's own but, very much a city girl, unfamiliar night noises soon brought her back to sleep in the main house and we liked that just as well.

The new chapter began, living part of the year in a village on Long Island. By myself, but by no means alone. When moved to this new world, I found it filled with familiar faces. Soon Marc and Amelia built their own house just across the Cove from mine and, for the first time in years, we had a day-to-day relationship. Amelia and I grew close and Friday evening dinners became a custom; we shared movies, graduations, birthdays and holidays. I would see a small sailboat coming across the bay: my grandson Jaan and his big black dog Dingo, coming for milk and cookies. His sister Tanya showed me her poetry or her prom dress. Friends lived all around. Mat Mallow and Ellen Chesler, whose son Jon was so close to Laura, had a house in Bridgehampton, Joe and Valerie Heller lived in Easthampton and Betty Friedan a few houses down our very street. Old friends like Barbara Riboud and Sergio Tosi crossed the ocean, Larry and Edith Malkin came from nearby New York to stay for weekends, as did Farley Granger and Bob Calhoun, my close friends and travel companions for years. Therefore, the house welcomed me, the light was beautiful, and the view greeted me like an old friend.

So all was well again? By no means. I had not really come to terms with yet another broken marriage and having to rebuild my world. I slipped into a depression, at first denied. When I took the prescribed medicine, it did not help me but instead altered my behavior. I began to withdraw, had mood swings and was rude to people. I distinctly remember getting up in the middle of dinner at close friends, without excuse or explanation, and driving home. When I realized that my children were worried about me, I stopped taking the pills, faced several unpleasant truths about myself, and started to reclaim my life. Commuting between France and Long Island, I began to restore the mill in Saché, filled the Sag Harbor house with things I loved and spent more time with my children. Family, work and travel the ultimate anodyne.

LIFE NOW

Arik and Laura, Alex and Lila

Marc, Amelia, Jaan, and Tanya

Mine is a full life, an ever-changing kaleidoscope, and I enjoy most of what it shows me, although of late it seems that the images spin by faster. Maybe it is that I am slowing down, but then, how does *anyone* deal with, or put out of one's mind, two hundred thousand people perishing in tsunamis, followed by nuclear catastrophes and earthquakes? Live, in detail, color and HD on our not so small screens, are war and wonder, agony and discovery, while everyday work, family, health issues and petty concerns continue to demand our attention. September 11 has forced people to accept that the impossible can happen and the unthinkable become reality. I had learned that in my childhood, I had also buried the consciousness so I could live without fear. Now, events are no longer just my own to accept or deny. I deal with it as I can, often settling for a donation in the hope it may help others. And will ease my conscience.

I spend about half of my time in Sag Harbor, surrounded by light and water. It was the first home I moved into without a husband and everything in it is there by my choice. For a while, some of my art and favorite objects moved back and forth with me until they found the place they liked best. In Deia, the house held Spanish antiques and Indian art. The Paris apartment needed art deco, while later Saché and Sag Harbor each asked for something else. Result of collecting and travels, a Tamayo now may hang next to a Thai Buddha, small Luba figures stand near Chinese ancestor portraits or a Lempiecka look across the room at Saul Steinberg's cat and a Vietnamese ginger pot. A mixed batch, it seems to be at home, as I am. Only, at times, I look up and see something quite different from what I expected to be there. As is in life.

Shuttling between two continents can create a curious lack of continuity in the small everyday things. Joining a gym, arranging doctor's appointments, magazine subscriptions or seeing an exhibition you promised yourself are not always obvious. Books you reach for, fresh spices you are sure you just bought or clothes you counted on wearing that evening often tend to live in a closet across the ocean. I remember when Laura was small we dragged a bulky American television set back to France, so she could follow Sesame Street on the video tapes faithfully recorded by the superintendent of our New York building. Thirty years later, we again make sure the DVDs will play overseas, for *her* children.

There are some things I have never been able to resolve: some of my children are always a continent or an ocean away. I miss them, for different reasons. My stepson Foster and his wife, Mary, have both died recently, moving beyond our reach at a cruel young age. The others, grown up and with families of their own, live hundreds or even thousands of miles apart from me and from each other. Cathy and Toni live on Mallorca and continue their careers as a photographer and journalist. Of my two grandsons, Fabian has become an up and coming young chef and Juan Antonio, whom I call John Anthony, is building a reputation as a sound engineer. We do see each other, as their island is fairly close to Saché, but it is half a world away from Sag Harbor.

Laura has married Arik, a delightful young man who was born in Israel, grew up in Istanbul and attended Northwestern University in Chicago. After a fairy tale wedding at the banks of the Bosporus, which we all attended, they moved to New York and on to Los Angeles. Arik is successful in his work, and Laura, after following a career as an actor, went back to school and got a degree in psychology. They have two beautiful children, Alex and Lila, and the small family is my heart's joy. Los Angeles may be closer to Sag Harbor than to Saché, but it is still a very long way.

Marc and Amelia's house stands just across Sag Harbor Cove, minutes away from mine. With Jaan, now a naval engineer, and Tanya with a career in advertising, they are following their path, but we keep in close touch. Amelia is a successful real estate broker. Of all, theirs is the only family that lives close to me for months at the time. That is, when *I* happen to be *there*. Sometimes it reminds me of Rubik's cube; I just can't seem to get all of us to turn the same color at the same time.

We do care, and we do get together. Summer belongs to the Hamptons, and Thanksgiving has become a sort of Sag Harbor tradition, when friends join family for a long weekend of cooking, eating and catching up. Children and grandchildren arrive from California, New York and Spain, and I could not imagine that day without them. Stanley brings his young son Paul from a second marriage; Fred's daughter Laura may join us, as does his widow Annie, as the friend she has become. The ages run from Alex and Lila, leaving a trail of toys and high, swooping children's voices, through young adults like Jaan, Tanya, Fabian, John Anthony and their companions, to the grown-ups and to myself, as the aged matriarch I have become. Everybody lends a hand, cleaning silver, setting tables, cutting, chopping, basting and stirring. I sit in my Chinese armchair next to the fireplace in the kitchen, sip my wine and watch it all. The house smells of baking, cooking and roasting, of tangerines and spiced wine. As always, the *who's who* tends to confuse newer acquaintances, but I look around the room and think how right it feels and the only regret is for the growing list of friends who are no longer with us. Among them Joe Heller, Marit Allen, Boris Carmeli, both Farley Granger as well as Bob Calhoun, Betty Friedan, Dallas Ernst and most recently, Catherine O'Neill.

Saché is still my other home, where I spend several months at the time. When I moved there by myself, I was well aware of what it would take to ready it for everyday living. After the breakup of my latest marriage, I had no great desire to restore yet another house, to struggle with masons, old stones, beams, furniture and gardens, but I ended up spending two years anyhow, making the main house comfortable and turning the mill into a bed-and-breakfast. Famous Balzac, sitting on our riverbank, once mused, "Imagine three mills built on their separate, charming islets adorned with clusters of trees, in an expanse of water. A valley like an emerald bowl in whose depth the Indre meanders in sinuous curves." He was right; they look beautiful. They also demand constant maintenance. For years, the river was mostly left to pass unhindered through the sluice gates, relentlessly scouring the walls and doing serious, albeit invisible, damage. During the restoration, frogmen reported cavernous holes that took literally tons of concrete to fill. It was the stuff of nightmares to imagine that solid-looking, monumental structure tottering on its undermined foundations.

Gerard, our Paris jack-of-all-trades, followed me to the country. He worked hard at the restoration and when we decided to open a bed-and-breakfast in the mill, he took it on with great gusto, which was something I was not prepared to do. He lives there full time now, and without someone like him, it would be difficult for me to leave for months at the time. Living with a French employee who has been part of the household for forty years brings its own situations. The first written account of the mill, chronicled in the late fourteen hundreds, was a disagreement between the miller and the tax collector. Six hundred years later, Gerard has the time of his life arguing with the local mayors, water authorities or neighbors, as well as lording it over the guests, the help, and at times, myself. *Plus que ça change.*

However, he knows how to repair anything that breaks down and charms the B/B guests, who send him Christmas cards and come back. As I am writing this I hear, somewhere below my window, a young couple from Vermont trying to check in. The husband explains earnestly that he is an important person at Ben & Jerry's, which leaves my man nonplussed. *Beeen and Cheerriis'?* As always, they come to an understanding and the clients are happily ensconced in their room. Along with regular French clients (yes, we do have a countess) and American ice cream royalty, we have accommodated Australian cattle breeders, German scientists and Dutch people on a bicycle tour, Belgians who made our life miserable, some very proper Swiss, and a Spanish antique dealer visiting the local *brocantes*. All confirming Gerard's set view of the outside world. It takes all kinds to fill a mill.

Life in that little corner flows along quietly; the only changes have been in the climate pattern. It has rained more than usual and the river floods the fields more often, while summer temperatures reach near-tropical heights. The Indre shrinks, the local cormorant dives from emerging rocks I never knew were there and a young heron struts through the shallow water spearing small prey. The early mornings now remind me of India: still cool, they carry the promise of heat, humid and muggy, that clings like a wet blanket. I see the flash of brilliant blue as a kingfisher flits down the river in long, swooping curves, leaving small ripples where it touches the surface. In the evening I sit by the river; moisture rises from the banks and slowly the earth begins to breathe again, every tree, bush, and flower releasing its smell. The August moon rises red, climbing to a distant silver disk. Along the banks beaver, mole, and ragondin make their home and the moon is so bright I can see a small furry creature slip from its hole into the stream. Bathed in the intense light my mill looks austere and forbidding; then an owl, touching a windowpane with its passing shadow, summons the magic.

As in Sag Harbor, I am surrounded by water. I have my studio, my books and my music, but there is less social life here, less interruption. Friends and children come to visit and sometimes say, "What do you do here? It is beautiful, but there is nothing to do." There are actually many things to do and Paris is a mere hour away by fast train, but I also remember Stendhal: "A few small white clouds, borne on a barely perceptive sirocco wind; delicious warmth filled the air and I was happy to be alive." Here, I often feel like that. Here I write. Every morning I can go back to my desk, stepping into yesterday's page. There is no stress or deadline, which suits me. It probably also means that it will take me longer than it should to put all my notes together. And when it is all done, I may just move and live across the ocean.

I woke up this morning in my mill on the river. A pale wintry sun rose through naked branches drawn with ink on a porcelain sky. Last year's ragged bird nests lingered in tree forks and a windswept crow scudded past my window. *Tous les matins du monde sont sans retour*. I am content.

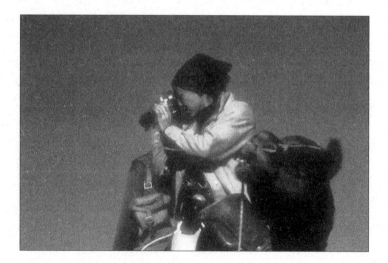